Library of
Davidson College

VOID

The Organ Preludes of
Johann Sebastian Bach

Studies in Musicology, No. 27

George Buelow, Series Editor
Professor of Musicology
Indiana University

Other Titles in This Series

No. 19 A History of Musical Americanism	Barbara Z. Achter
No. 20 The Songs and Motets of Alfonso Ferrabosco, the Younger (1575-1628)	John Duffy
No. 21 Johann Mattheson's Der Vollkommene Capellmeister: A Revised Translation with Critical Commentary	Ernest Harriss
No. 22 Beethoven's Early Sketches in the 'Fischhof Miscellany': Berlin Autograph 28	Douglas Porter Johnson
No. 23 Nicolò Jommelli: The Last Years, 1769-1774	Marita Petzoldt McClymonds
No. 24 Heinrich August Marschner, 1795-1861: His Life and Stage Works	A. Dean Palmer
No. 25 Francesco Corbetta and the Baroque Guitar, with a Transcription of His Complete Works	Richard T. Pinnell
No. 26 The Bass Viol in French Baroque Chamber Music	Julie Anne Sadie
No. 28 Luigi Cherubini: The Middle Years, 1795-1815	Stephen Charles Willis
No. 29 Liszt's Sonata in B Minor: A Study of Autograph Sources and Documents	Sharon Winklhofer

The Organ Preludes of Johann Sebastian Bach

by
George B. Stauffer

RESEARCH PRESS

Copyright © 1980, 1978
George B. Stauffer
All rights reserved

Produced and distributed by
UMI Research Press
an imprint of
University Microfilms International
Ann Arbor, Michigan 48106

Library of Congress Cataloging in Publication Data

Stauffer, George B   1947-
   The organ preludes of Johann Sebastian Bach.

  (Studies in musicology ; ser. 3, no. 27)
  Bibliography: p.
  Includes index.
  1. Bach, Johann Sebastian, 1685-1750. Preludes and fugues, organ. Preludes. 2. Bach, Johann Sebastian, 1685-1750. Works, organ. I. Title. II. Series.
MT145.B14S73   786.5'092'4   80-15519
ISBN 0-8357-1117-X

To my parents

Howard Hamilton Stauffer
Elizabeth Boyer Stauffer

Contents

Abbreviations — ix

Acknowledgments — xi

Introduction — 1

Chapter

    I.   The Sources of the Preludes — 5

            The Transmission of the Preludes
            The Question of the Lost Autographs
            The Notation of the Preludes in Early
                Manuscripts
            Two Aspects of the Sources:
                Titles and Variants

    II. The Chronology of the Preludes: — 25
          Preliminary Observations

            Manuscript Evidence
            Stylistic Evidence

    III. The Stylistic Development of the Preludes — 31

            The Through-Composed, Continuous Form
            The Ostinato-Variation Form
            The Through-Composed, Sectional Form
            The Hybrid Concerto Form
            The Concerto Form
            The ABAB Form
            Miscellaneous Forms

Contents

IV.	The Chronology of the Preludes: A Proposed Outline	91

        1700-1706
        1706-ca. 1712
        Ca. 1712-1723
        1723-1750
        Revised Versions of Earlier Works
        Special Cases

V.	The Pairing of Prelude and Fugue	127
VI.	The Function of the Preludes	137

        The Preludes and the Lutheran Worship Service
        The Preludes and Bach's Organ Examinations and Recitals
        The Preludes and Bach's Teaching

VII.	Two Aspects of Performance Practice: Registration and Manual Change	155

        The Registration of the Preludes
        The *Plenum* Combination
        The Use of Manual Change Within the Preludes
        The Use of a *Plenum* Registration Without Manual Change

Conclusion		173
Notes		177
Appendix I.	Source List	209
Appendix II.	Fantasia & Fugue in C Minor, BWV 562/1a & BWV 546/2a	233
Bibliography		247
Index		255

Abbreviations

BDok	*Bach-Dokumente*, issued under the auspices of the Bach-Archiv, Leipzig (Kassel: Bärenreiter; Leipzig: VEB Deutscher Verlag für Musik) Volume I, 1963, Volume II, 1969, Volume III, 1972.
Berlin, DStB	Deutsche Staatsbibliothek, East Berlin
Berlin, SPK	Staatsbibliothek Preussischer Kulturbesitz, West Berlin
BG	*Johann Sebastian Bach's Werke* (*Bach-Gesamtausgabe*), issued under the auspices of the Bach-Gesellschaft (Leipzig: Breitkopf und Härtel) 1851-1899.
BJ	*Bach-Jahrbuch*, 1904-
BR	*Bach Reader*, Hans T. David and Arthur Mendel, eds. (New York: W.W. Norton and Co.) 1945; Revised Edition, 1966.
BuxWV	*Thematisch-Systematisches Verzeichnis der Musikalischen Werke von Dietrich Buxtehude* (*Buxtehude-Werke-Verzeichnis*), Georg Karstädt, ed. (Wiesbaden: Breitkopf und Härtel) 1974.
BWV	*Thematisch-Systematisches Verzeichnis der Musikalischen Werke von Johann Sebastian Bach* (*Bach-Werke-Verzeichnis*), Wolfgang Schmieder, ed. (Wiesbaden: Breitkopf und Härtel) 1950.
DTB	*Denkmäler der Tonkunst in Bayern* (Leipzig: Breitkopf und Härtel) 1900-1931.

Abbreviations

Forkel	Johann Nikolaus Forkel, *Über Johann Sebastian Bachs Leben, Kunst, und Kunstwerke* (Leipzig: Hoffmeister und Kühnel) 1802; Modern Edition by Joseph M. Müller-Blattau (Kassel: Bärenreiter) 1942.
MBLpz	Musikbibliothek der Stadt Leipzig
MGG	*Die Musik in Geschichte und Gegenwart*, Friedrich Blume, ed. (Kassel: Bärenreiter) 1963
NBA	*Johann Sebastian Bach. Neue Ausgabe sämtlicher Werke* (*Neue Bach-Ausgabe*), issued under the auspices of the Johann-Sebastian-Bach-Institut, Göttingen, and the Bach-Archiv, Leipzig (Kassel: Bärenreiter; Leipzig: VEB Deutscher Verlag für Musik) 1954-.
NBA, KB	*Neue Bach-Ausgabe, Kritischer Bericht*
Peters Edition	*Johann Sebastian Bach's Kompositionen für die Orgel*, Friedrich Conrad Griepenkerl and Ferdinand Roitzsch, eds. (Leipzig: C.F. Peters) 1844-1852.
Spitta	Phillip Spitta, *Johann Sebastian Bach* (Leipzig: Breitkopf und Härtel) Volume I, 1873; Volume II, 1879.
Yale	Library of the School of Music, Yale University, New Haven, Conn.

Acknowledgments

I would like to express my gratitude to the Staatsbibliothek Preussischer Kulturbesitz in West Berlin, the Deutsche Staatsbibliothek in East Berlin, and the Musikbibliothek der Stadt Leipzig for allowing me to examine their collections of Bach manuscripts, and to the Johann-Sebastian-Bach-Institut in Göttingen for allowing me to use its extensive microfilm archive. I am equally indebted to a number of individuals for their assistance: to Dr. Alfred Dürr of the Bach-Institut for reading this work in its initial form and offering invaluable advice on certain points; to Dr. Dietrich Kilian of the Bach-Institut for counsel on source problems and for permitting me to read the manuscript of his *Kritischer Bericht* for volumes IV/5 and IV/6 of the *Neue Bach-Ausgabe;* to Hans-Joachim Schulze of the Bach-Archiv for advice on the *Möller Handschrift* and the *Andreas Bach Buch*; to Dr. Yoshitake Kobayashi of Göttingen for information on the scribes of the Bach circle; to Dr. Vernon de Tar of the Juilliard School for sharing with me his views on numerous performance problems; to Dr. Samuel Terrien of Union Theological Seminary and his wife Sara for editorial assistance; to Beatrice Terrien for typing, proofreading, and the calligraphic rendering of the examples; to Dr. Leeman Perkins of Columbia University for help in editing the final manuscript; and finally, to Dr. Christoph Wolff, formerly of Columbia University and now of Harvard University, for his active participation in this project from beginning to end and for his enthusiasm and encouragement each step of the way.

Introduction

Bach's preludes and fugues for organ have never suffered from neglect. While Bach's vocal works fell into eclipse soon after his death in 1750, his keyboard compositions continued to draw considerable approbation. The preludes and fugues, as part of this esteemed repertoire, remained in wide use throughout the eighteenth and nineteenth centuries. Consequently they number among the best-known and most-frequently discussed works of the baroque era. They were already available in several printed editions by the time the first volume of the BG appeared in 1851. They were treated at some length in the ground-breaking nineteenth-century biographies of Forkel, Hilgenfeldt, Bitter, and Spitta.[1] Since then they have been discussed in general terms in the numerous monographs dealing with the organ repertoire or Bach's organ compositions in particular.[2] Hence it is surprising that no one has singled out the preludes and fugues for a full-scale study, taking into consideration the sources, the style, the chronology, and other equally important aspects of the pieces.

The present volume focuses on half of this task, the detailed investigation of the preludes. Why should one choose to study the preludes to the exclusion of the fugues? It goes without saying that Bach made an immense contribution to the art of fugue writing. Still, his works represent the continuation of a tradition that was firmly established by his predecessors. C.P.E. Bach mindfully pointed out to Forkel that the composers his father studied in his youth—Buxtehude, Bruhns, and others—were "all strong fugue writers." If one compares a Bach organ fugue with a work by one of these "strong fugue writers," one sees that the two pieces have many basic features in common. Bach's fugue may be more sophisticated, but certain compositional precepts obtain in both works.

The tie with past convention is less clear in the case of Bach's organ preludes. When composing these pieces Bach was not bound by preexisting canons. On the contrary: like his predecessors, he was free to utilize the full resources of his own imagination. The prelude fell into the category of the *stile fantastico*, the style Walther termed "a manner of composing that is free from all constraint."[3] Perhaps it is for this reason that Bach's accomplishments in the field of the organ prelude are so remarkable. While his early efforts in this genre are derivative, his later works depart more and more from past tradition. One searches in vain in the seventeenth-century repertory for a piece that is even roughly comparable to the Toccata in F, BWV 540/1, or the Prelude in E♭, BWV 552/1. These compositions have no direct precedents outside of Bach's oeuvre. The goal of the present study is to examine in depth this unusual type of piece, the Bach free prelude for organ.

What constituted a free prelude in the baroque? The term "Praeludium" or "Praeambulum" was used loosely to designate an introductory piece whose main function was to establish the key of a work which would follow. The definition given by Johann Samuel Beyer in 1703 is typical of those found in contemporary lexica:

> A prelude is a short piece of music which an organist on the organ or instrumentalists on their instruments improvise in order to introduce the key of an ensuing work.[4]

The chief characteristic of the prelude was its free style, which called for improvisatory-like passages intended to exhibit the potential of both performer and instrument. The spontaneous nature of the prelude contrasted greatly with the more calculated design of stricter works such as canzonas, ricercars, and fugues. In general, these genres were considered less suitable for prefatory pieces.

In Germany one can observe two different trends in prelude writing leading up to the works of Bach. South-German composers—Pachelbel, J.K.F. Fischer, and others—wrote short *manualiter* preludes in a free style. These pieces were occasionally paired with fugues of an equally modest size. By contrast, north-German composers—Scheidemann, Tunder, and others—wrote *pedaliter* preludes containing contrapuntal as well as free material. This practice was continued by the next generation of north-Germans, whose large multisectional works often included extensive fugues. In spite of this, these compositions were still referred to as "Praeludia Pedaliter."[5] It was Bach who united the southern and northern traditions to produce a large, self-contained prelude with obbligato pedal—a prelude that normally served as the first half of a prelude-fugue pair.

In short, a prelude is defined more by function than by form. Under its heading come works entitled "Praeludium," "Toccata," and "Fantasia," terms used with considerable inconsistency by the composers themselves.[6] Included in this study will be all those compositions—called prelude, toccata, fantasia, or otherwise—which fulfill an introductory

Introduction

purpose. Thirty-three works fall into this category: nine single pieces and twenty-four preludes from prelude-fugue pairs.

Single pieces:

>Prelude in a, BWV 551[7]
>Toccata in d, BWV 565
>Toccata in E, BWV 566
>Prelude in G, BWV 568
>Prelude in a, BWV 569
>Fantasia in C, BWV 570
>Fantasia in G, BWV 572
>Fantasia in C (incomplete), BWV 573
>Passacaglia in c, BWV 582

Preludes of prelude-fugue pairs:

>Prelude in C, BWV 531/1
>Prelude in D, BWV 532/1
>Prelude in e, BWV 533/1
>Prelude in f, BWV 534/1
>Prelude in g, BWV 535/1
>Prelude in A, BWV 536/1
>Fantasia in c, BWV 537/1
>Toccata in d, BWV 538/1
>Prelude in d, BWV 539/1
>Toccata in F, BWV 540/1
>Prelude in G, BWV 541/1
>Fantasia in g, BWV 542/1
>Prelude in a, BWV 543/1
>Prelude in b, BWV 544/1
>Prelude in C, BWV 545/1
>Prelude in c, BWV 546/1
>Prelude in C, BWV 547/1
>Prelude in e, BWV 548/1
>Prelude in c, BWV 549/1
>Prelude in G, BWV 550/1
>Prelude in E♭, BWV 552/1
>Fantasia in c, BWV 562/1
>Fantasia in b, BWV 563/1
>Toccata in C, BWV 564/1

Not considered in this study are the Fantasia in a, BWV 561/1, the Prelude in C, BWV 567, and the Fantasia in G, BWV 571, works of doubtful authenticity omitted in the NBA, and the Canzona in d, BWV 588, and the Allebreve in D, BWV 589, works whose strict style suggests that they did not serve as preludes.

I
The Sources of the Preludes

The literary and archival documents pertaining to Bach's life reveal surprisingly little about the exact circumstances under which his compositions were written and performed. In view of this fact, the early sources of the works assume an unusually important role. They serve not only as the basis for textual criticism, but also as the primary reference for information about such central matters as stylistic development, chronology, function, and performance practice. A study of Bach's organ preludes, therefore, must begin with an examination of the sources themselves.

The Transmission of the Preludes

The sources of Bach's preludes can be divided into three categories: autographs, original prints, and manuscript copies.[1] Prints and copies must be considered primary material in many cases since the original autographs for most of the works have not survived.

Autographs

There are only six extant prelude autographs:[2]

Prelude & Fugue in G, BWV 541: complete autograph, New York: Hinrichsen Collection
Prelude & Fugue in b, BWV 544: complete autograph, Oxford: Rosenthal Collection[3]
Fantasia in C (incomplete), BWV 573: uncompleted autograph, Berlin, SPK: *P 224* (*Klavierbüchlein für Anna Magdalena Bach*, 1722), p. 40[4]
Prelude & Fugue in e, BWV 548: partial autograph (Prelude, plus mm. 1-20 of the Fugue written by Bach; remainder written by J.P. Kellner), Berlin, SPK: *P 274*, pp. 10-20[5]

Prelude & Fugue in g, BWV 535a: incomplete autograph (Prelude, plus mm. 1-65 of the Fugue), Berlin, SPK: Mus. ms. 40644 (the *Möller Handschrift*), Bl. 44ʳ-45ʳ⁶

Fantasia & Fugue (incomplete) in c, BWV 562: incomplete autograph (Fantasia, plus mm. 1-26 of the Fugue), Berlin, SPK: *P 490*[7]

The autographs of four other preludes can be traced into the late eighteenth or nineteenth centuries, but must now be considered lost:

Prelude & Fugue in A, BWV 536a: an autograph last reported (1844) in the possession of Capellmeister Karl Guhr in Frankfurt[8]

Prelude & Fugue in C, BWV 545: the so-called "Claussisches Autograph," last reported (1867) in the possession of Konsul Clauss in Leipzig[9]

Prelude & Fugue in E♭, BWV 552: an autograph last known (1774) to be in the possession of C.P.E. Bach in Hamburg[10]

Passacaglia in c, BWV 582: an autograph last reported (1844) to be in the possession of Capellmeister Karl Guhr in Frankfurt[11]

Original Prints

The Prelude & Fugue in E♭, BWV 552, issued as part of *Clavierübung* III in 1739, is the only one of Bach's free organ works to be published during his lifetime. The Prelude and Fugue are not printed as a pair. They frame, rather, the twenty-one chorale preludes (BWV 669-689) and the four duets (BWV 802-805) that make up the rest of the collection. The original edition of *Clavierübung* III, for which Bach himself wrote out many pages of the *Stichvorlage*,[12] must be considered the primary source for the Prelude & Fugue in E♭ since no autograph material has survived. All extant copies of the Prelude & Fugue appear to be derived from the 1739 print.[13]

Manuscript Copies

The remaining prelude sources, approximately 350 in number, can be classified as contemporary and posthumous copies.[14] The contemporary copies, to judge from the manuscripts whose writers have been identified, were written mainly by Bach's friends and students, as might be expected. The posthumous copies, dating from 1750 to about 1825 (the time printed editions began to supplant handwritten manuscripts), stem, in turn, from friends and students of the earlier scribes. Thus one finds that the preludes were handed down in distinct "traditions" which sprang up around individuals closely connected with Bach. For example, the "Kittel tradition" includes the prelude sources copied by Johann Christian Kittel, who studied with Bach from 1748-1750, and those written by Kittel's students, several of whom lived well into the nineteenth century.[15]

The recent handwriting studies undertaken in conjunction with the editing of the NBA have helped Bach scholars sort out the principal copyists of the organ works. This endeavor has shed new light on the use and dissemination of the preludes during Bach's lifetime and after his death. Thus it is important to note here, in approximate chronological order, the chief manuscript traditions that have been substantiated.[16]

The *Möller Handschrift* and the *Andreas Bach Buch*. The *Möller Handschrift*, Berlin, SPK: *Mus. ms. 40644*, and the *Andreas Bach Buch*, MBLpz: *III.8.4*, two collections named after former owners, number among the earliest surviving sources of Bach's keyboard music. To judge from diplomatic evidence, they were assembled during the period ca. 1703 to ca. 1710 by the same principal copyist, a person who worked in close contact with Bach (the *Möller Handschrift* contains the autograph entry of the Prelude & Fugue in g, BWV 535a) and had direct access to his works. The positive identification of this copyist has eluded scholars. Werner Wolffheim initially named Johann Gottfried Walther as the assembler of the two manuscripts.[17] Alfred Dürr later suggested Johann Bernhard Bach, the younger, rather than Walther.[18] Dietrich Kilian then proposed Johann Bernhard Bach, the elder, rather than Johann Bernhard Bach, the younger.[19] Most recently, Hans-Joachim Schulze has suggested that Johann Christoph Bach, brother of Johann Sebastian and father of Johann Andreas, may be the illusive scribe.[20] Until conclusive proof is presented, the matter must remain open.

The Walther-Krebs Circle. According to his own testimony Johann Gottfried Walther (1684-1748) had an extensive manuscript collection of keyboard music which included many works by Bach.[21] Presumably this collection was assembled by Walther during Bach's tenure in Weimar (1708-1717). Unfortunately, most of the collection has disappeared, rendering it impossible to assess accurately Walther's overall activity as a disseminator of Bach's keyboard works. One can trace Walther's role in the compilation of the manuscript complex Berlin, DStB: *P 801*, *P 802*, and *P 803*, however.[22] Containing over one hundred pieces by Bach, *P 801*, *P 802*, and *P 803* represent the most extensive source for the organ works of the Weimar period. The copying of the three manuscripts was apparently initiated by Walther when he began to assemble *P 802* around 1710. The work was aided by Johann Tobias Krebs (1690-1762), who studied first with Walther (about 1710-1714) and then with Bach (about 1714-1717).[23] After Bach's departure from Weimar, the writing was continued by Krebs and his son, Johann Ludwig (1713-1783), a student at the University in Leipzig from 1726-1735 and a copyist for Bach between 1729 and 1731. The two Krebses, together with several secondary scribes, completed *P 801* and *P 803*. Entries into *P 803* were made as late as 1751.

Kellner Circle. Johann Peter Kellner (1705-1772) was one of the most important copyists of Bach's keyboard compositions. According to his autobiography,[24] Kellner was a friend of Bach rather than his student. The close connection between the two men is attested by the fact that on at least one occasion they collaborated in copying out a work.[25] The most important of Kellner's prelude manuscripts are contained in Berlin, SPK: *P 274* and *P 804*. Both are *Konvolute* comprised of miscellaneous fascicles. Watermarks found in the two sources can be assigned to the period 1725-1750; certain pieces in *P 804* bear the dates 1725 and 1726. At least four other persons were copying in connection with Kellner: Leonard Frischmuth (?-1764), Wolfgang Nicolaus Mey (?-?), Johannes Ringk (1717-after 1772), and Johann Anton Wechmar (1727?-1799).

The Mempell-Preller Collection. The Mempell-Preller Collection is a group of manuscripts copied and collected by Johann Nicolaus Mempell (1713-1747) of Apolda and Johann Gottlieb Preller (1717-1785) of Oberrossla near Apolda.[26] The collection, located primarily in the Musikbibliothek der Stadt Leipzig, is especially noteworthy because most of the Bach organ works it contains are early compositions. No evidence connects either Mempell or Preller directly with Bach. The quality of some of their copies, however, indicates that both men relied upon sources close to the Bach circle. It is possible that Mempell was a student of Kellner. Preller, in turn, may have studied with Mempell or Johann Tobias Krebs or both. Preller apparently assembled the present collection by adding his copies, written about 1743-1749, to those made earlier by Mempell.

The Kittel Circle. Johann Christian Kittel (1732-1809) was one of Bach's last students. He became a famous organ teacher in his own right and played a central role in the dissemination of Bach's compositions. It is clear that Kittel copied many Bach works himself, though it has not yet been determined whether he was writing under Bach's supervision or whether he was writing independently. Much of his collection was destroyed in a fire in 1816;[27] other material, including an important manuscript that served as the *Vorlage* for Berlin, SPK: *P 320*, perished in World War II.[28] As a result, few of Kittel's copies of Bach preludes have survived. One that has been preserved is Berlin, SPK: *P 1009*, a manuscript containing the Toccata in F, BWV 540/1. Many other prelude sources once thought to have been written by Kittel have turned out to be copies made by his students, who include Johann Christian Rinck (1770-1846), Michael Gotthard Fischer (1773-1829), Johann Nicolaus Gebhardi (?-?), and Johann Andreas Dröbs (1773-1825).[29] Friedrich August Grasnick (1798-1877), an early nineteenth-century copyist, did not study with Kittel but obviously had access to many of his manuscripts (or possibly to those of his students?).

The Berlin Circle. The presence of several important Bach students during the period 1740-1780 made Berlin a center for the copying and distribution of Bach's works. Today this is reflected chiefly in the collection of the Amalien-Bibliothek, a library assembled in the second half of the eighteenth century for Princess Anna Amalia (1723-1787), youngest sister of Frederick the Great.[30] Between the years 1758 and 1783 the Amalien-Bibliothek was supervised by Johann Philipp Kirnberger (1721-1783), who had studied with Bach in Leipzig. Kirnberger is generally given credit for obtaining the numerous Bach works found in the collection. All of the Amalien-Bibliothek's prelude manuscripts are copies, neatly written by professional scribes. A distinctive feature of these manuscripts is the notation of pedal parts in red ink. The Amalien-Bibliothek prelude sources are of special interest because they frequently display texts of unusually high quality. It is likely, therefore, that they were derived directly from manuscripts owned either by Kirnberger or by the other Bach students in Berlin: C.P.E. Bach, W.F. Bach, or Johann Friederich Agricola.

The Hamburg Circle. Evidence suggests that Carl Philipp Emanuel Bach owned autographs or copies of his father's free organ works. Even though these manuscripts have disappeared without a trace (see discussion below), their former existence is substantiated by prelude copies that undoubtedly stem from them. These copies were written by individuals closely connected with Philipp Emanuel when he lived in Hamburg: Johann Stephan Borsch (ca. 1744-1804), C.F.G. Schwencke (1767-1822), Michel (a tenor who worked as copyist for Philipp Emanuel between 1780 and 1788), and Anonymous 303 (so named in the Tübinger-Bach Studien).

The Nuremberg Circle. A previously unknown group of prelude sources emanating from Nuremberg came to light recently during the editing of the free organ works for the NBA. Thus far three individuals connected with these sources have been identified, though their ties with J.S. Bach remain obscure.[31] Wilhelm Hieronymous Pachelbel (1686-1764), active as organist of the Sebalduskirche in Nuremberg, wrote out several Bach preludes, probably between 1729 and 1736. Pachelbel's manuscripts have not survived, but are known through copies made by

Lorenz Sichart, organist of St. Egidien in Nuremberg from 1744 to ca. 1754. Leonard Scholz (1720-1798), another Nuremberg organist, also wrote out several preludes, though often in corrupt or abridged form. Scholz may have drawn his material from Pachelbel's collection.

The Question of Lost Autographs

It is clear from the above that almost all the preludes have been handed down to posterity via copies. Only six autographs exist today. Of these manuscripts one is partially apograph, one contains an early variant, and two contain unfinished pieces. That leaves just two complete, definitive autographs for a repertory of thirty-three works. This curious situation elicits the intriguing question: What happened to the original sources of the Bach organ preludes?

The autographs of the preludes seem to have vanished immediately after Bach's death in 1750. Only one contemporary reference to the preludes—a statement appearing in the *Nekrolog* of 1754—might be construed as an allusion to a large body of autograph material. In the *Nekrolog* C.P.E. Bach and Johann Friedrich Agricola include the item "A large number of free preludes, fugues, and similar pieces with obligato pedal for the organ" on a list of "Unpublished Works of the Late J.S. Bach."[32] The autographs of other keyboard works mentioned, the Six Trio Sonatas for Organ, the *Orgelbüchlein*, and Well-Tempered Clavier I, are known to have been in Bach's possession at the time of his death. Considered within its *Nekrolog* context, the list presented by C.P.E. Bach and Agricola seems to be an inventory of the manuscript material in J.S. Bach's estate. If this is true, the autographs of the free organ works, like the original materials for the cantatas, Well-Tempered Clavier I, and others, were probably inherited by the Bach sons.

Contemporary documents, however, offer few traces of such a transaction. Wilhelm Friedemann, as the oldest son, undoubtedly had first choice of his father's manuscripts. He owned the autograph of one free organ work, the Concerto in d, BWV 596.[33] Whether or not he possessed others cannot be demonstrated. If he obtained prelude autographs, it is likely he squandered them as he did the cantata materials he inherited.[34]

According to the inventory of his estate, Carl Phillipp Emanuel, the second oldest son, owned only one organ prelude at the time of his death, a "Praeludium und Fuga für die Orgel aus dem C♯."[35] But the sudden appearance of many excellent prelude copies in Berlin in the 1750's and 1760's, the existence of prelude sources written by members of his circle, and his possession of his father's manuscript of *Clavierübung*

III suggest that Carl Philipp Emanuel owned other prelude copies or autographs. Since these were not listed as part of his estate, he may have sold them or given them away before he died.[36]

Johann Christoph Friedrich, the second youngest son, was a celebrated performer of his father's organ works.[37] He may have played from autographs given to him by his father (or by his mother after his father's death). It is also possible that Johann Christian, the youngest son, inherited several keyboard pieces, including the Prelude & Fugue in b, BWV 544, the Toccata in E, BWV 566, and an early version of the Prelude & Fugue in G, BWV 541. Dietrich Kilian has reasoned convincingly that manuscripts bequeathed to Johann Christian were inscribed "Christl" by his mother.[38] This inscription is quite visible on the title page of the autograph of the Prelude & Fugue in b.[39] It is also transmitted in extant copies of the Toccata in E and the Prelude & Fugue in G.

Thus at least two Bach sons, Carl Philipp Emanuel and Johann Christian, appear to have inherited prelude manuscripts. Two others, Wilhelm Friedemann and Johann Christoph Friedrich, also may have owned autographs of some pieces. The question remains: Why weren't these materials preserved? Carl Philipp Emanuel, for instance, went to great lengths to keep his father's manuscripts in the family.[40] Why didn't he retain the free organ works which seem to have been in his possession?

Several Bach scholars, including Walter Emery, contend that a large number of the autographs of the free organ works were gathered together and preserved as a collection after Bach's death. This collection either perished through an undocumented calamity in the late eighteenth or early nineteenth century or has remained hidden to the present day. A plausible alternative to this hypothesis can be proposed, however, and it is that the original sources of the free organ works, utilized for decades as performance scores, simply disintegrated after years of hard use. This explanation, though more mundane than the "lost cache" theory, is supported strongly by external evidence.

Bach's organ compositions, unlike most of his vocal works, were not relegated to obscurity after 1750. Championed by a small but enthusiastic group of organists trained in the Bach tradition, they remained popular throughout the eighteenth century. The extant sources show that Kirnberger, J.L. Krebs, Kittel, and other famous Bach students used the preludes as part of their repertoire. In addition, these men passed the works on to their students: Dröbs, Rinck, Fischer, and others. Thus there was no hiatus of interest in the preludes between Bach's death and the appearance of the first printed editions in the nineteenth century.

The fact that the preludes were perennial favorites accounts for the extraordinarily large number of copies that have come down to us. On the other hand, the popularity the pieces enjoyed in the eighteenth century is probably responsible for the demise of the original source material. As far as keyboard works are concerned it might be said: the more popular a piece, the less likely the chances for its autograph to survive. For example, the Fugue in g, BWV 542/2, specifically cited by Mattheson in 1731 and labeled "The very best pedal-piece by Mr. Johann Sebastian Bach" in two eighteenth-century scores, is transmitted in twenty-one sources, all copies. The autograph seems to have disintegrated long ago, perhaps even before Bach's death.[41]

The incomplete autographs of the Fantasia & Fugue in c, BWV 562, and the Fantasia in C, BWV 573, or the autograph of the Prelude & Fugue in g, BWV 535a, bound in a thick volume (the *Möller Handschrift*), were of limited practical value to an eighteenth-century organist. It is easy to understand why they survived. But other prelude autographs—undoubtedly unbound manuscripts, each containing a single work[42]—would have served as ideal performance scores. As a consequence they would have been subjected to hard use, which in turn would have caused disintegration.[43] The autograph of the Prelude & Fugue in e, BWV 548, though extant, shows the ravages of this process. On the other hand, the extant autographs of the Prelude & Fugue in G, BWV 541, and the Prelude & Fugue in b, BWV 544, are in excellent condition. Why did they survive when so many other prelude autographs disappeared? The answer might lie in the fact that they were both *Reinschriften* worthy of preservation. Other prelude autographs may have contained numerous emendations; for this reason they may have been deemed less sacrosanct by late eighteenth-century performers.

The Notation of the Preludes in Early Manuscripts

The notation of the preludes in early manuscripts provides certain clues about the dating and use of the repertoire. In the eighteenth century free organ works were usually written on two staves. The pedal part was not allotted a separate staff as it is today; rather, it shared the bass staff with the lowest manual voice or voices. Indications such as "Pedal," "Ped.," or simply "P," appearing at the entrances of the pedal part, distinguished it from the manual voices. In addition, rests and the direction of note stems helped to clarify the distribution of manual and pedal parts wherever confusion might occur. As a rule Bach adhered to this method of scoring and notated all his organ works, except trios, on two staves.[44] The opening of the Prelude in E♭, BWV 552/1, in *Clavierübung* III is representative of this procedure:

As far as clefs are concerned, the sources display two different combinations: a) soprano clef in the upper staff and bass clef in the lower staff, and b) treble clef in the upper staff and bass clef in the lower staff, e.g.:

a)

b)

Excerpts courtesy of Staatsbibliothek Preussischer Kulturbesitz, West Berlin

In general, all the sources of a given prelude use only one of these two possibilities. This fact leads to an interesting conjecture with regard to chronology. To judge from the extant autograph material, Bach invariably used the soprano clef to notate the upper staff of his keyboard works until the late-Cöthen–early-Leipzig years, i.e. the period around 1723.[45] From then on he began to employ the treble clef with increasing frequency. For example, the soprano clef appears throughout the autograph scores of the *Orgelbüchlein* (1714+) and the Well-Tempered Clavier I (1722). The treble clef, on the other hand, appears in the four *Clavierübung* prints (1726-1731, 1735, 1739, and ca. 1741-1742). Both the soprano and treble clefs are encountered in the *Klavierbüchlein für Anna Magdalena Bach* of 1722. For the most part, the initial entries in this collection are notated in the soprano clef, the later additions, in the treble clef.

Since a general pattern can be observed in Bach's usage of clefs, one might be tempted to employ it as a means of dating the preludes and the fugues paired with them: all those works consistently notated in the soprano clef would be assigned to the period before ca. 1723 and all those consistently notated in the treble clef to the years thereafter. If this method of dating were reliable, the following chronological picture would emerge.

Before ca. 1723 (i.e. notated in the soprano clef):

BWV 531	Prelude & Fugue in C
BWV 532	Prelude & Fugue in D
BWV 533	Prelude & Fugue in e
BWV 534	Prelude & Fugue in f
BWV 535	Prelude & Fugue in g
BWV 536	Prelude & Fugue in A
BWV 538	Toccata & Fugue in d
BWV 539/2	Fugue in d
BWV 540	Toccata & Fugue in F
BWV 542	Fantasia & Fugue in g
BWV 543	Prelude & Fugue in a
BWV 549	Prelude & Fugue in c
BWV 550	Prelude & Fugue in G
BWV 551	Prelude in a
BWV 562	Fantasia & Fugue (incomplete) in c
BWV 563	Fantasia con Imitazione in b
BWV 564	Toccata, Adagio, & Fugue in C
BWV 565	Toccata in d

BWV 566   Toccata in E
BWV 568   Prelude in G
BWV 569   Prelude in a
BWV 570   Fantasia in C
BWV 582   Passacaglia in c

After ca. 1723 (i.e., notated in the treble clef):

BWV 537   Fantasia & Fugue in c
BWV 539/1   Prelude in d
BWV 541   Prelude & Fugue in G
BWV 544   Prelude & Fugue in b
BWV 545   Prelude & Fugue in C
BWV 546   Prelude & Fugue in c
BWV 547   Prelude & Fugue in C
BWV 548   Prelude & Fugue in e
BWV 552   Prelude & Fugue in E♭
BWV 572   Fantasia in G
BWV 573   Fantasia in C (incomplete)

In the above list the Prelude & Fugue in G, BWV 541, and the Prelude & Fugue in C, BWV 545, might be shifted to the pre-ca. 1723 column, for in both cases a single reliable source transmits the work in the soprano clef. This implies that the two pieces might have been written before ca. 1723 and revised at a later date.

Unfortunately, several factors negate the reliability of a chronology based solely on clefs. First of all, Bach occasionally used the soprano clef for keyboard works written after 1723. It appears, for example, in the autograph (ca. 1748) and original print (ca. 1747) of the Canonic Variations on "Vom Himmel hoch," BWV 769, and in the so-called "London Autograph" of Well-Tempered Clavier II.[46] Thus allocating the keyboard works written in the soprano clef and the treble clef to early and late periods respectively cannot be taken as a hard and fast rule.

The second problem is the matter of revisions. A prelude transmitted in the treble clef might be a revised version of a piece originally notated in the soprano clef. As mentioned above, this may be true of the Prelude & Fugue in G, BWV 541, and the Prelude & Fugue in C, BWV 545. In the case of the so-called "Great Eighteen Chorales," BWV 651-668, for which plentiful source material is available,[47] Bach retained the original clefs of the Weimar versions when he revised them in Leipzig. The only exception to this is *Nun komm der Heiden Heiland*, BWV 661, in which the soprano clef of the Weimar version is replaced with a treble clef in the Leipzig version. This change undoubtedly was made in conjunction with the metric revision of the entire piece.

The third problem with using clefs as a chronological criterion is that most of the extant prelude sources are copies, not autographs. The copyists involved may have retained the clefs found in Bach's original manuscripts. On the other hand, they may have "updated" the scores by altering the notation from soprano to treble clef (a change in the opposite direction seems unlikely).[48] Since German organists in the eighteenth century could read the soprano and treble clefs with equal facility, such "updating" was not necessary from a technical standpoint and does not seem to have become prevalent until the nineteenth century. In the three instances where Bach's autograph is available for comparison with copies derived from it—the Prelude & Fugue in b, BWV 544, the Prelude & Fugue in e, BWV 548, and the Fantasia in c, BWV 562[49]—the clefs in the copies agree with the clefs in the autographs.

The fourth problem is the impossibility of knowing how many "early" versions of preludes may have existed. Who could have guessed, for example, that the Prelude & Fugue in g, BWV 535, represents a thorough reworking of the Prelude & Fugue in g, BWV 535a, if the only source of the latter, the *Möller Handschrift*, had not survived? Despite all these factors which call for caution, it remains noteworthy that only nine works are handed down without exception in the treble clef: the Fantasia & Fugue in c, BWV 537, the Prelude in d, BWV 539/1, the Prelude & Fugue in b, BWV 544, the Prelude & Fugue in c, BWV 546, the Prelude & Fugue in C, BWV 547, the Prelude & Fugue in e, BWV 548, the Prelude & Fugue in E♭, BWV 552, the Fantasia in G, BWV 572, and the Fantasia in C (incomplete), BWV 573. This point will be considered again in the discussion of chronology in Chapters II and IV.

With very few exceptions the preludes are laid out in a straightforward and economical fashion in the sources. In the case of prelude-fugue pairs, the fugue follows the prelude immediately unless it was written out at a different time. In many instances the prelude ends and the fugue begins on the same system, no doubt to conserve space. When the fugue begins on a new page, the preceding prelude often concludes with the cautionary remark "Fuga" or "Fuga sequitur," phrases reminding the performer to continue.[50]

The general appearance of the sources suggests that they had a utilitarian purpose. The preludes are written neatly, but not professionally.[51] In many instances the works are spatially arranged to facilitate page turns. A few manuscripts are *Auflagebogen*,[52] a practical arrangement that reduces or eliminates altogether the need for page turns. Many of the sources show signs of wear: page corners have been dog-eared and torn off, page edges are badly soiled, etc. These features lead one to conclude that most of the eighteenth-century writers and owners of the manuscripts were more concerned with performing Bach's preludes than preserving them for posterity.

Two Aspects of the Sources:
   Titles and Variants

The texts and variant readings of the individual prelude manuscripts are described in detail by Dietrich Kilian in NBA IV/5-6, KB. The present discussion will focus on two selected aspects of the sources of great importance for the later investigations of stylistic development and chronology: the titles of the pieces and the types and reliability of the variants that appear in the extant manuscripts.

For one attempting to establish definitive titles for the Bach preludes, the sources present more problems than solutions. The chief difficulty lies in the fact that the preludes simply are not handed down with uniform names. A prelude and fugue called "Praeludium et Fuga" in one source might be termed "Preludio e Fuga" or simply "Praeludium pedaliter" in another. Even more divergent are titles such as "Praeludium," "Praeludium concertato," and "Pièce d'Orgue" appearing in manuscript copies of works usually labeled "toccata" or "fantasia" today. The Toccata & Fugue in d ("Dorian"), BWV 538, for example, is called "Toccata con Fuge," "Preludium con Fuga," and "Preludio" in different sources. Since there is no autograph for this work, choosing a title becomes problematic. A glance at the Source List in Appendix I shows that the Toccata & Fugue in d is not an isolated case.

Faced with this dilemma, an editor must make a difficult choice: he must either consider each prelude as a separate piece and derive a suitable title from the available source material, or he must adopt a standard policy. Griepenkerl, Rust and Naumann, and Kilian, editors of the Peters Edition, the BG, and the NBA respectively, settled upon the latter solution and chose "normalized" Latin titles—"Praeludium et Fuga," "Toccata et Fuga," etc.—for the works in their editions. This approach, while bestowing admirable uniformity on a *Gesamtausgabe*, obscures the complex picture presented in the sources. As far as nomenclature is concerned, the sources are consistent only in their inconsistency. Several factors account for this.

Foremost is the fact that so little of the extant source material is autograph. Since eighteenth-century musicians apparently felt at liberty to update the names of pieces they copied, it is natural that the Bach preludes, which exist mainly as copies, were transmitted with a great variety of titles. Bach's musical texts, it seems, were generally regarded with respect and copied verbatim (see below). This is undoubtedly due to the fact that most of the people writing out the works were students. Bach's titles, on the other hand, were apparently deemed less "holy" by scribes and thus were more susceptible to embellishment. The extant sources of the Prelude & Fugue in b, BWV 544, make this clear. The title found on the initial page of Bach's autograph is "Praeludium pro Organo cum pedale obligato." Extant copies of the Prelude & Fugue, while preserving the same musical text as Bach's autograph, bear diverse labels:

> "Praeludium in H. Mol. pro Organo cum pedale obligato" (Berlin, SPK: *P 891*)
> "Preludio e Fuga per l'Organo" (Berlin, SPK: *P 276, P 560, AmB 60*)
> "Praeludium con Fuga in H mol. pro Organo cum pedale obligato" (MBLpz: *Ms. 1*)
> "Praeludium et Fuga in H moll pro Organo pleno cum Pedale oblig(ato)" (MBLpz: *Poel. Mus. ms. 24*)

Obviously phrases such as "Praeludium con Fuga" and "Praeludium" were used interchangeably, as were "pro Organo pleno" and "pro Organo." These differences frequently reflect individual or regional tastes. Kellner and his copyists, for instance, had a marked propensity for including the tonality of a piece in its title (cf. *P 891*, above). Copyists working in Berlin, on the other hand, customarily used short quasi-Italian names (cf. *P 276, P 560, AmB 60*).

Sometimes disparity is encountered even within a single source, for many manuscripts contain two titles, one located on the title page and another, a heading or *Überschrift*, located above the initial measures of the prelude. The wording of these two is seldom the same. In Bach's autograph of the Prelude & Fugue in b the *Überschrift*, "Praeludium in Organo pleno pedale," is only slightly different from the title-page title, "Praeludium pro Organo cum pedale obligato." Greater discrepancy appears in the partial autograph of the Prelude & Fugue in e, BWV 548 (Berlin, SPK: *P 274*). The title on the title page (in Kellner's hand) is "Praeludium et Fuga in E mol. pro Organo pedaliter" while the *Überschrift* reads "Praeludium pedaliter pro Organo." Which title is the correct one? Should the Prelude & Fugue in e be labeled "Praeludium et Fuga" or "Praeludium pedaliter" in a scholarly edition?[53] Even if the autographs of the preludes had survived, titling the individual works would still be a problem.

Bach himself seems to have taken a somewhat flexible attitude towards titling. The ambiguous title "Praeludium ô Fantasia Pedaliter ex D$^\flat$" that appears in the *Möller Handschrift* copy of the Prelude & Fugue in d, BWV 549a, most probably reflects Bach's own indifference. More striking are the name changes he instituted in two partitas printed in *Clavierübung* I (1731). The first movement of the Partita in a, BWV 827, titled "Prélude" in *Klavierbüchlein für Anna Magdelena Bach* (1725), was renamed "Toccata" in the *Clavierübung* I print. In a similar fashion, the first movement of the Partita in e, BWV 830, also titled "Prélude" in the *Klavierbüchlein*, was renamed "Fantasia" in *Clavierübung* I.[54] This suggests that Bach himself might have been responsible for the diverse titles applied to works such as the "Dorian" Toccata & Fugue.

Despite the inconsistencies inherent in the titling process, the sources do show an important tendency that is obscured by the standardized names used in modern editions. This tendency is the practice of referring to a prelude and fugue as a single piece, entitled "Praeludium." Over half of the works titled "Praeludium et Fuga" or "Toccata et Fuga" in the Peters Edition, the BG, and the NBA, are handed down in at least one source which gives them the more encompassing name, "Praeludium." As noted above, Bach himself called the Prelude & Fugue in b and the Prelude & Fugue in e "Praeludium pro Organo," a title he also used for the Prelude & Fugue in G, BWV 541. This shows that even after formalizing the prelude-fugue pair, he still viewed such compositions as belonging to the late seventeenth-century north-German tradition in which a multisectional free work was normally termed "Praeludium pedaliter."[55]

In light of the fact that only six autographs have survived, the important question arises: Do the many variants encountered in the prelude sources reflect changes made by Bach himself or are they the emendations of overly zealous copyists? While a definitive answer is precluded by the dearth of original material, a tentative hypothesis can be suggested from secondary evidence, from the nature of the prelude variants, and from our knowledge of Bach's working habits in other fields of composition.

The variants which occur in the prelude sources are of four principal types.

Revisions of Detail

Under this classification belong the small discrepancies in detail that do not alter the general shape of a passage. In some instances, a variant obviously constitutes a corruption of the original text and is most probably the result of a slip of the pen, i.e., a mistake made in the process of copying a text rapidly. In other cases a variant reflects a conscious revision, intended to improve or embellish the passage involved. Examples:

Passacaglia in c, BWV 582, mm. 143-144. B (= Bach's autograph, now lost, but used for the Peters Edition), while very similar to A (= MBLpz: *III.8.4*, the *Andreas Bach Buch*), is nevertheless a rhythmic refinement of it:

Prelude in C, BWV 545/1, penultimate measure. In this instance B (= the "Claussches Autograph," now lost, but used for the BG) represents a filling-in of A (= Stockholm, Stiftelson Musikkulturens främjande, written by Johann Caspar Vogler):

Sectional Expansion

This type of variant is more involved than a change of detail. It concerns the enlargement of a prelude through the expansion of one or more of its sections. The remaining sections are unaltered. Examples:

Prelude in C, BWV 545/1. BWV 545/1 represents the expansion of the early variant, BWV 545a/1, by six measures.[56] This expansion was accomplished by grafting three measures onto the beginning and three measures onto the end of BWV 545a/1 without changing the main body of the work.

Prelude in g, BWV 535/1. Besides the early variant BWV 535a (see below) there are three versions of this prelude. One contains 39 measures, one contains 42 measures, and one contains 43 measures. The differences in length stem from the middle section of the piece (mm. 14 1/2 - 36 1/2 of the NBA text), which is expanded from 18 mm. (=Berlin, SPK: *P 804 et al.*) to 21 mm. (=BG text) to 22 mm. (=NBA text). The outer sections of all three versions vary only in matters of detail.

Thorough Revision

The third and most extensive type of variant involves the revision of the entire prelude. Either the whole piece is rewritten, using the original only as a sketch for the new version, or the structure of the original is retained and the voices are comprehensively revised. Examples:

Prelude in g, BWV 535/1. The standard, 43-measure-long version of the prelude represents a complete transformation of the earlier 21-measure-long variant, BWV 535a/1.[57]

Prelude in A, BWV 536/1. The standard version represents a thorough revision of the part-writing found in BWV 536a/1.

Transpositions

Three preludes are handed down in more than one key: the Toccata in E, BWV 566, in E and C; the Prelude & Fugue in c, BWV 549, in c and d (=BWV 549a); and the Prelude & Fugue in C, BWV 545, in C and B^b (=BWV 545b). In the case of the latter two works, the alternate versions display differences that stem from considerations other than transposition.[58]

Do the four types of variants outlined above reflect Bach's method of composition and revision? Ample evidence suggests that they do.

Meticulous refinements similar to those appearing in the prelude sources are found throughout Bach's oeuvre, in the vocal works,[59] in the chorale preludes,[60] and in the newly discovered Goldberg canons,[61] to name just three examples. The technique of expanding pieces by sectional enlargement is also encountered outside the prelude repertoire, in the Art of Fugue[62] or the Well-Tempered Clavier.[63] The thorough reworking of a prelude has its parallel in the well-known revision of the first movement of the French Ouverture, BWV 831,[64] or in the revision of the Prelude & Fugue in a, BWV 894, which was transformed into the first movement of the Concerto in a, BWV 1044. Finally, transpositions occur frequently among Bach's other works, in the French Ouverture or the Well-Tempered Clavier, for instance.

Thus it is likely that most of the prelude variants, at least those involving a refinement of the musical text, reflect changes instituted by Bach himself. It is to be admitted that almost all the extant prelude sources were written by individuals other than Bach. But those individuals had no reason to alter intentionally the texts from which they copied.[65] In most cases the copyists were students, who were not in a position to make musical revisions. They were at liberty to change the title of a prelude or to delete or add ornamentation according to their own tastes. The musical text seems to have been quite another matter. One person who might have rejected this credo was Walther, who regarded Bach as a fellow musician rather than a mentor. Many of Walther's manuscripts of Bach's works have been lost.[66] The surviving prelude sources, copies of the Toccata & Fugue in d, BWV 538, the Prelude & Fugue in C, BWV 545, and the Fantasia in G, BWV 572, suggest even he did not feel compelled to change Bach's texts.[67]

The premise that most of the sources faithfully reflect Bach's originals receives support from the extant autographs. No copies are known to have been made of the autographs of the Prelude & Fugue in g, BWV 535a, the Fantasia in C, BWV 573, and the Prelude & Fugue in G (final version), BWV 541. But numerous copies stem from the autographs of the Prelude & Fugue in b, BWV 544, and the Prelude & Fugue in e, BWV 548, and they agree with Bach's text in all essentials. Discrepancies are limited to minor copying errors and changes in titles. The copyists involved, Kellner, Dröbs, Mempell, and others, adhered closely to the manuscripts in front of them. The case of the Fantasia in c, BWV 562/1, is even more striking. In this instance Bach revised the extant autograph (Berlin, SPK: *P 490*) several times. The copies of this autograph, made at different periods, reflect clearly the layers of revisions.[68] As was true of the Preludes & Fugues in b and e, the copies of the Fantasia contain slips of the pen and altered titles, but they display no intentional changes in the muscial text of Bach's original.[69]

Taking all these factors into account, one concludes that the variants in the prelude sources show Bach as the reviser of his own works. He employed many of the preludes as performance and teaching material over an extended period of time, in some instances, for forty or fifty years.[70] To judge from his working habits and the evidence in the sources, he made revisions, both large and small, when he used the preludes further. Slight emendations made over an extended period probably produced variants in the original scores. These accretions were picked up by students writing out the preludes for their own use.[71] In some instances multiple layers of revisions apparently obscured the original to the point where a new autograph was needed.

This process can be observed in the sources of the Prelude & Fugue in G, BWV 541. Bach used this work often, refining it several times. An early version, perhaps the earliest, appears in Berlin, SPK: *P 595*, where the piece is notated in the soprano clef. A later version appears in Berlin, SPK: *P 320*. Further additions, apparently obscuring certain passages in Bach's original, are mirrored in Berlin, SPK: *P 288*. Finally, the extant autograph (New York: Hinrichsen Collection), a *Reinschrift* made in the 1730's or early 1740's, reflects Bach's decision to write out a clean copy of the work. In the course of doing so, he made refinements which do not appear in any other manuscript.

Another example of a composition that developed by stages is the Prelude & Fugue in C, BWV 545, whose revisions are discussed elsewhere.[72] In other instances revisions were more abrupt and encompassing, as in the rewriting of the Prelude & Fugue in g, BWV 535a. It is natural that more variants are found in the earlier works than in the later pieces, since Bach wrote the latter with more assurance and had fewer years to revise them.

To summarize: the layers of variants in the prelude sources appear to be analogous to those found in the original materials of other Bach compositions. As a consequence, they can be put to use in the study of Bach's prelude style and in the establishment of a chronology for the repertoire. Nevertheless, since the variants are handed down in secondary manuscripts, they must be weighed with caution.

II
The Chronology of the Preludes: Preliminary Observations

In a study that investigates the way a composer treats a particular genre, chronology becomes a crucial issue. If the order in which the composer wrote his works can be determined, then it is possible to trace more accurately the development of his compositional style. Considerable strides have been made in the field of Bach chronology in the past twenty years. Alfred Dürr and Georg von Dadelsen have shown through a thorough investigation of source material that most of the dates traditionally assigned to Bach's vocal works were incorrect.[1] The chronology they established ended the century-long dominance of Philipp Spitta's scholarship and brought about a complete re-evaluation of Bach's activities in Weimar and Leipzig.

Unfortunately, similar progress has not been made with Bach's instrumental works. As far as chronology is concerned, they have remained solidly enshrouded in nineteenth-century views. This state of affairs is attributable principally to a source situation quite different from that of the vocal works. The autographs of most of Bach's instrumental pieces have been lost, and the pre-1750 copies that survive were not written in any discernible pattern. Therefore the dating techniques which Dürr and Dadelsen used for the vocal repertoire cannot be applied to instrumental compositions. As a result there has been no subsequent redating of works such as the organ preludes in the wake of Dürr and Dadelsen's revelations.

Yet without question existing prelude chronologies are far from satisfactory.[2] The most significant attempt to date the pieces was made by Spitta in his monumental Bach biography of 1873-1879. Spitta had extraordinary insight into Bach's oeuvre, and he consulted manuscripts whenever possible. In spite of this, his conclusions, especially those based purely on style, were frequently more subjective than systematic, and the dates he assigned to many preludes are highly suspect. Nevertheless, Spitta's chronology was adopted almost *in toto* by Wolfgang Schmieder in his *Bach-Werke-Verzeichnis* (1950). In this way it has been handed down practically as Holy Writ to the present generation.³

Recently several efforts have been made to date individual works by means of source criticism alone.⁴ These studies frequently ignore stylistic evidence, even when it suggests that pieces were written years before they were copied into surviving manuscripts. Such blind faith in the sources, an understandable reaction to nineteenth-century subjectivity, has only confused the issue.⁵ Other currently proposed solutions also have grave shortcomings. Hans Klotz suggested that Bach's organ compositions might be dated on the basis of manual and pedal compass.⁶ The problem with this method is clear: the exact range of many of the instruments Bach had at his disposal is unknown. Moreover, Bach may have written certain pieces for concerts or examinations on organs in Kassel, Gera, Halle, and other places.⁷ Klotz did not take these instruments into consideration. Shortly before he died, Walter Emery, who gave much thought to Bach keyboard chronology,⁸ attempted to settle the dating dilemma once and for all. He suggested Bach may not have written any free organ works after Weimar.⁹ Although this proposal represents an ingenious *deus ex machina* for modern historians, its likelihood of being correct is highly questionable.

It is obvious that additional work is needed in this area. Instead of using chronology as a guideline for style criticism, it is necessary to do precisely the opposite. Dates for the preludes can be established only through a thorough evaluation of the style as well as the sources of the repertoire. The state of the sources was discussed in Chapter I. Before turning to the style of the works it is important to outline the criteria that will later serve as the basis for the chronology proposed in Chapter IV.

Manuscript Evidence

Manuscript evidence concerns two matters: an inspection of the earliest sources and a consideration of Bach's notational habits.

Earliest Source

In a few instances manuscripts do supply vital chronological information. The six surviving autographs as well as several important pre-1750 copies can be dated with relative certainty. But since most of these sources are *Reinschriften*, they usually provide a *terminus ante quem*, not a date of composition. Hence even the chronological data provided by autographs and reliable early copies must be assayed carefully.¹⁰

Manner of Notation

Additional evidence can be derived from the manner in which a work is notated in eighteenth-century manuscripts.

Clefs. As it has been pointed out in Chapter I, in his early keyboard compositions Bach invariably used the soprano clef to notate the right-hand part. From the late-Cöthen–early-Leipzig years on, however, he frequently used the treble clef for this purpose. Thus with regard to chronology, works consistently handed down in the treble clef probably were written or revised after ca. 1723. It is also likely, though less certain, that works consistently transmitted in the soprano clef date before ca. 1723.

Dorian Notation. Up to and including the Weimar years Bach usually employed the so-called "dorian" notation when writing in the minor mode in keys requiring flats. This means such keys were notated one flat short of modern practice, i.e., D minor with no flats, G minor with one flat, and so forth. During the Cöthen years Bach abandoned this method and adopted the present-day system. In light of this, it is not unreasonable to assume that pieces consistently handed down in dorian notation were written in or before Weimar.[11]

To be sure, evidence derived from notational characteristics must be handled with caution. One must always take into account the vicissitudes of the copying procedure as well as the idiosyncracies of copyists and of Bach himself.[12] Still, notation provides a general guide that should not be ignored.[13]

Stylistic Evidence

Since it is impossible to date the preludes on manuscript evidence alone, a large number of chronological conclusions must be drawn from stylistic analysis. Bach's work in other genres suggests that he continually strove to improve his writing and to incorporate new ideas into it. The changes in his preludes undoubtedly follow a logical order of development. If one can trace this order of development, one gains important insights into chronology. Four stylistic aspects are especially significant: form, melodic material, part-writing, and harmonic design.

Form

Bach's preludes display a limited number of basic formal designs, ranging from highly derivative to highly innovative:[14]

1. Through-composed, continuous form (Ex: Fantasia in C, BWV 570)
2. Through-composed, sectional form (Ex: Prelude in g, BWV 535/1)
3. Ostinato-variation form (Ex: Passacaglia in c, BWV 582)
4. Hybrid concerto form (introduction + concerto-derived movement; Ex: Toccata in C, BWV 564/1)
5. Concerto form (Ex: Toccata in d, BWV 538/1)
6. A B A B form (Ex: Prelude in f, BWV 534/1)

The through-composed, continuous, the through-composed, sectional, and the ostinato-variation plans were used by Bach's predecessors. Consequently they appear in his early, derivative preludes. After expanding and refining these methods of organization, Bach turned to new possibilities: the hybrid concerto, the concerto, and the A B A B forms. Within each prelude type it is possible to trace developments that imply a chronological sequence.

Melodic Material

In his early compositions Bach used conventional melodic material, keyboard figures similar to those found in the organ works of contemporary composers. He gradually expanded the keyboard idiom, first by incorporating material drawn from Italian instrumental practice and then by using material derived from his own cantata writing. These developments can be dated, for they reflect changes that occur in other genres. Triadic, motoric instrumental figures first appear in Weimar, where Bach was strongly influenced by Vivaldi's writing. More flexible, cantata-derived melodic material replaces Italian instrumental figures in the early Leipzig years, when Bach was preoccupied with the weekly production of vocal works.

Part-writing

Part-writing provides important chronological data, especially with regard to early compositions. The earliest works often display faulty and inconsistent part-writing. Awkward voice leading, especially between the tenor (left hand) and the bass (pedal) is common. Because of Bach's gradual mastery of contrapuntal technique, later works show excellent part-writing in four and five real voices.[15] The *Orgelbüchlein*, begun around 1713, is an important terminus in this regard, for it reflects Bach's initial success with treating parts equally. As a chronological criterion, part-writing must be used with caution, however, since Bach undoubtedly "tidied up" the inner voices of some early preludes when using them again at a later date.[16]

For this reason the fugues of works originally planned as prelude-fugue pairs supply invaluable information.[17] Once written, these fugues were less easily altered than the preludes with which they were paired. For example, they often show with extreme clarity in the initial exposition Bach's ability — or inability, as the case may be — to maintain a four or five-voice texture. In early fugues the entrance of the pedal in the first exposition usually necessitated the deletion of one of the manual voices. In later works, parts do not begin to drop out until the theme has been presented in every voice, including the pedal.

Harmonic Design

The treatment of modulation, viewed from both a detailed perspective (individual modulations) and a general perspective (overall harmonic design), provides important chronological information. Bach's earliest works display few excursions outside the tonic and dominant. Those modulations that do take place are abrupt and proceed to their harmonic goal as directly as possible. In pieces written after Bach's espousal of Italian instrumental style the individual modulations are more extended, more firmly established, and more clearly set off by cadences. As a consequence the overall harmonic design is more ambitious and includes long passages outside the tonal spheres of the tonic and dominant.

The above criteria will be applied to the individual preludes in Chapter IV. Before an attempt is made to date the works, it is necessary to examine the stylistic development of the repertoire in order to clarify the trends which have important chronological implications.

III
The Stylistic Development of the Preludes

To judge from contemporary accounts, Bach wrote organ works from a very early age onwards. The extant sources, though giving an incomplete picture of his activity in this field,[1] verify that he composed free preludes intermittently over a span of more than three decades, from the Arnstadt period (the Prelude & Fugue in g, BWV 535a, in the *Möller Handschrift*) to the later Leipzig years (the Prelude & Fugue in E♭, BWV 552, in *Clavierübung* III). During this time Bach transformed the prelude by incorporating many new ideas into his writing. Less apparent is how this stylistic evolution is to be examined. How should the preludes be grouped for study?

Since most of the works cannot be dated objectively from external evidence, it is not possible to place them in chronological order and examine them from that point of view. Thus a discussion of the "Arnstadt compositions," the "Weimar compositions," and so forth is based on assailable *a priori* assumptions.[2] Another seemingly reasonable approach would be to study the preludes in terms of specific stylistic influences, i.e., to examine the "north-German-derived works," the "Italian-derived works," etc. Bach's eclecticism, however, was far too encompassing to allow such a narrow categorization of his compositions. Many preludes represent a synthesis of several styles and therefore are too cosmopolitan to be placed under a single heading.

A third possibility is adopted here. It is to focus on one fundamental aspect of the preludes, form, and to investigate the different ways Bach approached this specific compositional problem. In the baroque, the entire process of composing was commonly referred to as the *ars inveniendi* or *Erfindungskunst*. The *ars inveniendi* consisted of four specific aspects: *Dispositio (Einrichtung*, the laying-out of the piece), *Elaboratio (Ausarbeitung*, the working out of the musical ideas), *Decoratio (Schmückung*, the embellishment of the musical ideas), and *Executio (Ausführung*, the actual execution of the piece).[3] Of these procedures, *Dispositio* was viewed as the most elemental, for it determined to a large extent the direction the others would take. Mattheson described it as:

... the pleasing arrangement of all parts and particulars in a melody or in an entire musical work. It is similar to the way one plans and marks off a building, making a sketch or draft in order to show where a hall, a sitting-room, a bedroom, and so forth, are to be placed.[4]

Dispositio, then, corresponds to the organizational plan or form which a composer employs in a musical composition. The central question in this chapter will be: When writing a prelude, how did Bach organize his musical material? Unlike the composition of fugues, the composition of preludes did not presuppose set procedures or rules. In spite of this, Bach could turn to certain models established by his predecessors. What choices did he have initially and what new solutions did he himself fashion?

The works under discussion display six basic types of organizational schemes:

1. Through-composed, continuous form
2. Through-composed, sectional form
3. Ostinato-variation form
4. Hybrid concerto form
5. Concerto form
6. A B A B form

In the first three, procedure predominates over a clearly established architectonic plan: the opening material is elaborated in an ongoing fashion without literal repetition. Of these designs, the through-composed, continuous displays a fairly uniform texture throughout (Ex: the Fantasia in C, BWV 570), the through-composed, sectional exploits the principle of textural contrast (ex: the Prelude in g, BWV 535/1), and the ostinato-variation relies on the constant reiteration of a musical phrase (Ex: the Passacaglia in c, BWV 582). In the three other forms the repetition of extended segments of material is quite important. Of these plans, the hybrid concerto combines a free introduction with a concerto-derived movement (ex: the Toccata in C, BWV 564/1), the concerto displays the alternation of ritornello and episode (Ex: the Toccata in d, BWV 538/1), and the A B A B is based on the repetition of two contrasting sections (Ex: the Prelude in f, BWV 534/1). In addition, there are several miscellaneous designs which are difficult to classify (Ex: the Fantasia in g, BWV 542/1).

With the use of form as a basis of discussion, it is possible to follow the development of the preludes on two levels. On one level one can observe how Bach continually strove to extend and refine each type of structure. On another level one can see how systematically he moved on to a new design once he had explored fully the potential of an old. Therefore, it is best to begin with the forms Bach borrowed from his predecessors before turning to those in which innovations prevail.

The Through-Composed, Continuous Form

First to be considered is the through-composed, continuous form that appears in three preludes:

>   Fantasia in b, BWV 563/1
>   Fantasia in C, BWV 570
>   Fantasia in c, BWV 562/1

The first two works, the Fantasia in b and the Fantasia in C, are closely related and have many features in common: they are of modest size, imitative, and dominated by the same rhythmic figure, ♪♪♪ . In both pieces the pedal is treated in an *ad libitum* manner.[5] What is more striking is the similar way in which form is handled: rather than joining together several contrasting sections, Bach simply extended the opening material without making any significant textual or melodic changes. The Fantasia in b has a short coda (mm. 18-24), undoubtedly to create an appropriate transition to the "Imitatio" which follows. Other than this, the two works exemplify a prelude in which procedure — the ongoing *Verzierung* of the initial melodic material — takes precedence over formal design.

This technique was commonly employed by middle- and south-German composers in the late seventeenth and early eighteenth centuries. Johann Pachelbel and J. K. F. Fischer, to name two people whose work Bach "heard and studied,"[6] wrote very similar small-scale preludes, some of which even contain the same melodic and rhythmic figures that appear in the two Fantasias.[7] Indeed, it may have been Pachelbel's application of the term "fantasia" to works of this nature that led Bach to use the same title for his pieces. In short, when Bach wrote the Fantasia in b and the Fantasia in C he adhered rather closely to conventional models and did not go beyond them in any way.

The Fantasia in c represents a more ambitious approach to the through-composed, continuous form. It is not only larger and more carefully organized than the Fantasias in b and C, but it shows new stylistic influences on Bach's writing. The melodic material, the profuse and exactingly notated ornamentation, the five-part texture, and the tonal arrangement of the imitative entries reflect techniques used in classical French organ music. In particular, de Grigny's five-part fugues, published in his *Livre d'Orgue*,[8] seem to have been Bach's model. The Fantasia's harmonic plan, however, with its carefully spaced cadences, circle-of-fifth sequences, and clearly demarked modulatory areas was derived from a very different source, contemporary Italian instrumental practice. By combining French and Italian techniques, Bach was able to control and extend his materials in a manner not possible in the Fantasias in b and C. In so doing, he went beyond his prototypes and created a larger, more highly unified prelude based on a through-composed, continuous form.

The sources reveal that Bach was not completely satisfied with two aspects of the Fantasia in c. The first is the coda of the work (mm. 76-80 of the NBA text), which was revised at least once.[9] If the Fantasia was originally intended as part of a prelude-fugue pair, then its non-imitative, rhythmically free coda[10] was doubly important: it would not only bring the Fantasia to a conclusion; it would also serve as a bridge to the ensuing fugue. The second aspect is the Fantasia's role as the prelude of a prelude-fugue pair. To judge from the sources, Bach first paired the Fantasia with the five-part Fugue in c, BWV 546/2a. He then revised the Fantasia as an independent piece. Finally, he composed—or started to compose[11]—another five-part fugue for the work. The fact that the Fantasia in c existed in so many different states may well reflect Bach's changing attitude about the piece's role as prelude to a fugue.

The Fantasias in b and C show a similar ambivalence with regard to pairing. The Fantasia in C is handed down as an independent piece in the sources. The Fantasia in b, on the other hand, is paired, but with a modest "imitatio" rather than with a full-scale fugue. It may have been Bach's early propensity for writing extensive fugues and his desire to have appropriate pieces to pair with them that led him to abandon the Pachelbel-Fischer prelude style. But even the Fantasia in c—paired, unpaired, and re-paired during Bach's lifetime—apparently did not represent an entirely ideal alternative. Bach may have felt that a prelude with a through-composed, continuous design was not the best complement for a fugue, probably because it was too similar in style.[12] Perhaps it was for this reason that he pursued this type of prelude to a very limited degree.

The Ostinato-Variation

Bach turned to the ostinato-variation principle in just two works:

Prelude in a, BWV 569
Passacaglia in c, BWV 582

Viewed in terms of its structure, the Prelude in a is a unicum in the organ repertoire. It lacks the regular repetition of a firmly established melodic figure and in this way differs from works such as the Passacaglia in c. Still, it reflects the ostinato principle because it is based on the continual reiteration of a recognizable melodic pattern. The first thirty-two measures of the Prelude, for example, consist of six periods of three, five, five, four, nine, and six measures, respectively. Even though these periods are of different length, they are perceived equally as variations. They are all based on a descending scale and they are clearly demarked by cadence and changes of figuration. Thus the classification of the Prelude as an ostinato-variation form, albeit an unorthodox one, seems justified.

In other respects the Prelude in a is much more conventional. A glance at Pachelbel's Ciacona in d or Buxtehude's Ciaconas in c and e or Passacaglia in d (all four of which appear, significantly, in the *Andreas Bach Buch*) reveals that Bach was following well-established traditions both in using certain standard types of variations and in merging several related variations into groups of two or three. In spite of this, the Prelude in a seems to fall far short of its prototypes. Its ostinato figure, never firmly established, shifts from manual to pedal in random fashion. Its harmonic structure, though encompassing, is more digressive than direct. Its variations, however different, do not show a logical and carefully planned progression. Taking all these facts into account, one is tempted to conclude that the work is a written record of an early improvisation in which spontaneity prevailed over calculated design.[13]

Why is the Prelude in a consistently labeled "prelude" in the sources? There is no reason to assume that this title meant the work was to be paired with a fugue. As a rule, contemporary ciaconas and passacaglias were independent pieces, and the Prelude, based on a similar form, undoubtedly was included in the same category. Bach may have decided to call this work "prelude" rather than "ciacona" or "passacaglia" simply because it did not fit into the usual ciacona or passacaglia scheme.

The Passacaglia in c represents a more orthodox approach to the ostinato-variation form. The work begins with an eight-measure-long theme which Bach derived from a "Trio en Passacaille" by André Raison.[14] This theme is followed in a straightforward manner by twenty variations arranged in a carefully graduated progression. Certain of the variations are interrelated, a fact that has led to a great deal of interesting speculation about the overall plan of the work.[15] Siegfried Vogelsänger has recently proposed that the variations be grouped in the following manner.[16]

Group: I   II   III   IV   V   VI   VII
Variations: 1+2   3+4+5   6+7+8   9+10+11+12   13+14+15   16+17+18   19+20

Christoph Wolff agrees with Vogelsänger about the general organization of the Passacaglia, but has suggested that the variations are related to one another in a slightly different way:[17]

Group: I   II   III   IV   V   VI   VII
Variations: 1+2   3+4+5   6+7+8+9   10+11   12+13+14+15   16+17+18   19+20

The fact that the analyses differ underlines the point that the variations are not as easily categorized as one might assume. Certain groupings are obvious: 1-2, 3-4-5, 6-7-8, 10-11, 13-14-15, 16-17-18, and 19-20. But variations 9 and 12 are of a transitional nature in the sense that they bridge the material which precedes and follows them. Therefore they might be viewed as individual links in Bach's plan:

Group: I   II   III   IV   V   VI   VII
Variations: 1+2   3+4+5   6+7+8 ← 9 → 10+11 ← 12 → 13+14+15   16+17+18   19+20

No matter which way one analyzes the Passacaglia's structure, it is clear that Bach superimposed a remarkable degree of symmetry and order on the ostinato-variation.

As was true of the Prelude in a, the Passacaglia in c shows Bach's indebtedness to existing models. The fragmentation of the ground, the grouping of variations, and the controlled use of diminutions are techniques employed by Buxtehude and Pachelbel, as mentioned above. In the Passacaglia in c, however, Bach went beyond his prototypes. The Passacaglia is longer, more complex, and more sophisticated than any contemporary ostinato movement. In the twenty variations Bach summarized the art of the ostinato form in a manner analogous to his exhaustive treatment of chaconne in the final movement of the Partita in d, BWV 1004, for unaccompanied violin.

This fact must be kept in mind when one considers the role of the Passacaglia as a prelude. Does the Passacaglia function as a prelude to the fugue which follows it? A close look at the two reveals that Bach did not treat them as a prelude-fugue pair but rather as an unusually large, highly unified ostinato form. First, the subject of the Fugue is taken note for note from the first half of the Passacaglia ostinato.[18] Second, the Passacaglia and the Fugue actually overlap with one another, since the c′ in the final chord of the Passacaglia is also the first note of the Fugue subject. Third, the Passacaglia and the Fugue are not separated by a double bar.[19] Fourth, the entire work is consistently called "Passacaglia" (or "Passacalio") rather than "Passacaglia *con Fuge*" or "Passacaglia *et*

Fuga" in the sources. All these factors imply that Bach viewed the Fugue as an extension—one might even venture to say the twenty-first variation—of the Passacaglia.

Seen in this light the Passacaglia represents a large, sophisticated ostinato form rather than a prelude-fugue pair. This point is important, for it supports the view that Bach did not consider the ostinato-variation as an ideal complement to a fugue. It may have been for this reason that he focused most of this attention on more progressive forms with greater potential for development.

The Through-Composed, Sectional Form

A design of greater consequence for Bach's prelude writing is the through-composed, sectional form that appears in twelve works:

> Prelude in C, BWV 531/1
> Prelude in c, BWV 549/1
> Prelude in A, BWV 536/1
> Prelude in e, BWV 533/1
> Prelude in G, BWV 550/1
> Prelude in g, BWV 535/1
> Prelude in a, BWV 543/1
> Prelude in a, BWV 551
> Toccata in d, BWV 565
> Toccata in E, BWV 566
> Prelude in D, BWV 532/1
> Fantasia in G, BWV 572

The first seven works, the Preludes in C, c, A, e, G, g, and a, display a single basic plan. They begin with *passaggio*,[20] or passagework, which acts as an introduction and firmly establishes the tonic. This is followed by an extended elaboration of a motive (or motives) derived from the opening material. This second section contrasts with the first by its denser texture and stricter rhythm. It is invariably the modulatory part of the prelude and either brings the work to a close or leads to free material which acts as a conclusion. This type of structure can be summarized as follows:

	Introduction	Principal Section	Conclusion
Texture:	sparse	dense	sparse
Rhythmic nature:	free	strict	free
Harmonic activity:	establishment of tonic	modulation	re-establishment of tonic

The manner in which Bach used this through-composed, sectional form can be observed in the Prelude in C. The opening pedal solo (mm. 1-10) serves as the introduction, clearly establishing the tonic. The contrapuntal elaboration of this material, first in the tonic (mm. 10-18) and then in the subdominant (mm. 18-22), constitutes the principal section. The free material which follows (mm. 34-40) acts as the conclusion. How the other six preludes fit into this pattern is shown by the following chart, which compares the contents of all seven works. In some cases the introduction can be divided into *passaggio* and transitional material; in others the closing section is absent. Nevertheless, the works are very similar in formal outline:

	Introduction		Principal Section	Conclusion
	Passaggio	Transition		
Prelude in C	mm. 1-10	–	mm. 10-34	mm. 34-39
Prelude in c	mm. 1-9	–	mm. 9-29	–
Prelude in A	mm. 1-3	mm. 4-14	mm. 14-32	–
Prelude in e	mm. 1-5	mm. 6-11	mm. 11-32	–
Prelude in G	mm. 1-23	–	mm. 23-59	–
Prelude in g	mm. 1-3	mm. 3-14	mm. 14-36	mm. 36-43
Prelude in a	mm. 1-24	mm. 24-35	mm. 35-47	mm. 47-53

The relationship between the Prelude in g, BWV 535 and its early variant, BWV 535a, demonstates how consciously Bach manipulated the through-composed, sectional form. BWV 535a, though short and perfunctory, can still be divided into an introduction (mm. 1-6, specifically labeled "passaggio" in Bach's autograph), principal section (mm. 4-15), and conclusion (mm. 15-20). When Bach transformed BWV 535a into BWV 535 he took advantage of its tripartite nature and enlarged each of its three segments:

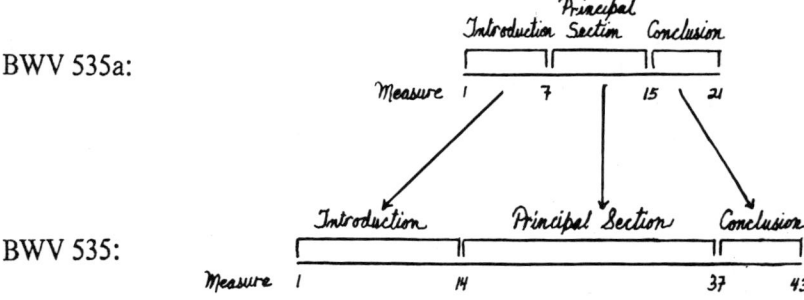

The outer sections of BWV 535 represent a reworking of the outer sections of BWV 535a. The principal section of BWV 535, while not directly derived from that of BWV 535a, is based on a similar figuration, the arpeggio. Thus in the revision Bach must have wanted to preserve the through-composed, sectional design, for he not only retained it but also expanded and formalized its parts.

The extent to which he refined the through-composed, sectional form can be seen by comparing the Prelude in e with the Prelude in a. The same formal gestures appear in both works, but they are handled with considerably more skill in the Prelude in a. For example, in both cases the introduction consists of a manual *passaggio*, a *trillo longo*, and a pedal solo. In the Prelude in e these elements are related to one another motivically, but they are separated temporally by rests. In the Prelude in a the three are skillfully tied together. The manual *passaggio*, much more extensive than that of the Prelude in e, shows a carefully graduated increase in motion (♫ → ♫♫ → ♫♫♫)[21] that forms a natural transition to the *trillo longo* (m. 23). The *trillo longo*, in turn, leads directly into the pedal solo. In the Prelude in a manual *passaggio*, *trillo longo*, and pedal solo evolve out of each other and become one extended phrase. In the Prelude in e they remain three separate entities.

The principal section of the Prelude in e consists of homophonic material presented in a series of redundant progressions. By contrast, the imitative writing in the principal section of the Prelude in a is much more concise and carefully organized. In addition, this material emerges quite naturally out of the introduction, which is not the case in the Prelude in e. Of further interest in the Prelude in a is the way Bach incorporated varying stylistic elements. The arpeggios in the introduction reflect harpsichord practice (cf. the Chromatic Fantasy in d, BWV 903/1). The imitative material in the principal section, on the other hand, is characteristic of instrumental music. By amalgamating these contrasting styles Bach was able to increase the effectiveness of the through-composed, sectional form to a degree unobtained in the Prelude in e.

What works served as models for the Preludes in C, c, A, e, G, g, and a? The through-composed, continuous compositions of middle- and south-German composers such as Pachelbel and Fischer probably did not play an important role in this case. It is more likely that north-German works, especially those of Böhm, Bruhns, and Buxtehude, stimulated Bach in the direction of the through-composed, sectional form. Böhm's *Praeludium* in C, for example, resembles Bach's preludes not only in terms of external features (cf. the Prelude in C), but also in terms of formal design. Like Bach's works, Böhm's composition displays an unmistakable prelude-fugue character. The form of the Prelude is even more significant: an introductory pedal solo is followed by a modulatory principal section. In short, the same fundamental elements which Bach used in his preludes are found in Böhm's *Praeludium.* For this reason it is especially lamentable that so few of Böhm's free organ works have survived.[22] If the *Praeludium* in C is representative of a type of form Böhm regularly employed, then his influence on Bach's prelude writing was far greater than it is generally considered today.[23]

Buxtehude's organ works obviously played an important part as well. In several of Buxtehude's multisectional *Praeludia Pedaliter*[24] the introductory material — i.e., the material that precedes the first fugue — is quite extensive and can be broken down into distinct sections. The introduction of the *Praeludium* in f# (BuxWV 146), for example, consists of three sections. The first (mm. 1-13) contains free *passaggio* and arpeggio material, the second (mm. 14-27), chordal material, and the third (mm. 27-29), cadential material. It is easy to see how Bach might have adapted the formal outline of Buxtehude's introduction for use in his own preludes. By increasing the dimensions of the sections while retaining the general design, Bach would have obtained a prelude of suitable proportions for pairing with a large and extensive fugue.

Just such an evolution can be observed in the three works Bach modeled after Buxtehude's multisectional *Praeludia Pedaliter:* the Prelude in a, BWV 551, the Toccata in d, BWV 565, and the Toccata in E, BWV 566. These compositions represent the type of *Praeludium* in which fugal material is incorporated directly into the overall design. The Prelude in a and the Toccata in E have five-part plans: free material, fugue, free material, fugue, free material. The Toccata in d, by contrast, has a three-part design: free material, fugue, free material.

Of interest here is the introductory segment of these pieces (i.e., the initial section of free material), which roughly corresponds to the "prelude" of a prelude-fugue pair. In the Prelude in a and the Toccata in d this material bears little resemblance to Bach's well-organized through-composed, sectional pieces. The introduction of the Prelude in a (mm. 1-11) is nothing more than an extended *passaggio.* The introduction of the Toccato in d (mm. 1-30), although somewhat larger, represents a chain of improvisatory gestures rather than a carefully planned prelude form.

The introduction of the Toccata in E (mm. 1-30), however, approaches the scope of an independent prelude. It can be divided into four sections: *passaggio* material (mm. 1-4), chordal material (mm. 5-8), *passaggio* material (mm. 9-13), and chordal material (mm. 14-30). Even though the part-writing in the chordal sections is somewhat chaotic, the fact that these sections are calculated to contrast with the *passaggio* is important. The textual control and the carefully rounded form mark a considerable advancement over the Prelude in a and the Toccata in d. In terms of size and independence, the introductory section of the Toccata in E could almost qualify as the prelude of a prelude-fugue pair. It is not entirely surprising to discover that Kittel or one of his students converted the Toccata in E into a prelude and fugue by writing out only the first half of the work (mm. 1-122) and labeling it "Prelude & Fugue in E"![25] This procedure would not have been possible with the Prelude in a or the Toccata in d.

One cannot assume that Bach began with the north-German multisectional *Praeludium Pedaliter* and gradually evolved the through-composed, sectional prelude from it. Several through-composed, sectional preludes—the Prelude in C, the Prelude in c, or the Prelude in e, for example—undoubtedly predate the Toccata in E.[26] Indeed, the well-developed introductory section of the Toccata in E was most probably the result of Bach's experience with the through-composed, sectional form rather than vice versa.

The final degree to which Bach expanded and formalized the through-composed, sectional form can be seen in the Prelude in D, BWV 532/1, and the Fantasia in G, BWV 572. Both works display a design that is fundamentally the same as that used in the Preludes in C, c, A, e, G, g, and a. What differs is the three sections—the introduction, the principal section, and the conclusion—are much more extensive and fully developed. They contrast not only in terms of texture, rhythmic flexibility, and harmonic activity, but also in terms of tempo (*tempo ordinario*, "allabreve," and "adagio," in the Prelude in D; "très vitement," "gravement," "lentement" in the Fantasia in G).

Equally important is the appearance of new stylistic influences. In the through-composed, sectional preludes discussed up to this point Bach adhered to north-German practice in his choice of melodic material and harmonic scheme. The melodic material reflects figurations found in Buxtehude, Bruhns, or Böhm. The harmonic plans are conservative, with little movement outside the tonic, dominant, and subdominant. In the Prelude in D, however, Bach turned to Italian practice: the melodic material and harmonic sequences of the principal section bear the stamp of Corelli's writing. In the Fantasia in G he turned to French practice: the strict five-part texture of the principal section is characteristic of French string writing. These features suggest that Bach wished not only to enlarge the through-composed, sectional form, but to expand the organ idiom as well.

The Prelude in D and the Fantasia in G represent the last stage in Bach's development of the through-composed, sectional design. In these compositions he created a type of prelude that is very large and fully independent. The Fantasia, as far as can be determined, was never paired with a fugue. The Prelude, to judge from the sources, also seems to have originated as an independent composition and was paired with the Fugue in D, BWV 532/1, at a later date.[27] In these two pieces Bach extended the through-composed, sectional design to unparalleled proportions: the Prelude is 107 measures long, the Fantasia 202 measures long. After these works he was compelled to look for new organizational possibilities.

The Hybrid Concerto Form

In Weimar Bach first had the opportunity to become well acquainted with contemporary Italian instrumental music. Through the study and transcription of Italian works available to him during those years[28] he readily assimilated the new style, quickly incorporating it into his own compositions.[29] In the realm of prelude writing this encounter was especially propitious, for it not only furnished him with a new means of treating melody, rhythm, harmony, and texture, but it also provided him with an entirely new method of organization, the concerto principle. Bach used the concerto in two different ways. He usually employed it *in toto* to produce a prelude whose overall design resembles that of a concerto movement. In other instances he combined a concerto or concerto-derived movement with a lengthy *passaggio* or *passaggio*-like introduction to create an unusual hybrid form. This form appears in three works:

Toccata in C, BWV 564/1
Toccata in F, BWV 540/1
Prelude in G, BWV 541/1

These compositions are discussed here because they stand midway between the preludes with a through-composed, sectional form and those with a straightforward concerto design. In the process of amalgamating these two types Bach faced an unusual compositional problem: how could the seemingly disparate elements, the free introduction and the strict concerto movement, be integrated in order to produce a unified work?

In the Toccata in C the division between introduction and concerto movement is quite clear. The introduction (mm. 1-32) is composed of a manual *passaggio* and a pedal solo. As noted above, manual *passaggii* and pedal solos frequently appear as opening material in through-composed, sectional preludes. Hence the presence of these elements in the Toccata in C does not represent an innovation in itself. What is unusual is the manner in which both are treated.

The manual *passaggio* is no longer a short introduction, a few measures of free material leading directly into the principal portion of the prelude. Rather it constitutes a large, carefully planned section complete in itself. In order to extend and draw out the *passaggio* material it was necessary for Bach to rely on new organizational principles, all of which were to be found in Italian instrumental music. The first of these is the treatment of rhythm. Within its original context, the *passaggio* was a rhythmically free figure. In the Toccata in C such rhythmic freedom is significantly curtailed by the use of a constant 32nd-note pulse. In this instance the 32nd-note pulse does not represent a strict rhythmic "motorization"; that is a more extreme step taken in the two other works with a hybrid concerto form, the Toccata in F and the Prelude in G. Nevertheless, it is an important change in the direction of formalizing what would normally be a rhythmically free element.

The rhythmic flexibility which does appear in the *passaggio* is written directly into the music. For example, the grouping of 32nd notes into units of six in mm. 9-10 temporarily obscures the prescribed meter, 4/4, and produces the effect of 9/16:

Mm. 9-10, as written:

Mm. 9-10, effect created:

This creates a sudden and unexpected shift in meter and thus produces the sense of freedom and flexibility one would expect to find in such a *passaggio*. It can be seen that this effect results from careful calculation on Bach's part.

The second decisive organizational factor is the underlying harmonic plan. The *passaggio* begins in the tonic, modulates towards the subdominant, and finishes back in the tonic. Thus a closed-ended harmonic structure is produced. The unequivocal full cadences at the beginning and end emphasize this tonal design and establish the tonic as a reference point for the central modulatory section. One need only compare the tentative opening of the Prelude in A, BWV 536/1, to recognize the new harmonic precepts at work in the *passaggio* of the Toccata in C.[30]

Important changes can also be observed in the pedal solo. Like the *passaggio*, it constitutes an independent section with a fully rounded harmonic plan: it begins in the tonic, modulates towards the dominant and subdominant, and ends in the tonic. In this respect it resembles the extended pedal solos of the Prelude in C, BWV 531/1 and the Prelude in c, BWV 549/1, which were discussed in connection with the through-composed, sectional form. What distinguishes the pedal solo of the Toccata from those of the other works is the unusual musical material it contains. The standard type of north-German passagework — figures in disjunct motion, tailor-made for performance by alternate feet[31] — has been significantly modified by the introduction of material of a purely melodic nature, the triplet and 32nd-note figures in conjunct motion. Moreover, the dialogue effect created at the beginning of the pedal solo is drawn directly from melodic practice. One need only compare mm. 10-12 of the Toccata with mm. 14-16 of the Adagio which follows to see the melodic origin of the pedal solo:

Adagio (melody only), mm. 10-12:

Pedal solo, mm. 14-16:

Buxtehude, Böhm, and other north-German composers incorporated pedal solos into their free *Praeludia*. Bach's attempt to make this material more cantilena-like was something quite new.

Stylistic Development

The manual *passaggio*-pedal solo introduction leads directly into the concerto movement of the Toccata. While Bach's decision to include a concerto movement in an organ prelude represents a remarkable innovation, the step seems logical in retrospect. In works such as the Prelude in a, BWV 543/1, and the Prelude in D, BWV 532/1, Bach attempted to expand the principal section of a sectional prelude while at the same time preserving its unity. The concerto form provided him with an alternative solution to this problem.

The concerto section of the Toccata in C is the most conventional concerto movement found in Bach's preludes. Its structure can be summarized as follows:

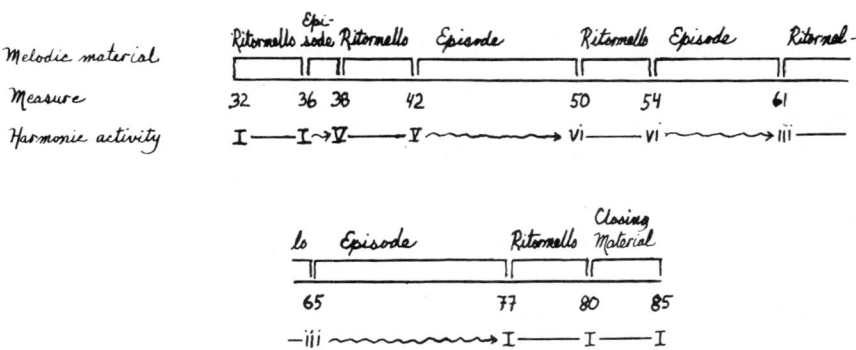

The modest proportions of the ritornello (4 mm.) and the episodes (2-12 mm.) and the orthodox nature of the form (the ritornello is never altered) suggest that this movement is one of Bach's earliest keyboard adaptations of the concerto. A strikingly similar structure is found in the first movement of the Toccata in G, BWV 916, a keyboard work whose presence in the *Andreas Bach Buch* implies an early origin. The ritornello of the G-major movement is 4 mm. long and likewise appears a total of five times (in I, V, vi, iii, and I, respectively). In addition, the episodes correspond in length almost exactly to those of the Toccata in C.

Noteworthy in the concerto movement of the Toccata in C are the motoric, sequential instrumental figurations. The principal motives of both the ritornello and the episodes are not idiomatic keyboard figures, but stem rather from Italian instrumental practice.[32] The ritornello motive is especially typical of string writing:

Ritornello motive:

Episodic motive:

What binds together the *passaggio*, the pedal solo, and the concerto movement of the Toccato? The chief unifying factor is the thematic connection between the pedal solo and the concerto movement. The motives of both ritornello and episode are introduced initially in the pedal solo, a fact that helps to explain why Bach abjured normal pedal figurations, inserting in their place melodic material that could be used in the concerto movement. Thus the introduction (or at least part of the introduction) and the principal section of the Toccata are related thematically, a characteristic that recurs to the through-composed, sectional prelude.

Aside from this, the form of the Toccata is somewhat like a pasticcio. The manual *passaggio*, the pedal solo, and the concerto movement are skillfully constructed, but they remain independent of one another. Each begins and ends in the tonic and hence has a closed harmonic plan. Each has a different rhythmic pulse: the manual *passaggio* is dominated by the thirty-second note, the pedal solo by several rhythmic units, and the concerto movement by the sixteenth note. In addition, both the manual *passaggio* and pedal solo are to be interpreted freely, *senza battuta*, while the concerto movement is to be performed *a battuta*. The rhythmic segregation of *passaggio*, pedal solo, and concerto movement and the dichotomy of free introduction and strict principal section are matters left to be resolved in the Toccata in F and the Prelude in G.

The Toccata in F can be considered a logical sequel to the Toccata in C. On the one hand the two works display a strikingly similar design, consisting of a lengthy introduction (which can be subdivided into manual and pedal sections) and a long concerto movement. On the other hand the Toccata in F represents a refinement of the compositional principles set forth in the Toccata in C. The melodic material of the Toccata in F is more clearly Vivaldi-derived, its introductory and concerto sections are more carefully unified, and its concerto section, though Italianate, departs significantly from Italian models.

Bach's new approach can be detected in the initial section of the Toccata, a manual canon (mm. 1-55). To a certain extent this passage is closely related to a manual *passaggio*, for it has a similar prefatory function. But Bach has subjected the material to such rigid melodic, rhythmic, and contrapuntal control that it can no longer be called a *passaggio* by any broadening of the term. The melodic and rhythmic nature of the passage reflect Vivaldi's influence. The melodic contour of the opening figuration, for instance, has been determined by the triad. In m. 1 the tonic is outlined, in m. 2 the dominant, in m. 3 the tonic, in m. 4 the dominant, and in m. 5 the tonic:[33]

The strict adherence to the triad and the measure by measure alternation of tonic and dominant harmonies show that in the Toccata, strong down-beat progressions determine the shape of the melodic material. As far as rhythm is concerned, the opening figuration establishes the motoric pulse that is maintained throughout most of the piece. By establishing this pulse at the beginning of the Toccata, Bach was able to use it to unite the introductory section with the concerto movement. This technique represents a significant change from the Toccata in C, in which manual *passaggio*, pedal solo, and concerto movement do not share a common atomic note value.

Forceful motoric pulses and incisive, triad-oriented melodic figures are two of the most distinctive features of Vivaldi's mature concerto writing. Bach's keyboard transcriptions reveal that he was well acquainted with three of the publications which helped to establish the Vivaldi style on the continent: *L'Estro armonico* (Op. III, 1711), *La Stravaganza* (Op. IV, 1714) and *Concerti a cinque stromenti* (Op. VII, 1716-1721).[34] Bach undoubtedly assimilated the melodic and rhythmic principles that dominate the Toccata in F from these collections.

In terms of counterpoint the entire opening passage, except for a brief 8-measure lapse, is a strict canon at the octave. Bach may have had one or both of two works in mind when he decided to remodel the traditional *passaggio* in this fashion: Buxtehude's *Praeludium* in g (BuxWV 150) or Vivaldi's Concerto in d (L'Estro armonico, #1).[35] Both compositions begin with an extended passage of imitation over a pedal point. Of the two, it seems more likely that the Vivaldi concerto served as the prototype since stylistically it is so much closer to the Toccata than is the Buxtehude *Praeludium*.

One must also take into account Bach's own penchant for contrapuntal devices, an interest that comes to the fore in Weimar in works such as the *Orgelbüchlein* chorales "In dulci jubilo," BWV 608 (a double canon), "Christe, du Lamm Gottes," BWV 619 (a canon "alla Duodecima") and "Gott, durch deine Güte," BWV 600 (a canon "all Octava").[36] The melodic, rhythmic and contrapuntal tendencies seen in the first section of the Toccata in F represent an extraordinary effort to bring the opening manual *passaggio* into tight structural control. The modicum of rhythmic freedom in the *passaggio* of the Toccata in C is totally eliminated in the canonic material of the Toccata in F.

The pedal solo, mm. 55-82, emerges directly out of the pedal point of mm. 1-55. In this way Bach provided an organic link between it and the manual canon. Moreover, the pedal solo is based on the same melodic and rhythmic motives as the canons and thus serves as an extension of the manual material. This approach is markedly different from that taken in the Toccata in C, where Bach made no attempt to link the pedal solo with the manual *passaggio*, rhythmically or melodically. In the Toccata in F both the manual canon and the pedal solo are repeated in the dominant, the former measure for measure (though in inverted counterpoint), the latter in an extended form.

Important innovations also have been made in the concerto movement of the Toccata. This movement, unlike that of the Toccata in C, is not composed of conventional ritornello and episodic sections, as it is frequently assumed.[37] The material usually cited as the ritornello (mm. 176-219, inter alia) has a much denser texture (4-7 parts) than the material usually referred to as the episode (mm. 219-238, inter alia). Indeed, the two alternate in ritornello-episode fashion. But to call the former a ritornello and the latter an episode on this basis alone does not seem entirely satisfactory since the usual harmonic roles of ritornello and episode have been reversed. The "ritornello," which should remain in one key, is modulatory, while the "episode," which should modulate, is harmonically stable. Thus Bach made a radical modification in the standard concerto form, rendering the normal terms "ritornello" and

Stylistic Development 49

"episode" invalid. For the present purpose "tutti" and "solo," respectively, will be used since they describe more accurately the nature of the material involved.

The solo sections are trios based on the motive used in the opening canons and pedal solos. In retrospect this figure (illustrated above) can be called the solo motive since it clearly represents the solo elements of the Toccata. Its transformation into a trio reflects Bach's interest in trios and trio texture, a concern that also appears to stem from his exposure to Italian music in Weimar. The Mühlhausen cantatas, for instance, do not contain trio movements while the earliest datable Weimar cantatas do.[38]

Bach's appropriation of trio texture for organ writing represents an extraordinary innovation. One does not find this crucial element of concerto style, the manipulation of two treble lines over a continuo-like bass, in the organ works of his predecessors. Among the preludes it plays an unusually important role in the Toccata in d ("Dorian"), BWV 538/1, and the Fantasia in g, BWV 542/1, as well as the Toccata in F. The Walther and Tobias Krebs copies of the so-called "Great Eighteen Chorales"[39] and Walther's copy of the Largo from Trio Sonata #5 in C, BWV 529,[40] verify that this development occurred during the Weimar years.

In the Toccata in F the trio sections refer back to the introductory material and represent a compression of the manual canons and the pedal solos. In the introduction the solo motive is presented first in the manual voices, then in the pedal alone. In the trios this material is introduced imitatively in all three parts. Thus the trios repeat in capsule form the procedures that took place in the introduction.

The tutti sections, more heterogeneous than the trios, are made up of three distinctive elements. The first is the arpeggiated figure (m. 177ff.) that marks the beginning of each section. This figure, always presented in imitation, appears only in the tutti and thus helps to set it off from the soloistic segments of the Toccata. It might well be called the tutti motive. The second element is the detached chords (mm. 197-203, inter alia) which initially appear at the conclusion of each pedal solo. The third element is the solo motive which stems from the introduction and solo sections. In the tutti the solo motive appears as a closing sequential figure. Through the use of these three diverse elements Bach constructed a tutti section which contrasts with the solo and introductory material and yet at the same time is related to it.

The above discussion can be summarized in the following diagram, which outlines the form of the Toccata in F:

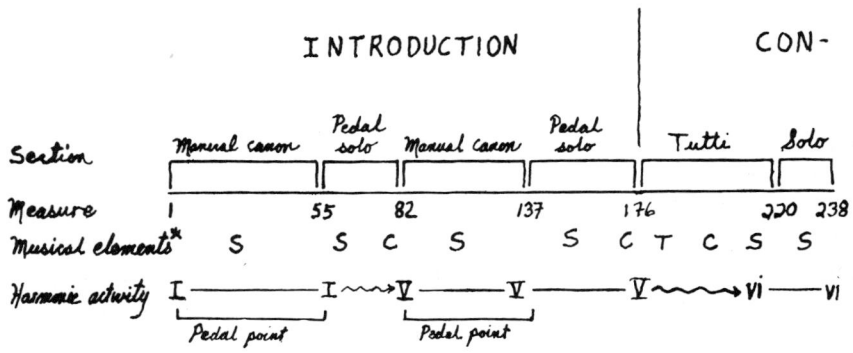

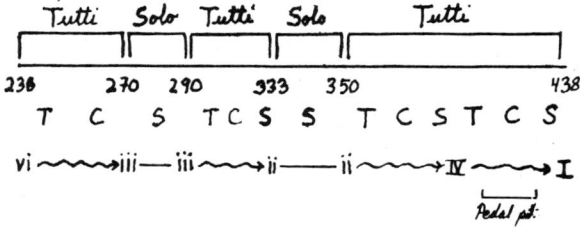

The diagram shows the remarkable extent to which the various sections and subsections of the piece are interrelated: the manual canons, the pedal solos, the tuttis, and the solos are bound together by common motives. It is also obvious that the introduction plays a crucial role in the overall harmonic design. The tonic is established in the initial manual canon rather than in the concerto movement, which begins in the dominant. Thus it would not be possible to remove the introductory material—as it would be in the Toccata in C—and have a concerto movement that is complete in itself. The integral role of the initial manual material in the overall form is also reflected in the final tutti section, where the extensive pedal point (mm. 394-416) is obviously intended to mirror the long pedal points of the introduction.

The Toccata in F represents a considerable advancement over the Toccata in C and unquestionably stems from a later date. The piece shows Bach not only had assimilated Vivaldi's concerto style and Italian trio writing, but also was able to modify these techniques for his own purposes. The form of the Toccata, while superficially reflecting that of the Toccata in C, represents an entirely new synthesis. The Toccata in C is a composite of exisiting forms. The concerto movement, separated from the introduction, would form a satisfactory composition. This would not be possible in the Toccata in F, where the concerto movement begins in the dominant. In the Toccata in F the introduction and the concerto movement have become interdependent.

The process of integration seen in the Toccata in F is carried one step further in the Prelude in G, BWV 541/1. In this work one can observe the last vestiges of the hybrid form, a concerto movement preceded by *passaggio*. But the material in the Prelude is so concise and so thoroughly integrated that the work is best described in terms of contrasting musical elements rather than in terms of introductory, ritornello, and episodic sections.

There are three principal elements in the Prelude in G. The first is the *passaggio*, represented by the opening measures (mm. 1-11). Like the solo motive of the Toccata in F, this *passaggio* displays the triadic orientation and the motoric pulse typical of Vivaldi's concerto themes. The "motorization" of the *passaggio* is confirmed by the remark "Vivace," which Bach probably added[41] as a cautionary note to remind contemporary performers to play the passage *a battuta* rather than *senza battuta*, as the line itself might have initially suggested. The "Vivace," therefore, reflects Bach's organizational intention: in order to incorporate the *passaggio* successfully into the principal section of the Prelude (m. 12ff.) it was absolutely necessary that both share the same motoric pulse as well as the same tempo.

The degree of formalization and sophistication in the Prelude in G can be seen immediately if one compares its *passaggio* with that of a work written under the influence of north-German style. The *passaggio* of the Prelude in A, BWV 536/1, for example, is quite static. It is based on a potentially strong progression (I→II→V), but it seems tentative because the rhythmic and harmonic accents obscure the downbeat. Moveover, rests interrupt the forward movement. The *passaggio* of the Prelude in G, by contrast, creates an extraordinary forward momentum. The steady flow of sixteenth notes, the carefully placed strong accents, and the effective manipulation of range produce an opening that leads forcefully into the principal material of the piece.

The following figures are the second and third elements of the Preludes:

Tutti motive:

Sequential motives:

The "tutti motive" is so named because it generally appears amidst dense, five-part texture and acts in much the same fashion as a ritornello. Here again Bach shows his indebtedness to Vivaldi, who frequently used short, concise figures with distinctive rhythmic patterns as the focal point of his concertos. Bach used a figure similar to the tutti motive in the G-Major Fugue which is paired with the Prelude and in the opening chorus from Cantata #21, *Ich hatte viel Bekümmernis* (1714).[42]

The sequential element is represented by two closely related figures. The first is derived from string writing as the following excerpt from Vivaldi's Op. III, #12, demonstrates:

The second sequential figure is a variant of the first; it is a typical pedal motive and appears only in the pedal voice in the Prelude. Both sequential figures are usually accompanied by tremolo chords (mm. 16-17, inter alia).

Stylistic Development

Taking into account these principal elements, the overall organization of the Prelude in G can be diagrammed as follows:

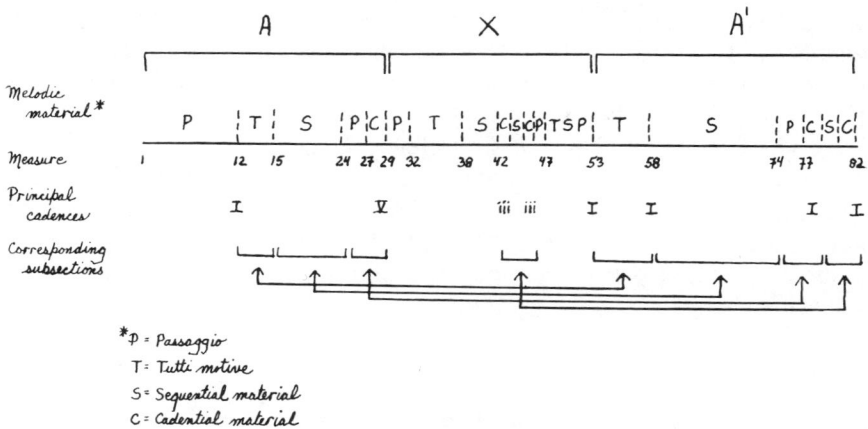

This schema shows that the form of the Prelude, while ostensibly *passaggio*-concerto movement, is, in fact, something quite different. The thorough integration of *passaggio*, tutti, and sequential elements produces instead a large three-part structure, A-X-A'. The basic arrangement of the material in A and A' is a logical one: tutti motive→sequential material→*passaggio*→cadential material. These same elements appear in X, but the cadence occurs in the middle, surrounded by tutti, sequential, and *passaggio* material. The end result is a form which displays remarkable symmetry. If one includes the opening *passaggio* in A, the two outer sections are evenly balanced: A = 29 mm., A' = 30 mm. This balance is emphasized by the fact that A' is an elaborated version of A, with the cadential material transposed from the dominant to the tonic. The corresponding subsections of A and A' are marked in the diagram.

In addition, the two cadences (both in iii) which occur in the middle of X bracket the center of the Prelude and emphasize the axial nature of the overall structure. The resulting tripartite design is not unlike that of the first movement of Brandenburg Concerto No. 4 in G. The Brandenburg movement is much more expansive than the Prelude in G; furthermore, it is a literal da capo form. Nevertheless, the tendency towards a symmetrical plan is the same in both works.

The degree to which the various elements of the Prelude are integrated is remarkable. The changes in texture are extremely subtle, and this helps to create a sense of homogeneity. In the Toccata in F the tutti sections were characterized by a 4-7 voice texture and the solo sections by a 3-voice texture. No such distinctions are possible in the Prelude in G, where the texture constantly vacillates between 1-, 3-, 4-, and 5-part writing. It is the *passaggio* element and the repeated chords—both equally ubiquitous—that enable Bach to shift textures so quickly. The chief organizational factor is the cadence, which dictates a tripartite division of the work.

The Prelude in G is one of the few preludes for which it is possible to follow Bach's minute revisions over an extended period of time.[43] These revisions do not involve the overall form of the work, which apparently satisfied the composer from the start. Rather, they concern matters of detail. For example, the chords in mm. 21-24 show the following change:

The alteration illustrates Bach's efforts to improve the part-writing in the Prelude, even to the point of imbuing chords with a contrapuntally interesting part (bracketed above). The motive created by the change appears elsewhere (m. 49, m. 73) and thus reflects his concern for unifying the work as much as possible.

The Toccata in C, the Toccata in F, and the Prelude in G demonstrate Bach's shift from Buxtehudian to Vivaldian precepts in the course of refining the hybrid concerto form. The principal problem posed by this design, the integration of a *senza battuta* introduction with an *a battuta* concerto movement, was solved effectively in the Toccata in F and the Prelude in G by "motorizing" the introductory material and incorporating it into the concerto movement itself. At the same time the traditional ingredients of the concerto, ritornello and episode, were reinterpreted in order to accommodate the material drawn from the introduction. While the Toccata in C reflects certain prototypes, the Toccata in F and the Prelude in G point in an entirely new direction. In the Toccata in F, introduction and concerto movement are carefully integrated in a large, expansive structure. In the Prelude in G, introduction and concerto movement are reduced to quintessential gestures and merged to such a degree that the hybrid form is transformed almost beyond recognition into an unusually concise three-part plan.

The Concerto Form

The Toccata in C, the Toccata in F, and the Prelude in G illustrate how Bach combined the concerto with a free introduction to produce a prelude whose general design shows remnants of the through-composed, sectional form. In seven other works he abandoned this amalgamative plan and focused his attention on writing a concerto movement *per se*. The preludes which reflect this procedure are:

> Prelude in G, BWV 568
> Toccata in d ("Dorian"), BWV 538/1
> Prelude in C ("9/8"), BWV 547/1
> Prelude in e, BWV 548/1
> Prelude in b, BWV 544/1
> Prelude in c, BWV 546/1
> Prelude in E♭, BWV 552/1

The feature which all these works have in common is a concerto-derived construction: a distinct ritornello, stated at the outset of the piece, alternates with episodic material. Aside from this, the preludes are remarkably individual and represent quite different approaches to one basic formal design.

The Prelude in G is somewhat of an enigma as far as placement within Bach's prelude oeuvre is concerned. The careless doublings, the parallel octaves, and the overly abrupt modulations imply that the composition is one of Bach's very early works. In addition, the typically north-German manner of handling the pedal and the clavier-derived manual figurations, characteristic of Reinken or Böhm, indicate that the piece predates Bach's adoption of the Italian instrumental idiom in Weimar. Still, the Prelude is organized along the lines of a concerto movement. The opening material (mm. 1-6), used to establish the tonic at the beginning of the work, returns three more times, in the dominant, the sub-dominant, and once again in the tonic. In doing so, it functions as a ritornello. The material in between, derived from this ritornello, is modulatory and episodic. Thus the Prelude in G adheres to the structural tenets of the concerto, as can be seen in the following diagram of the piece:

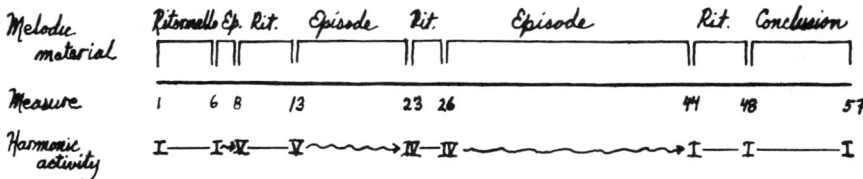

Whence did Bach derive the technique seen in the Prelude in G? Vivaldi was certainly not the source, for the Prelude displays the type of north-German organ idiom which Bach abandoned after encountering Vivaldi's works in Weimar. In the years preceding that time, however, he must have been familiar with the instrumental music of the pre-Vivaldi generation of Italian composers: Corelli, Torelli, Legrenzi, and others. In the Fugue in c, BWV 574, Bach used a theme by Legrenzi as the basis for a piece written in a typically north-German fashion.[44] In a similar manner, when writing the Prelude in G he may have borrowed the ritornello principle from the pre-Vivaldi Italians without adopting their instrumental idiom.

An alternative explanation would be that the form of the Prelude in G represents an extension of the technique used by Pachelbel in his pedal toccatas. For instance, Pachelbel's Toccata in C,[45] a work probably known to Bach,[46] is built upon three extended pedal points, on the tonic, the dominant, and the tonic respectively. The principal thematic material appears at the beginning of each pedal point to mark the arrival of a new tonal center, much in the same manner as the ritornello of a concerto form. By expanding the tonal plan of such a piece and by adding episodic material, Bach would have ended up with a work not unlike the Prelude in G. The frequent use of pedal points in the Prelude lends a certain credence to this hypothesis.

Stylistic Development 57

It is also possible that the Prelude in G is not a work by Bach. It is difficult to reconcile chronologically the piece's disparate elements. The compositional shortcomings and north-German figurations suggest the pre-Weimar years. The concerto form, however, points to a later period. These incongruities have no parallel in Bach's oeuvre. For the moment this matter will be left open. Firmer conclusions about the Prelude's authenticity will be drawn in Chapter IV, where the source material will also be taken into account.

The Toccata in d, the so-called "Dorian," represents another stage in the development of the concerto form. The work is quite unlike the Prelude in G. The part-writing alone suggests that it is a far more mature composition. More specifically, the presence of instrumental figurations, the reliance on a motoric pulse, and the handling of ritornello and episode indicate that it was written at a period when Bach was working under the immediate effect of Vivaldi's style.

The melodic material, for example, has an unmistakably Vivaldian stamp. The opening motive displays all the distinctive characteristics of Vivaldi's themes: it is concise, rhythmically incisive, harmonically unambiguous, and motivically fecund:

Similar figures appear in the Toccata in F, BWV 540/1, and the Prelude in G, BWV 541/1, as noted above. In the Toccata in d, however, Bach practiced extraordinary economy, for the single 1/2-measure-long motive provides the melodic kernel that serves as the basis for all the ritornello and episodic material. This motive appears in almost every measure of the piece. Combined with an unceasing 16th-note pulse, it unifies the entire prelude and provides an unusual degree of homogeneity.

The Toccata is a pivotal work as far as form is concerned, for many of its structural features reappear in the remaining concerto-derived preludes, even in those written long after Bach had turned away from Vivaldi's direct influence. The structure of the Toccata can be outlined as follows:

Melodic material	Ritornello	Episode	Ritornello	Episode	Ritornello	Episode	Ritornello	Closing Material
Measure	1	13	25	37	47	66	81	99 99
Harmonic activity	i	i →v	v	v →iv →vii→VI →V			i	i — i

The ritornello, 13-1/2 measures long in its initial form, is considerably larger than that of the Toccata in C, BWV 564/1. By expanding this opening material, Bach was able to enlarge the entire prelude while at the same time reducing the overall number of ritornello sections. In the Toccata in d the ritornello appears four times. At the beginning and end of the work it establishes the tonic. In mm. 25-37 it establishes the dominant. In mm. 47-66, however, it touches on several keys: G minor, C minor, and B♭ major. The structural pattern thus created—ritornello in the tonic, ritornello in the dominant, ritornello in several keys (i.e., a modulatory ritornello section), and ritornello in the tonic—becomes the standard for the other preludes with a concerto form. It is used unchanged in the Preludes in e and b, and with slight modifications in the Preludes in C, c, and E♭.

Certain formal features of the episodes are equally significant for Bach's later style. The most striking of these is the creation of distinct segments of episodic material. After being established in one episode, these segments are repeated note for note at a different pitch level in another. Two such segments can be observed in the Toccata. The first, labeled e^1 in the diagram above, appears in mm. 37-43 and again in mm. 66-73. The second, labeled e^2 in the same diagram, appears in mm. 43-47 and mm. 73-78. Although both segments move sequentially through the circle of fifths, they contain distinctly different elaborations of the principal motive of the Toccata.

Like the expansion of the ritornello, the repetition of entire segments of episodic material facilitated the enlargement of the prelude. Moveover, it added new possibilities for unification. On one level the Toccata is united through the use of motor rhythm and a ubiquitous melodic motive. On a second level it is unified through the use of recurrent ritornello sections. But on still another level it is united by the repetition of distinctive segments of episodic material.

In terms of structure of Prelude in C ("9/8"), BWV 547/1, represents the logical continuation of the principles set forth in the Toccata in d. The Prelude contains one additional ritornello section and one additional episode. Nevertheless, the overall design of the piece closely parallels that of the Toccata. With regard to the ritornello, the first and last sections establish the tonic, the second establishes the dominant, and the third and fourth (rather than just the third) are modulatory. This can be seen in the following diagram of the work:

The episodes of the Prelude also follow the pattern found in the Toccata in d. The first episode, based on ritornello motives, is quite short (5 measures) and modulates quickly to the dominant. The second episode is longer and contains a new series of sequences (mm. 25-30). This segment of sequential material, labeled e^1 in the above diagram, is used again at a different pitch level in the third and fourth episodes. Hence the same method of construction used in the Toccata in d — short episode (free), long episode (sequential segment established), long episode (sequential segment repeated) — is employed in the Prelude. The introduction of corresponding segments or blocks of episodic material has important ramifications in the preludes yet to be discussed.

A third feature that links the Prelude in C to the Toccata in d is the unusual harmonic coloring created by the use of parallel modes. In the Toccata both C major and C minor are used. In the Prelude this technique is expanded, with the result that several pairs of keys are touched upon: C major and C minor, F major and F minor, and G major and G minor. As representatives of the tonic, subdominant, and dominant, respectively, C major, F major, and G major naturally would receive emphasis in a piece in C major. The parallel minors of these keys would not, however. Consequently they represent steps outside the normal baroque hierarchy of related tonalities.

While reflecting the Toccata in d in general outline, the Prelude in C differs significantly in detail. This can be seen most clearly in the construction of the ritornello. The ritornello of the Toccata consisted of a somewhat free expansion of a short motive over a space of 13 measures. The ritornello of the Prelude is much more concise and tightly knit. It is based on a series of four motives, here termed w, x, y, and z, initially presented in the soprano:

Each of these four motives has its own distinctive rhythmic and melodic character and for this reason maintains its own identity throughout the piece. Nevertheless, the motives complement and reflect one another in a most remarkable way. For example, the first and third, w and y, move in conjunct motion. The second and fourth move in disjunct motion. Both y and z stem from the initial motive, w: y is an elaboration of the scale, while z emphasizes the pivotal notes, c, e, and g.

The construction of a relatively compact ritornello from a chain of short motives is a technique Bach used elsewhere. The most analogous example, perhaps, is the first movement of Brandenburg Concerto No. 2 in F, whose ritornello is similarly built upon a series of different but closely related motives, x, y, and z, presented one after another:

The ritornello of the Prelude in C has yet another element of sophistication. In addition to the melodic interrelationships in its thematic material, the entire chain of motives is constructed so that it forms invertible counterpoint with itself at the distance of one measure and at the interval of an octave. In short, the ritornello of the Prelude in C displays a degree of melodic and contrapuntal subtlety that surpasses that of Toccata in d.

Another refinement can be observed in the treatment of rhythmic pulse. In the Toccata in d a sixteenth-note pulse is relentlessly maintained. In the Prelude in C rhythmic subdivisions are handled more flexibly, with the smallest unit constantly shifting back and forth between the eighth note and the sixteenth note. For a brief period, mm. 77-79, even these values are suspended in favor of the quarter note.

Stylistic Development

The type of melodic material used in the Prelude in C can be found in several of Bach's other keyboard works, invariably pieces in 6/8 or 9/8 meter. One of the earliest of these, the Prelude of English Suite No. 6 in d, BWV 811, contains figurations very similar to those of the Prelude in C. The period of composition for the Suite, Cöthen or early Leipzig, as well as that of Brandenburg Concerto No. 2, ca. 1719, reinforce the view that the Prelude in C, which resembles these two works in crucial details, represents a slightly later phase of writing than the purely Vivaldi-oriented Toccata in d.[47]

The Preludes in e and b, BWV 548/1 and 544/1, mark a more radical change in Bach's approach to the concerto form. The two preludes rely on the ritornello principle and in this way show an indebtedness to the concerto-derived works discussed thus far. They are separated from these works by two important factors, however. The first is the type of melodic material they contain and the second is the manner in which their ritornello and episodic sections are organized.

In both preludes Bach turned away from the motoric triadic themes associated with Vivaldi's instrumental works. Replacing them are figures which are more suggestive of vocal writing. This is especially evident in the Prelude in e, which begins not with incisive imitation, as do the Preludes in C and d, but rather with a four-measure-long melody accompanied by homophonic chords. The result is a cantilena opening uncharacteristic of instrumental ritornelli. The Prelude in b begins in a quasi-imitative fashion, but here, too, a melody soon emerges in the soprano voice (m. 3ff.), accompanied by chordal material in the lower parts.

The melodic lines in both preludes have a recitative-like flexibility, and indeed, many Baroque composers labeled this type of instrumental writing "recitativo."[48] One finds this distinctive style in the instrumental parts of Bach's Leipzig vocal works. The solo violin in the aria "Erbarme dich" from the St. Matthew Passion (1729 or possibly 1727[49]), for instance, displays figurations quite similar to those of the Preludes in e and b:

Other examples include the arias "Stürmt nur, stürmt, ihr Trübsalswetter" from Cantata #153, *Schau lieber Gott, wie meine Feinde* (1724), and "Ich traue seiner Gnaden" from Cantata #97, *In allen meinen Thaten* (1734). The above-illustrated idiom, appropriated for use in a keyboard work, is not unique to the Preludes in e and b. It also appears in the Allemande of Partita No. 3 in a (1725) and the 25th variation of the *Goldberg Variations* (ca. 1742), to name two well-known examples. Among the other free organ works it appears in one notable case, the Fantasia in g, BWV 542/1.[50] But in all these keyboard pieces the recitative-like melody is either maintained throughout or segregated sectionally from other material. In the Preludes in e and b it is immediately integrated with figures more typical of keyboard writing. Such a combinatorial process—something quite foreign to the preludes discussed up to this point—represents a most unusual synthesis of idioms.

A close look at the ritornello of the Prelude in e reveals precisely how this is achieved. Initially (A, below) the opening melody, x, appears with chordal accompaniment. Next (B, below), x is fragmented and presented imitatively in the soprano and alto. Below this imitation continues the octave pedal figure, now inverted, joined by a new descending scalar figure, y, in the tenor. The sequential pattern of y suggests an instrumental origin, and in point of fact similar figures can be found in Vivaldi's concertos, in the instrumental ritornelli of Bach's concerto-derived keyboard works (cf. the Prelude of English Suite No. 3 in g, BWV 808). Finally (C, below), the soprano melody, stripped of its sixteenth notes, is transformed into a typical instrumental motive and combined with yet another figure, z, which is idiomatic of organ writing:

Similar stages can be observed in the Prelude in b.

The metamorphosis of idiom seen within the ritornelli of the two preludes was undoubtedly brought about by the exigencies of the concerto form. It would have been extremely difficult to sustain a cantilena texture for an entire concerto movement. By combining the opening melody with figures having more contrapuntal and sequential potential Bach was able to create an expansive and motivically rich ritornello.

The second aspect of the preludes to be considered is the manner in which the ritornello and episodes are constructed. The ritornelli of both works are strikingly large. These augmented proportions are the result of an unusual segmented design. The ritornello of the Prelude in e (mm. 1-19, illustrated above), is divided into two main segments, r1 (mm. 1-7) and r2 (mm. 7-19). R1, which contains the principal thematic material (i.e., the recitative-like melody), establishes the tonic and ends on a half cadence. The half cadence bridges r1 with r2, which contains sequential material that moves through the circle of fifths to a strong cadence in the tonic.

The opening ritornello of the Prelude in b (mm. 1-17) exhibits a similar construction. R1 (mm. 1-7), which contains the principal melodic material, establishes the tonic and ends on a half cadence. R2 (mm. 7-17), comprising sequential material, moves through the circle of fifths to a full cadence in the tonic. Diagrammatically the ritornello of both works can be summarized in the following way:

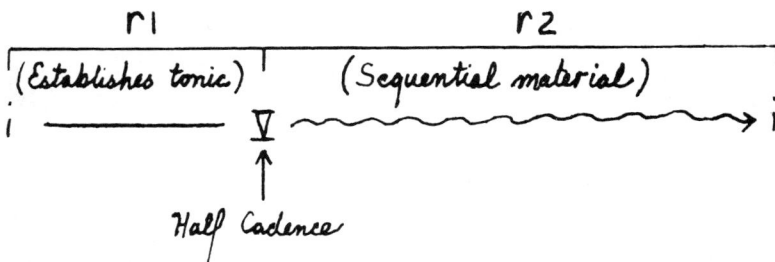

The division of the opening ritornello into two main segments, each with differing melodic material and harmonic function, has important consequences in the remainder of the prelude. After it has been presented in the initial measures the ritornello can be represented by any one of three forms: its complete form (r1 + r2), an abbreviated form (r1 or r2), or a reshuffled form (r2 + r1, etc.). This block-like manipulation can be seen most distinctly in the Prelude in e, in which the ritornello appears as follows:

Measure	Ritornello Form	Key(s)
1-19	Complete: r1 + r2	e
33-51	Complete: r1 + r2	b
81-90	Abbreviated: r1, r1	G, a
125-137	Abbreviated: r2	e

The above tabulation also reveals that the modulatory ritornello section, a feature of the Toccata in d and the Prelude in C, is retained in the Prelude in e.

The handling of the ritornello in the Prelude in b is slightly more complicated because some of the sequential material in r2 is altered during the course of the work. Nevertheless, the overall plan is remarkably similar to that of the Prelude in e:[51]

Measure	Ritornello Form	Key(s)
1-17	Complete: r1 + r2	b
27-43	Complete: r1 + r2'	f#

50-73	Reshuffled: r2″ + r1 + r2″	D, e
78-85	Abbreviated: r2‴	b

The result of this procedure is expansion by amalgamation. By joining together different but closely related segments of material, Bach succeeded in enlarging the ritornello without producing the type of monothematic repetition that characterizes a work such as the Toccata in d. Using this method of organization, he could achieve variety either by altering the melodic material or by shifting the individual ritornello segments.

A block-like construction also obtains in the episodes of the two preludes. In the Preludes in e five distinct types of episodic material—each derived from the ritornello—can be distinguished: e1 (mm. 19-24), e2 (mm. 24-27), e3 (mm. 27-33), e4 (mm. 51-55), and e5 (mm. 51-61). The three episodes of the Prelude, all quite extensive, result from stringing together these short episodic segments in bead-like fashion. The exact makeup of each episode can be summarized as follows:

	Measure	Contents
Episode #1	19-33	e1,e2, e3
Episode #2	51-81	e4,e1,e5,e4,e1,e4,e3′
Episode #3	90-125	e4,e2,e3,e2,e1,e4,e1

In the Prelude in b a single six-measure-long segment of material (mm. 17-23), here labeled e, serves as the basis for all three episodes:

	Measure	Contents
Episode #1	17-27	e, plus four measures of sequential material
Episode #2	43-50	e
Episode #3	73-78	e

The formal consolidation of episodic material was not initiated in the Preludes in e and b. The technique is foreshadowed in the Toccata in d and the Prelude in C, where sequential material established in episode #2 reappears in subsequent episodic sections. But in both these compositions the degree of unification between episodic sections falls far below that in the Preludes in e and b. Hence the Preludes in e and b represent the logical extension of an earlier procedure and reflect Bach's desire to bring episodic as well as ritornello material under tighter thematic control.

Whence did Bach derive the constructional technique that appears in these works? The most obvious prototype can be found among Vivaldi's concertos, many of which rely upon a remarkably similar procedure. For instance, the first movement of the Concerto in a for Two Violins and Strings (Ryom 522), a work Bach transcribed for organ (=BWV 593), has a ritornello composed of five segments: r1 (mm. 1-3), r2 (mm. 4 and 5), r3 (mm. 6-8), r4 (mm. 9-13), and r5 (mm. 14-16).[52]

The first two segments, r1 and r2, are closely related to one another (by the metamorphosis of the rhythmic figure ♪♫♪ into ♪♫♪) and establish the tonic. The third, r3, consists of sequences. R4 and r5, which contain similar material, re-establish the tonic and bring the ritornello to a conclusion. The episodes also display distinct segments of material, e1 and e2, which reappear intermittently in the movement. The overall structure of the piece can be diagrammed as follows:

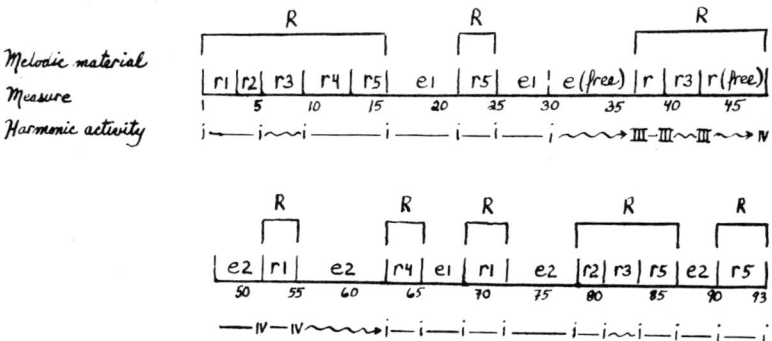

It is obvious from the above that Vivaldi's more sophisticated works such as the A-minor Concerto provided Bach with a model for the constructional technique found in the Preludes in e and b. It is equally clear that Bach's two compositions, in addition to containing an entirely different type of thematic material, also represent a refinement of Vivaldi's scheme. In both works the initial ritornello consists of two large segments, opening and sequential, rather than several small ones. Moreover, the total number of ritornello sections in the entire piece has been reduced to four, and each of these is proportionately larger than those in Vivaldi's movement. In short, Bach consolidated Vivaldi's sectional ritornello in order to unify its internal structure and at the same time to set it off more clearly from the episodic material.

The refinements found in the two organ preludes undoubtedly stem from Bach's experience in other genres. His own instrumental concertos must have provided him with numerous models, though the influence is not as direct as might be expected. The ritornelli of the Brandenburg Concertos, for example, are not constructed along precisely the same lines: either they are much more concise, composed of a chain of short motives (cf. the ritornelli of the first movements of Concertos No. 1, 2, 3, 5, and 7), or they are much more expansive on account of the immediate elaboration of material by the concertino instruments (cf. the ritornello of the first movement of Concerto No. 4). In either case the ritornelli do not exhibit the same inner design found in the preludes.

The Leipzig cantatas, on the other hand, hold a more important clue to Bach's development of this particular type of form. Because of the demands of his position as *Thomaskantor*, Bach produced cantatas at a rate of approximately one per week during his initial years in Leipzig.[53] Considered in its entirety, this repertoire contains an extraordinary number of ritornello forms. Indeed, the weekly production of cantatas in the initial Leipzig years must have provided Bach with experience in the art of ritornello writing that far exceeded that gained from the composition of instrumental works *per se*. Within this enormous corpus of ritornello movements, the opening choruses of the cantatas shed important light on the Preludes in e and b.[54]

Many of the opening choruses of the so-called chorale-cantatas[55] of *Jahrgang* II (1724-1725) exhibit lengthy ritornelli[56] that are constructed quite like those of the Preludes in e and b. Such cantata ritornelli, appearing especially in conjunction with *cantus firmus* technique, are similarly composed of two or more segments, each containing closely related but distinctive melodic material. Moreover, the segments have different harmonic functions: invariably the first, r1, establishes the tonic while those following it, r2, r3, etc., present a series of sequences.

The advantage of this type of ritornello within the framework of a *cantus firmus* movement is obvious. Once the complete ritornello is presented at the beginning of the piece, any or all of its segments can be used almost without change as interludes between phrases of the chorale. After the entire chorale is presented the ritornello is repeated in its full form. The following scheme is produced by this procedure:

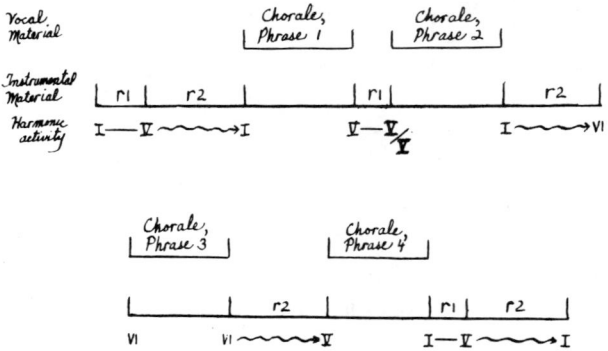

The factor that usually determines precisely which segment or segments are called into play in a particular interlude is the harmonic direction of the interlude itself. If an interlude is to begin and end in the same key, the stable segment of the ritornello, r1, is used. If an interlude is modulatory, a sequential segment, r2, r3, etc. is employed.

Two specific examples should help clarify the way this technique works in practice. The 16-measure-long ritornello of the opening chorus of Cantata #140, *Wachet auf ruft uns die Stimme* (1731),[57] is made up of three segments, r1 (mm. 1-4), r2 (mm. 5-8), and r3 (mm. 9-16). R1 is harmonically stable, whereas r2 and r3 are sequential. Within the opening chorus, whenever an interlude begins and ends in the same key, either r1 or the entire ritornello is employed. Whenever a modulatory interlude is called for, r2 or r2 + r3 is used.[58]

Another piece, the opening chorus of Cantata #3, *Ach Gott, wie manches Herzeleid* (1725), has a ritornello that can be broken down into two parts, r1 (mm. 1-5), and r2 (mm. 6-11). R1 establishes the tonic (mm. 1-3) and quickly modulates to the dominant (mm. 4-5), while r2 moves through a series of sequences, eventually making a cadence back in the tonic. The general construction of this ritornello, its inner proportions (r1:r2 equals approximately 1:2), and the formal gestures used in r1 (melodic material presented over a tonic pedal) all reflect to an extraordinary degree the ritornelli of the Preludes in e and b. In the opening chorus of the Cantata the ritornello appears in just two forms: r1 + r2 and r1 alone. In all cases the harmonic function of the two segments remains intact—i.e., r1 always establishes a key and r2 always modulates sequentially back to the tonal center established in r1. Schematically the opening chorus of Cantata #3 looks like this:

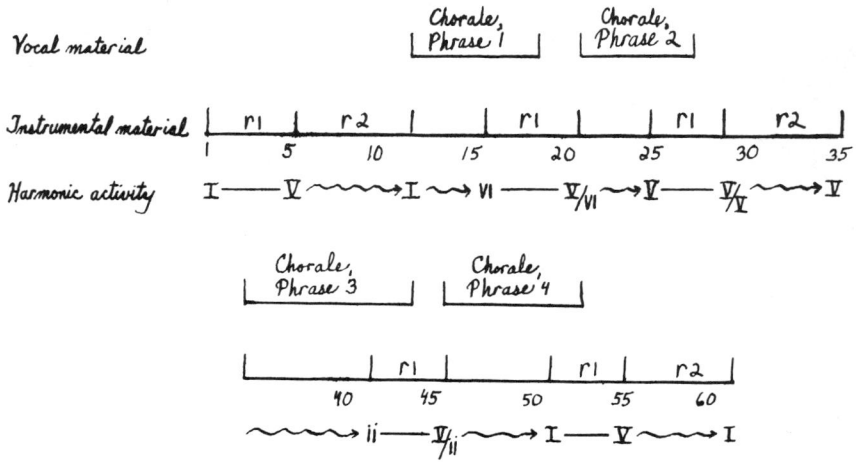

Obviously the analogy between the opening choruses and the organ preludes has its limits. In the cantatas, episodes are replaced by vocal material, which adds a new dimension to the genre and determines to a great extent the melodic and harmonic shape of the ritornello. Nevertheless, it may well be that the expansive, segmented ritornello which Bach developed in his cantatas served as the prototype for the ritornelli of the Preludes in e and b. As pointed out above, much of the melodic material in the preludes reflects an instrumental style appearing in the Leipzig vocal works. It does not seem illogical that Bach also would have turned to his cantatas for certain refinements of prelude design.

The Preludes in e and b represent a remarkable shift in Bach's treatment of the concerto form. In these two compositions the effect of the Italian concerto, so pervasive in the Toccata in d, is tempered by the influence of vocal writing. In the last two preludes having a concerto form, the Prelude in c, BWV 546/1, and the Prelude in E^b, BWV 552/1, the movement away from Italian instrumental practice is even more pronounced.

The Prelude in c, like the Preludes in e and b, has melodic material which reflects vocal practice. The opening measures of the composition are derived from double chorus writing, a style Bach seems to have employed during just one period of his life, the initial six years in Leipzig. *Singet dem Herrn ein neues Leid,* BWV 225, *Der Geist hilft unsrer Schwachheit auf,* BWV 226, *Fürchte dich nicht, ich bin bei dir,* BWV 228, and *Komm, Jesu, komm,* BWV 229, the only motets Bach wrote for double chorus, can be assigned with assurance to the period 1723-1729.[59] The St. Matthew Passion, of course, dates from this time as well.

The precise technique adopted in the Prelude in c — the dialogue-like alternation of chordal material between two different choruses — appears most straightforwardly in the opening measures of *Komm, Jesu, komm*, possibly the earliest of the six motets, and in *Ich lasse dich nicht,* BWV Anh. 159, a work for double chorus which Bach apparently studied as preparation for his own efforts in this genre.

It is worth noting that the double-chorus dialogue technique used in *Komm, Jesu, komm* and *Ich lasse dich nicht* can also be observed in the opening chorus of Cantata #47, *Wer sich selbst erhöhet, der soll erniedriget werden* (1726), whose initial measures closely resemble the beginning of the Prelude in c. In the motet *Komm, Jesu, komm* a dialogue is created by the use of two choruses. In the cantata movement the same effect is produced by split orchestration, i.e., by distributing the

70   *The Organ Preludes of J. S. Bach*

chordal material between two contrasting instrumental groups, the strings and the woodwinds. In the prelude a similar result is gained by the use of different ranges of the same manual:

Komm, Jesu, komm:

Cantata 47:

Prelude in c:

The close relationship of these three passages has chronological implications which will be considered in the next chapter.

A second melodic feature linking the Prelude in c with vocal practice is the "sigh" or "lamentation" motive which also appears in the work's opening measures. This motive, termed *suspiratio* by baroque theorists, was one of the standard rhetorical figures used in vocal music throughout the seventeenth and eighteenth centuries. Although initially a vocal motive employed for the purpose of text painting, it was also employed as an expressive device in instrumental accompaniments of vocal works. This can be seen, for example, in the chorus "O Mensch bewein dein Sünde gross" from the St. Matthew Passion. Transferred to the keyboard, the *suspiratio* also proved to be an excellent means of textual exegesis in chorale preludes such as *Nun komm der Heiden Heiland*, BWV 659, or *Dies sind die zehn heil'gen Gebot'*, BWV 678. It also appears in a purely programmatic context in Bach's Capriccio in B♭ "sopra la lontananza del suo fratello dilettissimo," BWV 992, where it is used to portray sadness in the Adagissimo movement, a "general Lamento of the friends."

In Bach's free organ works the *suspiratio* appears less frequently. It can be found in only two pieces, the Prelude in c and the Fantasia in c, BWV 537/1. Although it is significant that both the Prelude and the Fantasia are in C minor, the key Mattheson termed "extremely sweet as well as also sad,"[60] it does not follow that Bach wished to imbue the two compositions with programmatic overtones. It is more logical to ascribe the appearance of the *suspiratio* to his desire to expand the prelude idiom, a trend already observed in the Preludes in e and b.

Equally important in connection with the choice of melodic material is the manner in which rhythm is treated. The Preludes in e and b, it has been noted, reflect Bach's attempt to loosen the rhythmic constraints imposed by motoric figures. In the Prelude in c he further escapes the monorhythmic approach by introducing within the first twenty measures of the piece an extraordinary range of rhythmic units: the half note and the quarter note in mm. 1-4, the eighth note in mm. 5-9, the triplet in mm. 10-12, and the sixteenth note in mm. 19-20. Since most concerto-derived compositions are limited to one or two rhythmic subdivisions, the sudden appearance of five different rhythmic units in the Prelude in c can only betoken Bach's conscious attempt to bring unprecedented rhythmic flexibility to the concerto-derived prelude.[61] Within the ritornello the five rhythmic units create a remarkable accelerando effect:  . This is a very unusual technique and does not seem to have been used to the same extent in any of Bach's other keyboard ritornelli.[62]

In the episodes the center of rhythmic interest is shifted from the horizontal to the vertical. Horizontally a constant triplet motion is maintained throughout and therefore no accelerando is created. Vertically, however, three of the rhythmic units presented in the ritornello, the half note, the quarter note, and the triplet, are juxtaposed in a new manner. In this way the episode is clearly set off from the ritornello even though it is derived from the same note values:

Ritornello:

Episode:

This type of rhythmic integration represents a refinement that cannot be found in any other Bach prelude.

The structure of the Prelude in c reflects the technique employed in the Preludes in e and b. Once again a segmented ritornello is used: r1 (mm. 1-5), r2 (mm. 5-12), and r3 (mm. 13-25). R1, containing the double chorus material, establishes the tonic. R2, containing the *suspiratio*, ends on the dominant. R3, containing sequential material, brings the section to a close in the tonic. It should be noted that the proportions of the ritornello in so far as harmonic structure is concerned are slightly different from those of the Preludes in e and b. In the ritornelli of the Preludes in e and b the dominant is reached or emphasized at the one-third mark. In the Prelude in c this occurs at precisely the half-way point, producing a perfectly balanced, symmetrical harmonic plan:

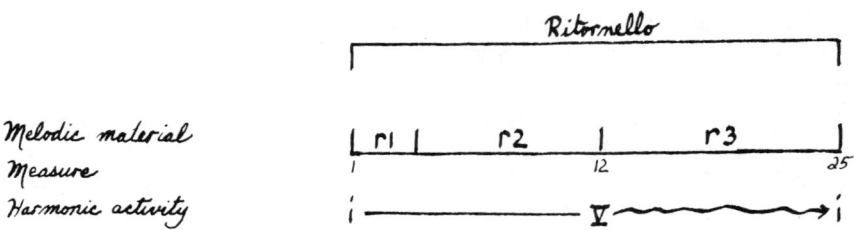

This same design is used in the ritornello of the Prelude in E♭, which will be discussed shortly.

The manipulation of the ritornello within the Prelude in c is also slightly different from the procedure followed in the Preludes in e and b. The full ritornello appears twice, at the beginning and end of the piece. In between, r1, r2, and r3 appear separately, framed by episodic material:

Measure	Ritornello Form	Key
1-25	Complete: r1, r2, r3	c
49-53	Abbreviated: r1	g
70-78	Abbreviated: r2	g
85-97	Abbreviated: r3	f
120-144	Complete: r1, r2, r3	c

Even though the distribution of the ritornello segments differs from the scheme used in the Preludes in e and b, the overall emphasis on four tonal areas, i, v, iv, and i, is quite similar.

The episodes of the Prelude in c show a more significant change in construction. The three episodes of the Prelude in b, aside from the order of imitative entries, are almost identical, and the three episodes of the Prelude in e reflect the process of agglutination. Hence there is very little development within the episodes of either work. In the Prelude in c, on the other hand, the episodes are based on the fugue-like expansion of a single motive. The imitative and developmental nature of these episodes contrasts greatly with the nonimitative and nondevelopmental character of the ritornello. This produces an important shift of emphasis in the form of the Prelude in c: the episodes, whose material is constantly subjected to fugal elaboration, become the main point of interest rather than the ritornello, whose material remains quite constant. The formal contrast between an unchanging ritornello and developmental episodes becomes even more striking in the Prelude in E♭.

In the Prelude in E♭ Bach turned to yet another source for melodic material, the French overture. The standard French overture, as codified by Lully in the 17th Century, consists of a slow, stately, dotted-rhythm introduction followed by a brisk, imitative allegro. In the Prelude in E♭ these two contrasting elements are incorporated into the framework of a concerto form. The slow introduction of the overture serves as the basis for the ritornello of the Prelude, and the allegro of the overture serves as the model for the larger of the Prelude's two episodic segments (e2, below). The other episodic segment (e1, below), though not patterned after the overture *per se*, nevertheless displays certain French characteristics. Its trio texture is typical of that employed in interludes in French orchestral suites, and its echo passages are a feature frequently connected with French style.[63] The distribution of the ritornello and the two episodic segments within the Prelude can be summarized as follows:

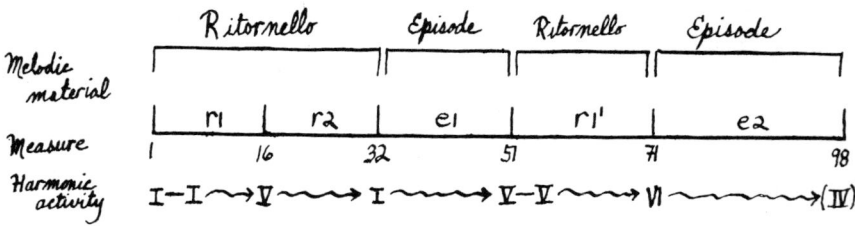

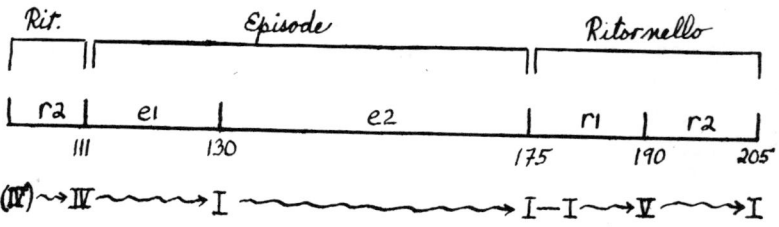

The diagram also shows that the Prelude in E♭, like the Preludes in e, b, and c, has a segmented ritornello. R1 (mm. 1-16) establishes the tonic (mm. 1-4) and then modulates to the dominant (mm. 5-16). R2 (mm. 17-32) begins in the dominant and moves sequentially back to the tonic. The symmetrical harmonic design thus produced resembles that found in the ritornello of the Prelude in c, where the dominant is also reached at the midpoint. Another feature the Prelude in E♭ shares with the Prelude in c is the arrangement of the ritornello segments: the complete ritornello appears twice, at the beginning and end of the work. In between, each of the segments appears once, framed by episodic material. The keys touched upon by the ritornello are the same four emphasized in the Prelude in c: the tonic, the dominant, the subdominant, and the tonic:

Measure	Ritornello Form	Key
1-32	Complete: r1 + r2	E♭
51-71	Abbreviated: r1'	B♭
98-110	Abbreviated: r2'	A♭
174-205	Complete: r1 + r2	E♭

The episodes of the Prelude combine features found in the Preludes in e, b, and c. The shorter episodic segment, e1, is similar to the episodic segments in the Preludes and e and b because its contents remain constant. Appearing initially at mm. 33-50, e1 is repeated almost note for note at a different pitch level in mm. 111-130. E2, on the other hand, shows the type of fugal development seen in the episodes of the Prelude in c. In the first appearance of e2 this development proceeds for twenty-eight measures, in the second appearance, forty-eight measures. Hence in the Prelude in E♭ Bach incorporated the two types of episodes he explored in his earlier works, placing them side by side in startling juxtaposition.

It is this element of juxtaposition and formal contrast that distinguishes the Prelude in E♭ from the other preludes with a concerto form, for in the work ritornello and episode are differentiated from one another to an unprecedented degree. One can detect a motivic bond holding the entire piece together: the ritornello and both episodic segments are based on the same melodic figures, the descending scale (x, below) and the appoggiatura (y, below):

Ritornello:

Episode 1 (e1):

Episode 2 (e2):

In addition, e1 and e2 both display the distinctive syncopated rhythm ♪ ♩ ♪ ♫ ♫ . The prevailing impression produced by ritornello, e1, and e2, however, is one of textural and figural change. The ritornello, in 5-part texture, is both melodic (mm. 1-4) and imitative (mm. 13-15). It is dominated by dotted rhythms. E1, in 3-part texture, is purely melodic and contains flowing quarter- and sixteenth-note motion. E2, in 3-part and 4-part texture (mm. 71-98 and mm. 130-174 respectively), is fugal and contains predominantly sixteenth-note motion. As a result, the episodic segments and ritornello are distinguished from one another not only by changes in texture and melodic material, but also by alterations in the basic rhythmic pattern employed. In no other prelude does Bach go to such extremes to emphasize the sectionalized nature of the concerto design.

The fact that the Prelude in E♭ was printed as the first piece in *Clavierübung* III helps to explain Bach's choice of melodic material as well as form. The French overture was the ideal source for the melodic material because of its traditional role as a large introductory piece. The Italian concerto was the appropriate model for the form; in choosing it Bach was able to display for the first time in print the remarkable adaptations and refinements he had made in transferring this design to the organ. Finally, in amalgamating the French overture and the Italian concerto in the opening piece of *Clavierübung* III Bach produced a remarkable sequel to *Clavierübung* II. In *Clavierübung* II the overture and the concerto are presented as two distinctly different archetypal forms. The antithesis they represent is emphasized by the fact that the Italian Concerto is written in F and the French Overture in b, two unrelated keys symbolically separated by the interval of a tritone, the "diabolus in musica."[64] In *Clavierübung* III Bach went one step further by demonstrating that it was indeed possible to amalgamate these seemingly irreconcilable forms in a single piece, the Prelude in E♭. Seen in this context, the Prelude represents one of the most remarkable syntheses in Bach's keyboard oeuvre.

In summary, several distinct trends can be observed in the seven preludes with a concerto form. First, there is a gradual formalization of structural detail. The ritornello, rather loosely constructed in the Preludes in G and d, becomes more highly organized in the Prelude in C. In the Preludes in e, b, c, and E♭ a very formal segmented design emerges. In the latter two works the balanced proportions of the ritornello as well as its use as a framing element within the prelude reflect the preclassical symmetry that is a feature of Bach's late writing.[65] The episodes of the preludes undergo a similar transformation. Those in the Prelude in G show few, if any, interrelationships. In the Preludes in d and C, however, certain segments of episodic material are repeated. In the Preludes in e, b, c, and E♭ a block-like construction is used extensively to unify the various episodic sections.

Second, one can observe a metamorphosis of idiom in the seven works. Beginning with north-German clavier-derived figurations, Bach turned successively to Vivaldi, to his own vocal works, and then to the French overture for new types of melodic material. The result was an incredible expansion of the traditional organ idiom.

Third, it is possible to see an important shift in the relationship between prelude and fugue. This change was brought about mainly by the extraordinary enlargement of the prelude through the use of the concerto form. In the Toccata & Fugue in d, prelude and fugue are motivically related, a feature that has antecedents in the north-German multisectional *Praeludium Pedaliter*. In the Preludes & Fugues in C, e, and b this direct connection is gone, and prelude and fugue stand as equal though thematically independent partners. With the Prelude & Fugue in c, however, the balance begins to tip in favor of the prelude. In this work the prelude was composed on a grand scale, while a less substantial, pre-existing fugue was paired with it as a matter of convenience.[66] Finally, in the case of the Prelude in E♭, the fugue becomes almost superfluous. As an extensive overture with its own imitative sections, the Prelude in E♭ has no need of a fugue. Indeed, the tradition of pairing the two together, promoted by Mendelssohn in the nineteenth century, may have begun with Forkel rather than Bach.[67] In *Clavierübung* III some sixty pages of music stand between the Prelude in E♭ and the Fugue in E♭. This spatial separation symbolizes the amount of independence which Bach granted the organ prelude in the process of adopting the concerto form.

The A B A B Form

In several preludes Bach used a type of sectional, repetitive form that can be outlined as A B A B (Closing Material). The preludes which are constructed in this manner are:

                Prelude in C, BWV 545/1
                Prelude in f, BWV 534/1
                Fantasia in c, BWV 537/1

The first two works, the Preludes in C and f, are especially similar to one another in terms of overall design and melodic material. The early version of the Prelude in C, BWV 545a/1, displays the A B A B design in its most embryonic form. The initial A, which establishes the tonic, consists of 3-part imitation over a pedal point. The initial B, a series of sequences, modulates to the dominant. The second A, a slightly embellished version of the first, is a fourth lower, in the dominant. The second B, likewise an elaboration of its counterpart, is also transposed down a fourth. This B is extended by means of a short dominant pedal point, which leads directly to the closing material. In its earliest form then, the Prelude in C can be summarized as follows:

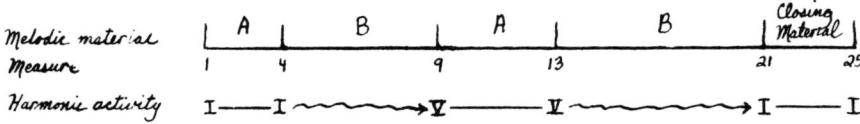

The Prelude in f adheres to this plan exactly. The pedal points, the imitation, and the sequences all occur at the same places within the form. The polarization of tonic and dominant is also identical. The chief difference lies in the fact that the material in both the A and B sections is drawn out and extended considerably, producing a prelude of substantially larger proportions than the Prelude in C:

	A	B	A	B	Closing Material	Total
Prelude in C (early version, BWV 545a; 4/4):	3 mm.	5 mm.	4 ½ mm.	8 mm.	4 ½ mm.	25 mm.
Prelude in f (3/4):	10 mm.	21 mm.	11 mm.	28 mm.	6 mm.	76 mm.

The diminutive size of the Prelude in C was undoubtedly the factor which motivated Bach to enlarge the work into its present form, BWV

545/1. He accomplished this expansion by attaching three measures (Y, below) to the beginning and three similar measures to the end of the work, thereby adding a new element of symmetry to the A B A B design:[68]

$$\underset{\underline{}}{Y\ A\ B\ A\ B\ X^*\ Y}$$

*Closing Material

In the present discussion of structure, however, it is important to keep in mind that the above represents an ingenious afterthought rather than Bach's original concept of the piece.

What was Bach's model for the type of design found in the Prelude in f and early version of the Prelude in C? No exact prototypes exist, but the rudiments of the form can be seen in the works of Pachelbel and Fischer. Pachelbel's Toccatas in C and g,[69] for example, consist of imitative material reiterated over two prolonged pedal points, the first on the tonic and the second on the dominant. The Preludes in C, G, and B♭ of Fischer's *Ariadne Musica* display a similar structure, albeit on a more modest scale. It is quite likely that Bach derived the A sections of his preludes, also based on tonic and dominant pedal points, from these pieces. The B sections, whose sequences resemble the episodes of an Italian concerto, appear to be Bach's addition to the plan used by Pachelbel and Fischer. Thus the A B A B form may represent another extraordinary synthesis on Bach's part: an amalgamation of the south-German pedal toccata and the Italian instrumental concerto!

It is curious to note that the A B A B design does not appear in Bach's keyboard works outside of the organ preludes. It cannot be found among the forty-eight preludes of the encyclopedic Well-Tempered Clavier or among Bach's other free pieces for keyboard. This fact might be explained by the integral role that extended pedal points play in the form. Technically, these pedal points can be performed successfully only on the organ. Therefore, the A B A B design, unlike several others used in the preludes, seems to have been viewed by Bach as suitable to the organ alone.

The melodic material of the Prelude in C reflects the direct influence of Italian instrumental style. The principal motive of the Prelude is triadic, and it outlines a strong harmonic progression in which chordal change occurs consistently on the quarter note. The forward motion caused by such a regular harmonic accent gains additional impetus from the sixteenth-note motoric pulse initiated by the motive itself:

This short but incisive figure permeates the Prelude to an extraordinary extent: it occurs in one form or another in almost every measure of the piece. Even those bars added by Bach at a later date are derived from it. The motivic economy of the Prelude, reminiscent of the "Dorian" Toccata, was undoubtedly the result of Bach's exposure to Vivaldi's concertos, in which similarly concise themes are treated in the same way.

The Prelude in f is somewhat more complex because its melodic material can be traced to diverse sources. The opening figuration is typical of keyboard writing. Bach used this exact motive at the beginning of another work, the Toccata in e, BWV 914, for harpsichord. A second important figure appears at m. 8 of the Prelude. This motive, with its repeated leaps of a tenth, is derived from violin writing, as can be seen by comparing it with the solo line from the first movement of Bach's Concerto in d for Two Violins, BWV 1043:

Prelude in f:

Concerto in d:

Another manifestation of violin style is the cadenza that appears at the end of the Prelude. This cadenza, written for a single voice, is characteristic of violin rather than keyboard music. Strikingly similar passages can be found in contemporary violin works such as Bach's own unaccompanied violin sonatas. The Fugue of the Sonata in a, BWV 1003, for example, concludes with virtually the same cadenza.

Vivaldi's instrumental writing also played a determining role in shaping the melodic material of the Prelude in f. The figure (mm. 16-22, soprano voice) that dominates the B sections of the Prelude is drawn directly from Vivaldi's concertos. This motive appears in the Prelude in G, BWV 541/1, and, in a slightly varied form, in the Toccatas in d and F. In these works it serves as the basis for sequential passage work. This is its function in the Prelude in f as well.

The variegated nature of the melodic material in the Prelude in f reflects once again Bach's effort to expand the traditional organ idiom by drawing on sources other than contemporary organ works. The ingenious amalgamation of motives borrowed from keyboard, violin, and concerto practice cannot conceal certain awkward passages in the piece, however. The most obvious of these it the written-out retard that occurs at the end of the initial B section, where the sixteenth-note motoric pulse is abruptly suspended for two measures (mm. 30-31). This passage strikes one as a not-altogether-successful structural joint, perhaps the result of Bach's attempt to relieve the motoric regularity found in the Prelude in f as well as the Prelude in C. This problem is resolved in the third work to be discussed, the Fantasia in C.

The Fantasia in c, while constructed along the same lines as the Preludes in C and f, contains several refinements which add a new level of sophistication to the A B A B form. First, the A and the B sections, both imitative, are based on distinctly different motives (labeled x and y below). This sectional segregation of melodic material, which helps to clarify the underlying structure of the piece, does not occur to the same extent in the Preludes in C and f. Second, the texture of the Fantasia, except for the addition of a voice at cadences, is four-part throughout. As a consequence, the unnecessary doublings that occasionally occur in the Preludes in C and f are eliminated. Third, the number of thematic entries is almost tripled in the final B section, creating a stretto effect that adds an element of culmination to an otherwise balanced form. Fourth, the two A sections end with a half cadence, thus producing a harmonic bridge that leads impellingly to the B sections. The distribution of the melodic material, the part writing, and the imitative and harmonic structure of the Fantasia can be summed up in the following linear diagram:

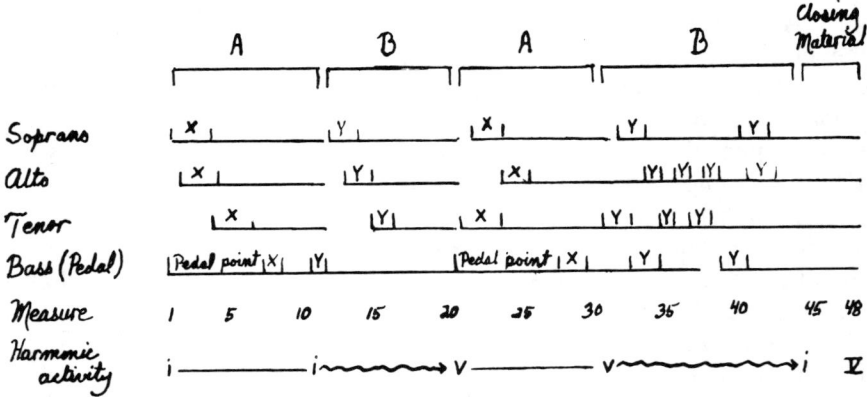

The fifth refinement, not easily diagrammed but clearly observable in the score of the Fantasia, is the subtle treatment of rhythmic pulse. The A sections begin with quarter-note motion which quickly changes to predominantly eighth-note and then sixteenth-note motion. The B sections begin with eighth-note motion which gradually changes to predominantly sixteenth. Thus in each section of the work there is a graduated rhythmic accelerando which is arrested only by the advent of the next section. The sixteenth-note motion produced in the final B section is sustained in the closing material:

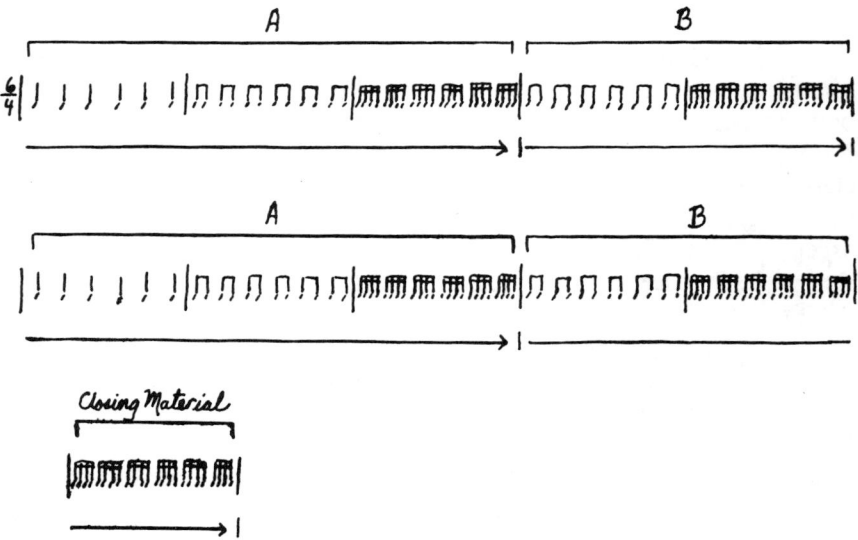

The gradual rise and fall of motion in the Fantasia produces a rhythmic flexibility that is completely absent in the Prelude in C and only implied in the Prelude in f. This rhythmic flexibility resembles that of the Prelude in c, BWV 546/1, and, in a similar fashion, probably reflects Bach's desire to avoid the type of motoric pulse that occurs in the Preludes in C and f. In addition, it may also account for the title "Fantasia," which frequently, though not always, implies a certain amount of metrical freedom.[70]

Considered together, the five refinements outlined above suggest that the Fantasia is one of Bach's later compositions. The figurations appearing in the work support this supposition. As in the Preludes in e, b, and c, the melodic material comes from vocal rather than instrumental or keyboard practice. The two principal motives of the Fantasia, x of the A section and y of the B, are both rhetorical figures standardly exploited in seventeenth- and eighteenth-century vocal music. X is a form of *exclamatio*, which Walther described as "a rhetorical figure used when one cries out in anguish; in music it can be produced very appropriately by means of a leap of an ascending minor sixth."[71] Bach frequently employed the *exclamatio* in his vocal works to express despair, grief, and similar emotions, and he often relied — as he does in the Fantasia — on the interval of the ascending sixth. For instance, the aria "Erbarme dich" from the St. Matthew Passion contains an *exclamatio* much like x of the Fantasia:

"Erbarme dich"

Prelude in c:

The motive y is a form of *suspiratio*, the "sigh" or "lamentation" figure used to express sighing, weeping, and similar moods of affliction. The *suspiratio* has already been discussed in connection with the Prelude in c, BWV 546/1, the only other free organ work in which it appears.

Bach was able to combine the *exclamatio* and the *suspiratio* in one work because they portray compatible affects. Nevertheless, the idea of employing two different but complementary rhetorical figures to delineate the sections of an A B A B form was an ingenious innovation. Bach undoubtedly turned to vocal writing for melodic material because he wished to avoid—in a fantasia—the type of rigid instrumental figures used in the Preludes in C and f.

One additional feature distinguishes the Fantasia from all other preludes, and that is the "attacca" conclusion that links it with the Fugue in c. The Fantasia is the only fully developed Bach prelude to end on the dominant. This harmonic bond is further heightened by a thematic connection: in the last measure of the Fantasia the alto voice presents an ascending chromatic line that later becomes the theme of the middle section of the da capo fugue.[72] This organic tie is indicative of the unusually close musical relationship between the Fantasia and the Fugue: both are approximately the same length, both contain two contrasting themes, both have balanced, sectionalized forms (Fantasia: A B A B; Fugue: C D C′), both are written in four real parts. In this instance, Bach must have viewed the prelude and fugue as one compositional entity and attempted to unify the two in ways not encountered elsewhere in the repertoire.

In conclusion, one can observe two general trends in the preludes with an A B A B form. First, there is a gradual change in the type of melodic material used: the instrumental-derived motives of the Preludes in C and f are replaced by rhetorical figures in the Fantasia in c. Second, there is a constant refinement of the A B A B design itself: it is established in the Prelude in C, expanded in the Prelude in f, and given new levels of sophistication in the Fantasia in c.

Miscellaneous Forms

Three preludes remain to be discussed:

>Fantasia in g, BWV 542/1
>Fantasia in C (incomplete), BWV 573
>Prelude in d, BWV 539/1

Because these works are difficult to classify, it will be necessary to deal with each on its own terms.

The Fantasia in g is unique among Bach's preludes. It has an unusual form that exploits the principle of sectional contrast: three sections of free, improvisatory material frame two other sections written

Stylistic Development 85

in a strict, imitative manner. The result is a five-part structure which can be outlined: Free, Strict, Free, Strict, Free.

The obvious model for this general plan is the north-German multisectional *Praeludium Pedaliter*, which often displays the form: Introduction (free), Fugue (duple meter), Interlude (free), Fugue (triple meter), Conclusion (free).[73] The Fantasia is an idealization of this form. The essence of the *Praeludium Pedaliter*, the alternation of strict and free material, has been retained, but the overall plan has been so sharply compressed that an entirely new type of composition emerges: a concise, self-contained prelude that can be performed alone or in conjunction with an independent fugue.[74]

In addition, the Fantasia is unified by a method quite different from that used in the *Praeludium Pedaliter*. The *Praeludium Pedaliter* is essentially a through-composed form, even though its fugues, and sometimes its free sections as well, are often based on transformations of the same theme. The Fantasia in g, on the other hand, displays certain features of a repetitive design. The two strict sections are composed of the same sequences (x, below), and even the free sections contain certain corresponding passages (y and z, below):

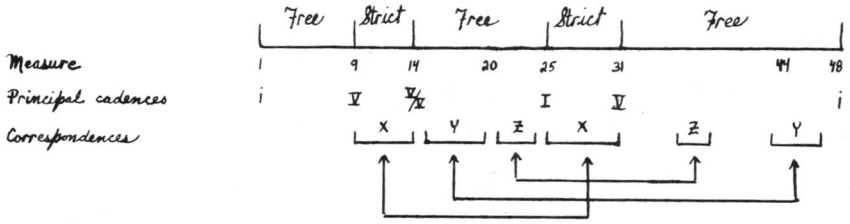

The melodic material of the Fantasia is as innovative as its form. The strict sections, in four-part imitative style, are based on conventional keyboard figures. The free sections are derived from something altogether different, the vocal recitative. The influence of the vocal recitative on the Preludes in e and b has already been discussed. In these works Bach incorporated highly stylized recitative- or aria-like melodies into the ritornello of a concerto form. In the Fantasia in g he fashioned a keyboard recitative that is much closer to vocal practice: it preserves the *senza battuta*, dialogue-like declamation of *recitativo secco*. Similar writing appears in the Chromatic Fantasia & Fugue in d, where an extended section of extremely free keyboard recitative acts as a bridge between the first part of the Fantasia (*passaggio* and arpeggios) and the Fugue.[75] The stark contrast between recitative and fugue in the Chromatic Fantasia & Fugue is much like the juxtaposition of free and imitative writing in the Fantasia in g.

The harmonic vocabulary of the free sections of the Fantasia in g heightens the effect of the recitative-derived melodic material by adding an additional element of drama. The bold dissonances, the abrupt harmonic shifts, and the enharmonic changes rival those of the Chromatic Fantasia and are unique among Bach's free organ works. Bach modulates as far afield as E♭ minor, a key rarely used in baroque organ compositions because of the limitations of mean-tone tuning. A constant state of flux is created through the extensive use of unstable chords such as the augmented-sixth chord and the diminished seventh chord.

The combination of keyboard recitative and startling harmonic progressions produces the type of free, daring fantasia that was frequently described by Baroque theorists. Walther, for instance, states the following about the fantasia:

> Fantasia is the result of playing according to one's humor, *ex tempore*. One performs or writes down that which strikes one's fancy at the moment, without being bound to the confining nature of the beat.[76]

C.P.E. Bach, although representing a younger generation, basically agrees with Walther. He goes further, however, by specifically pointing out the close relationship between fantasia and recitative:

> Improvising without a strict beat seems to be an especially appropriate way to express affects, for every meter carries with it a certain amount of constraint. At all events one can see from accompanied recitative that tempo and meter must often be modified in order to excite and still a series of emotions. In such instances meter is frequently employed merely as a notational convention, and is not something to be interpreted strictly. We can achieve this effect without ceremony on our instruments by improvising freely, without observing a regular beat. This type of playing, therefore, has a decided merit.[77]

It seems safe to assume that free fantasias were frequently improvised by performers but rarely written down, perhaps because the pieces sounded much better than they actually looked on paper.[78] In the Fantasia in g Bach laid aside such inhibitions and succeeded in producing those qualities most admired in a fantasia: drama and spontaneity. But using a sectional form, he went beyond the normal fantasia and imposed a degree of contrast and order not mentioned by the theorists. The strict sections of the Fantasia contain conventional melodic material and straightforward, predictable harmonic progressions. They lend an unexpected modicum of order to the piece and render the free sections all the more free by contrast.

The Fantasia in g represents still another Bach synthesis, a combination of the north-German multisectional *Praeludium Pedaliter* and the free fantasia. Moreover, one can observe the influence of Italian instrumental writing, for the strict sections of the work display the type of texture associated with the trio sonata: independent treble parts supported by an animated bass line that delineates strong harmonic progressions. This blending of so many different stylistic elements is characteristic of Bach's Weimar compositions, a point which will be pursued further in the discussion of chronology in the next chapter.

The Fantasia in C, BWV 573, has been handed down as a 12-measure-long fragment. Even in this incomplete state it is a very important composition, because it is one of the few free organ works that can be dated with assurance. It appears as a *Konzeptschrift* in the first *Klavierbüchlein für Anna Magdalena Bach* and consequently illustrates the type of prelude Bach was capable of writing during the years 1722-1723.

The melodic material is clearly concerto derived. The concise, triad-oriented motives reflect the influence of Vivaldi's instrumental style. Very similar writing can be found in other concerto-oriented works in C major: the Concerto in C, BWV 595 (a transcription of an orchestral movement by Johann Ernst), or the Prelude in C, BWV 545/1. Without a doubt both the Concerto in C and the Prelude in C were written in the wake of Vivaldi's publications. Like these works, the Fantasia displays another Vivaldian feature, a sixteenth-note motoric pulse.

What distinguishes the Fantasia as one of Bach's more mature compositions is the masterful treatment of part-writing. The work is written in five real parts which are maintained throughout the surviving twelve measures, even at important cadences. The imitative entries are extremely well handled, much more so than the only other prelude with strict five-part texture, the Fantasia in c, BWV 562/1. The controlled part-writing of the Fantasia in C represents a new level of order imposed on concerto-derived melodic material.

Much more difficult to assess is the structure of the work. In its existing state the Fantasia is a fragment, and from this fragment it is hard to determine exactly what type of form Bach had in mind. The Fantasia starts with two measures of ritornello-like material (labeled A, below) that begins and ends in the tonic. This is followed by a quick modulation to the dominant, which in turn is followed by two different sets of sequences, the first coming to a cadence in the dominant and the second to a cadence in the mediant. As a result the Fantasia has an open-ended design that can be summarized as follows:

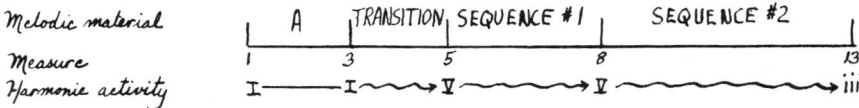

How is the piece to proceed? Even though the Fantasia is incomplete, enough music has been presented to show that the work does not follow any standard prelude design. It is unlikely that Bach had a concerto form in mind. Otherwise A, as a ritornello, would have been presented in the dominant at m. 5 or m. 8. It is equally improbable that an A B A B form was planned, for the same reason. Perhaps Bach intended the work to be through-composed. The fact that the opening material is so distinctive and so clearly set off from the sequences that follow it rules against this possibility. The most likely choice would be a bogen form, with A appearing in the tonic at the beginning and end of the work. The minute proportions of A infirm this hypothesis, however.

This perplexing situation makes sense only if one assumes that the structural ambiguity of the Fantasia is intentional. In this regard it is essential to consider the original context of the work. Within the *Klavierbüchlein für Anna Magdalena Bach* the Fantasia begins on the verso side of leaf 20 and ends about one-third of the way across the bottom system. The following page, the recto side of leaf 21, is ruled but otherwise empty. Thus Bach could have continued the Fantasia if he had so chosen. But he stopped writing at the E-minor cadence that marks the end of a modulatory sequence. Why?

The title of the work provides a clue. The term "fantasia" had several meanings in Bach's time. It frequently was used for works of an improvisatory character: pieces such as the Fantasia in g, BWV 542/1, which were rhythmically free and harmonically daring. The Fantasia in C with its rather rigid, concerto-derived melodic material and straightforward progressions does not seem to fall into this category. The term fantasia was also applied, in a slightly different sense, to works intended to stimulate one's compositional imagination or "Phantasie." Bach's three-part Inventions, written to demonstrate the formation and development of "gute Inventiones," belong to this category. They were originally titled "Fantasie" in the *Klavierbüchlein für Wilhelm Friedemann Bach*. The Fantasia in C may have been intended for a similar didactic purpose.

Within the three *Klavierbüchlein* intended for family use, Bach left many pieces incomplete. This may not reflect lethargy or indifference on his part, but rather his desire to induce his sons to finish the fragments.[79] According to T.L. Pitschel, Bach himself often relied on the works of others to stimulate his own imagination when he was improvising:

> You know, the famous man who has the greatest praise in our town in music, and the greatest admiration of connoisseurs, does not get into condition, as the expression goes, to delight others with the mingling of his tones until he has played something from the printed or written page, and has thus set his powers of imagination in motion.[80]

The incomplete Fantasia may have been intended for the same purpose, that is, to set Wilhelm Friedemann's "powers of imagination in motion." Friedemann had already begun composing in his own *Klavierbüchlein* in 1720. By the time the Fantasia fragment was written he would have been almost thirteen years old and ready for such a compositional challenge.

Viewed in this light, the form of the Fantasia becomes understandable. The structure is intentionally vague in order to encourage improvisation. In no other prelude do so many different things occur in the initial twelve measures. For improvising, one is given a great deal of material: the ritornello-like A section and two different types of sequential patterns. How these musical fragments are applied to finish the piece is determined solely by one's ingenuity. The Fantasia in C, therefore, may have been "complete" from Bach's viewpoint. If this is true, the work stands alone in the prelude repertoire as a unique example of a composition exercise.

While Bach may never have intended the Fantasia in C as a finished composition, it is possible that he never viewed the Prelude in d, BWV 539/1, as an organ work at all. Both the style and the provenance of the piece make its position in the prelude repertoire very tenuous.

Most obviously, the complete lack of a pedal part renders the work suspect. Obbligato pedal is an integral facet of Bach's prelude style. It is lacking in only two compositions, the Fantasia in C, BWV 570, and the Fantasia con Imitazione in b, BWV 563, both early pieces of modest proportions. The former is an independent composition; the latter is paired with an unpretentious, pedal *ad libitum* fughetto. The Prelude in d, by comparison, seems awkwardly matched with a lengthy fugue that calls for pedal obbligato throughout.

The melodic material of the Prelude raises more questions. The figurations used in the work are better suited to the harpsichord or clavichord than to the organ. For instance, the *arpègements* or broken chords that appear throughout the Prelude are not characteristic of organ style. They cannot be found in other organ preludes except for the Toccata in d, BWV 565, where they are used for special effect. The *arpègement* is a feature of harpsichord and clavichord playing and is frequently called for in works such as the Prelude & Fugue in C♯, BWV 872a, or the Fantasia & Fugue in a, BWV 904. Melodically, the Prelude in d resembles these pieces, not Bach's free organ preludes. To judge from its style, then, the Prelude in d appears to be a typical harpsichord or clavichord composition.

The sources shed no light whatsoever on this matter. The Prelude is handed down in just one manuscript, Berlin, SPK: *P 517*, which dates from the early nineteenth century. The Fugue in d, transmitted with the Prelude in *P 517*, appears as a separate piece in four other manuscripts.[81] Therefore the pairing of the Prelude with the Fugue also can be brought into question.[82] Forkel listed the two as prelude and fugue in his biography of 1802, but this is the earliest reference to the combination.

Since comparable pieces can be found among Bach's works, there seems to be no reason to question the authenticity of the Prelude in d. The Prelude's role as an organ composition is another matter, however. Stylistic and philological evidence suggests that the piece was appropriated from Bach's keyboard repertoire for use with the Fugue in d. Even if this appropriation reflects the composer's wishes, which it probably does not,[83] the Prelude in d cannot be considered representative of Bach's organ prelude writing.

IV
The Chronology of the Preludes: A Proposed Outline

Now that the stylistic development of the preludes has been traced, it is appropriate to return to the matter of dating. In the preliminary discussion of this topic,[1] criteria were proposed for establishing a more reliable prelude chronology. It was suggested that the works could be dated only through a careful consideration of manuscript as well as stylistic evidence. Manuscript evidence includes: 1) dates of pre-1750 sources and 2) manner of notation. Stylistic evidence includes: 1) form, 2) melodic material, 3) part-writing, and 4) harmonic design. The systematic application of these criteria—the task of the present chapter—produces a fairly clear picture of the relative order in which the preludes were composed.

Assigning specific dates to specific pieces poses still another challenge. For instance, it is obvious from stylistic evidence that certain pieces stem from a very early period. Exactly how early, however, is difficult to determine. The sources which might yield the answer to this question are lost. Comparison with other compositions is of little avail, for most of the preludes seem to have been written during or before the Weimar years, that is to say, during the period for which lamentably few works—keyboard or otherwise—can be dated precisely. Biographical data is of limited help. The material describing Bach's activity as an organ composer is quite general in nature and focuses mainly on the two periods which reportedly were the most productive, Arnstadt and Weimar.

Given these circumstances, one must aim at best to narrow down the time span in which a particular work might have been written. The stylistic changes in the repertoire can be traced. It is primarily a matter of determining when these changes most probably took place. The central question is: What are the important chronological termini with regard to the composition of the preludes? The biographical periods of Bach's life—Lüneburg, Arnstadt, Mühlhausen, etc.,—do not serve as ideal dividing lines in this respect, for it cannot be assumed that Bach abruptly altered his prelude style each time he moved from one location to another.

Other factors must have produced a more tangible effect on his writing. In the case of the preludes, one can identify three crucial events which determined significantly the shape of the works. Since these events are datable, they may serve as pivotal termini for chronology. The first was the visit with Buxtehude during the winter of 1705-1706. This visit marks the culmination of Bach's study of north-German keyboard style — a study that can be traced back to the Lüneburg years. The second event was the encounter with Vivaldi's instrumental works around 1712, an experience which immediately provided Bach with a new means of treating form, melody, harmony, and rhythm. The third event was Bach's preoccupation with vocal writing during the initial Leipzig years. This concentrated involvement with vocal style tempered the influence of Vivaldi's works and ushered in yet another phase of prelude writing.

By weighing the available manuscript and stylistic evidence and by using the above termini as guidelines, one is able to propose the following chronology for the preludes and the fugues paired with them. Each work is considered on two levels. First, it is assigned to the general period within which it most probably was written: 1700-1706, 1706-ca. 1712, ca. 1712-1723, or 1723-1750. Second, it is ranked in relation to the other compositions which fall within the same general time span. The second procedure produces a more specific, though naturally more hypothetical date for each piece. Below the chronology are grouped the revised versions of earlier compositions and other special cases: works that appear to be spurious and works that do not seem to have been intended for organ.

I. 1700-1706

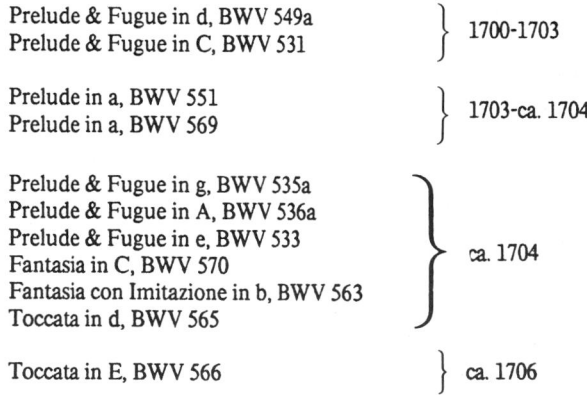

II. 1706-ca. 1712

Prelude & Fugue in G, BWV 550
Prelude & Fugue in a, BWV 543a } 1706-1708

Fantasia & Fugue in c, BWV 562/1a &
 BWV 546/2a
Passacaglia in c, BWV 582
Prelude & Fugue in D, BWV 532
Fantasia in G, BWV 572
Toccata, Adagio, & Fugue in C, BWV 564
Fantasia in g, BWV 542/1 } 1708-ca.1712

III. Ca. 1712-1723

Prelude & Fugue in C, BWV 545a
Prelude & Fugue in f, BWV 534
Toccata & Fugue in d, BWV 538
Toccata in F, BWV 540/1
Prelude & Fugue in G, BWV 541 } ca. 1712-1717

Prelude & Fugue in C, BWV 547
Fantasia in C (incomplete), BWV 573 } 1717-1723

IV. 1723-1750

Prelude & Fugue in e, BWV 548
Prelude & Fugue in b, BWV 544
Prelude & Fugue in c, BWV 546 } 1723-1729

Prelude & Fugue in E♭, BWV 552
Fantasia & Fugue in c, BWV 537 } 1729-1750

Revised Versions of Earlier Works — **Possible Date**

Prelude & Fugue in g, BWV 535 (Revision of BWV 535a) — After 1717
Prelude & Fugue in A, BWV 536 (Revision of BWV 536a) — Between ca. 1704 and ca. 1725
Prelude & Fugue in a, BWV 543 (Revision of BWV 543a) — After ca. 1730
Prelude & Fugue in C, BWV 545 (Revision of BWV 545a) — Between ca. 1712 and 1717
Prelude & Fugue in c, BWV 549 (Revision of BWV 549a) — After 1717
Fantasia in c, BWV 562/1 (Revision of BWV 562/1a) — Ca. 1730

Spurious Works

Prelude & Fugue in e, BWV 533a (Variant of BWV 533) — ---
Prelude in G, BWV 568 — ---

Works Intended for Harpsichord or Clavichord Rather Than Organ

Prelude in d, BWV 539/1 — After ca. 1723

1700-1706

This period includes Bach's formative years from his stay in Lüneburg up to and including the time of his extended visit with Buxtehude in the winter of 1705-1706. Lamentably little is known about Bach's earliest organ training. After the death of his father in 1695 he was sent to Ohrdruf to live with his brother Johann Christoph, who gave him his first formal clavier instruction. Five years later, in March, 1700, he entered the Michaelsschule in Lüneburg. He remained at this institution for three years, singing in the choir while at the same time gaining his secondary education.[2] During this period he apparently exhibited unusual interest in organ playing, for he traveled to Hamburg several times in order to hear Reinken perform in the Katharinenkirche. In the spring of 1703 Bach himself suddenly emerged as an organist of sufficient accomplishment to be invited to test and dedicate the organ of the Neue Kirche in Arnstadt.

From these known facts one concludes that Bach must have acquired some skill in organ playing during the Lüneburg years. Circumstantial evidence strongly suggests he studied with Georg Böhm, the organist of the Johanniskirche in Lüneburg. In view of his insatiable interest in music, Bach would hardly have failed to contact Böhm during his stay in Lüneburg, for Böhm was one of the better-known organists and composers of the day. Moreover, Bach had regional ties with the famous musician: Böhm was not a native north-German, but stemmed rather from Ohrdruf, the village in which Bach had lived for five years. Since Böhm later served as an agent for the sale of Bach's Partitas,[3] it can be assumed that the two men were friends. That this friendship grew out of a student-teacher relationship is implied by a comment C.P.E. Bach made to Forkel in a letter of 1774.[4]

The two chorale partitas, *Christ, der du bist der helle Tag*, BWV 766, and *O Gott, du frommer Gott*, BWV 767, also suggest that Bach studied with Böhm. These early works are modeled directly after the *manualiter* partita, a form that Böhm in particular promoted. It seems most unlikely that Johann Christoph Bach in Ohrdruf, Reinken in Hamburg, or Buxtehude in Lübeck would have induced Bach to write this type of piece during his formative years.

Bach spent the summer of 1703 working as a violinist at the court of Prince Johann Ernst in Weimar. In July he was called to Arnstadt to test and "play for the first time" the new organ in the Neue Kirche. One month later he was named organist of the same church. Once installed in the new post he turned his full attention to playing and composition. The *Nekrolog* of 1754 describes the Arnstadt years as follows:

> Here he really showed the first fruits of his application to the art of organ playing, and to composition, which he had learned chiefly by the observation of the works of the most famous and proficient composers of his day and by the fruits of his own reflection upon them. In the art of the organ he took the works of Bruhns, Reinken, Buxtehude, and several good French organists as models. While he was in Arnstadt he was once moved by the particularly strong desire to hear as many good organists as he could, so he undertook a journey, on foot, to Lübeck, in order to listen to the famous Organist of the Marien-Kirche there, Diedrich Buxtehude. He tarried there, not without profit, for almost a quarter of a year, and then returned to Arnstadt.[5]

To judge from the available biographical information, the preludes which Bach wrote during the years 1700-1706 must have been highly derivative, displaying the direct influence of north-German and French composers. The only datable work from this period is the Capriccio in B♭ "sopra la lontananza del suo fratello dilettissimo," BWV 992, which can be assigned to the year 1704.[6] The Capriccio reflects the level of Bach's compositional technique at that time and therefore serves as an important guide for dating the early preludes. The work contains six movements. All are modest in size and all are based on conventional keyboard figures. The "Fuga all'imitazione dela cornetta di postiglione" in particular is pertinent to the organ works. It reveals that in 1704 Bach could write three-part counterpoint well, but it also shows that he had difficulty expanding this texture to four parts. The movement is ostensibly a three-part fugue, yet a fourth voice appears five times, at m. 16, m. 37, m. 42, m. 44, and m. 55. In the first four instances one of the sounding parts immediately drops out when the fourth voice enters, thus reducing the texture back to three parts. Only at the end of the Fugue, m. 55ff., do all four voices come into play for more than one measure. Since the fourth part is not sustained consistently, its role in the movement is rather equivocal.

Another salient feature of the "Fuga all'imitazione della cornetta di postiglione" is its modest harmonic design. Except for one brief modulation (mm. 44-55) to the mediant, D minor, all thematic entries and episodes occur in the tonic or dominant. The excessive amount of time spent in these keys and the abruptness and brevity of the single modulation outside that sphere distinguish this piece from Bach's later fugues.

It should also be pointed out that the earliest copy of the Capriccio appears in the *Möller Handschrift* (Berlin, SPK: *Mus. ms. 40644*). This collection and its companion, the *Andreas Bach Buch* (MB Lpz: *III.8.4*) represent the two most important sources of Bach's earliest surviving keyboard works.[7] The one Bach autograph they contain has been dated "vor 1707" by Dadelsen.

Among the preludes, six works share a close stylistic affinity with the Capriccio and therefore appear to date from approximately the same time.

Prelude & Fugue in g, BWV 535a

Comment:[8] The only source for the Prelude & Fugue in g is the autograph contained in the *Möller Handschrift*. Using handwriting and watermarks as a guide, Dadelsen has assigned this autograph to the Arnstadt years, "before 1707."[9] It is difficult to arrive at a more precise date because very few samples of Bach's pre-1707 handwriting are available for comparison. As one might expect, the work is written in soprano clef and dorian notation.

The derivative style of the Prelude suggests an early origin. The melodic material is drawn from conventional keyboard figures. The form is through-composed and sectional, a design used by Buxtehude and Böhm. The introductory *passaggio* is somewhat perfunctory, but the five-part material (m. 15ff.) matches the best writing of the Capriccio in B♭.

As Krüger has already demonstrated,[10] the four-part Fugue also shares a close relationship with the Capriccio. It may be longer than the Capriccio's "Fuga all'imitazione della cornetta di postiglione," but it shows similar limitations in its part-writing and harmonic design. Four-part texture is seldom maintained because one of the manual voices invariably drops out when the pedal enters. This can be seen clearly in the initial exposition: the soprano presents the subject and is joined in turn by the alto and tenor. When the pedal enters, however, the tenor drops out. It returns only when the pedal exits several measures later. As has been mentioned, in Bach's more mature fugues the texture is not reduced until the subject has been presented in every voice.

As for the Fugue's harmonic design, an excessive amount of time is spent in the tonic and dominant. The only excursion outside this tonal sphere is the short modulation to the mediant which occurs near the end of the movement. The abruptness of this passage is revealing: the modulation from tonic to mediant is accomplished in three measures and the modulation from mediant back to tonic in one measure. In a later work Bach would have used intermediary keys to extend the tonal transition and make it smoother.

Since the Prelude & Fugue in g is so similar to the Capriccio in B♭ in terms of compositional technique, one surmises that it stems from the same period, ca. 1704. The strong contrast between the carefully worked-out Fugue and the rather cursory Prelude suggests that the two movements may have been written under different circumstances. In all likelihood Bach planned out the Fugue—the most challenging part of the composition—before he entered it into the *Möller Handschrift*. The Prelude, on the other hand, seems to have been composed on the spot, a process that would help to explain its unambitious scope.[11] If this is true, the Prelude & Fugue demonstrates two facets of Bach's early compositional activity. The Fugue is an example of a piece carefully planned in advance, and the Prelude is an example of a piece produced "aus dem Stegreif." The Prelude obviously was not entirely satisfactory, for Bach revised it extensively at a later date (see under Revised Versions, below).

Prelude & Fugue in A, BWV 536a

Comment: The sources are of no avail in dating this work. The manuscript (supposedly autograph) used by Griepenkerl for the Peters Edition (Volume II, Anhang) disappeared in the nineteenth century. The only other sources, the four recently discovered Scholz copies (Göttingen, Johann-Sebastian-Bach-Institut) stem from the second half of the eighteenth century. Three of these are corrupt arrangements. The fourth agrees precisely with Griepenkerl's text and presents the Prelude & Fugue in the soprano clef.

Stylistic considerations place the work in the period ca. 1704. The Prelude displays the same through-composed, sectional design used in the Prelude in g, BWV 535a/1. This form as well as the melodic material of the work is derived from north-German practice. The Prelude in A is more highly unified than the Prelude in g, but in terms of part-writing it is noticeably inferior: the lack of independence between pedal and left hand produces awkward voice-leading, including parallel octaves (mm. 19-20).

The Fugue, too, displays clumsy part-writing. A great effort is made to sustain four-voice texture, but once again difficulties arise between the pedal and the left hand. For example, in the initial exposition the tenor (left hand) leaps up into the alto range when the bass (pedal) enters, thereby avoiding a clash between the two voices. In a later fugue Bach would have preserved the ranges of individual parts more carefully and not taken the tenor up into the tessitura of the alto.

The harmonic structure of the Fugue reminds one of the Capriccio in B♭. Most of the movement is spent in the tonic and dominant. A substantial middle section, however, includes thematic entries in the submediant, supertonic, and subdominant. Although this appears to be an advanced feature, the abruptness of the individual modulations reflects perfectly the style of the Fugue in g, BWV 535a/2, and the "Fuga all'imitazione della cornetta di postiglione" of the Capriccio.

Spitta assigned the Prelude & Fugue in A to the year 1716.[12] He chose this date primarily because of the Weimar cantata *Tritt auf die Glaubensbahn* (Cantata #152).[13] It is clear that Bach revised the Prelude & Fugue in A at some point, possibly in Weimar around the time the Cantata was written (see under Revised Versions, below). The style of the work, however, points to an origin of ca. 1704.

Prelude & Fugue in e, BWV 533

Comment: The oldest surviving sources for this work are the copies of Johann Caspar Vogler and Johann Ringk contained in Leipzig, Bach-Archiv: *Mus. ms. 2* (Fugue only) and Berlin, SPK: *P 425*, respectively. Both of these were written during Bach's Leipzig years at the earliest.

The style of the work suggests an origin of ca. 1704. The Prelude has the same through-composed, sectional form as the Prelude in g, BWV 535a/1, and it is almost as modest in size. The melodic material, which includes the *trillo longo*, reflects the influence of Buxtehude. The Fugue is also limited in scope and compositional technique. It is a five-part piece, and yet in the initial exposition two voices drop out when the fifth voice, the pedal, enters. The harmonic plan of this movement is even less ambitious than that of the Fugue in g, BWV 535a/2: no modulations whatsoever are made outside the tonic and dominant.

The great variety of readings that have been handed down show that the Prelude & Fugue in e was revised by Bach several times. Even the earliest surviving version (= the 31-measure-long BG text)[14] may have benefited from post-compositional emendations, especially with regard to part-writing. Enough early characteristics remain, however, to show that the work belongs to the same formative period as the Prelude & Fugue in g, BWV 535a, and the Prelude & Fugue in A, BWV 536a.

Toccata in d, BWV 565

Comment: The sources are of little avail in dating this work. The oldest surviving manuscript is a copy, written by Johann Ringk, in Berlin, SPK: *P 595*. This copy was undoubtedly made sometime after 1730. The Toccata was surely composed before then since it is notated in the soprano clef and dorian notation in all eighteenth-century sources.

To judge from its style, the work belongs to the period ca. 1704. The overall design—free introduction, fugue based on the introduction, free conclusion—points directly to north-German prototypes. The Böhm-like melodic material and improvisational finale are features which appear in the Prelude & Fugue in d, BWV 549a, and the Prelude & Fugue in C, BWV 531, two pieces which seem to have been written during the Lüneburg years (see below). The more skillful treatment of the pedal clearly separates the Toccata from these compositions, however.

The harmonic plan and part-writing of the fugue ally the Toccata with the Capriccio in B♭. The central modulatory section touches on the mediant, subtonic, and subdominant. These keys are established with the same abruptness observed in the "Fuga all'imitazione della cornetta di postiglione." Ostensibly the Fugue is a four-voice movement, but all the parts sound together in only five of ninety-eight measures. This lack of sustained four-part texture links the work with the Capriccio and the Prelude & Fugue in g, BWV 535a, and suggests an origin of ca. 1704.

Fantasia in C, BWV 570

Comment: the oldest source of this work is the manuscript copy contained in the *Andreas Bach Buch*. Since the Fantasia is part of this collection, it undoubtedly dates from an early period.

The highly derivative nature of the piece supports this reasoning. The form is a through-composed, continuous design that appears in the works of Johann Pachelbel and J.K.F. Fischer. The melodic material and ad libitum use of pedal also reflect the style of these composers. The part-writing is slightly better than that of the Prelude & Fugue in g, BWV 535a. The *manualiter* setting helps to account for this, however, since the pedal, the most difficult voice to handle, is virtually eliminated. Harmonically the Fantasia remains in the tonic and dominant.

In terms of general technique the Fantasia is not far removed from the Arioso of the Capriccio in B♭ and therefore can be assigned to the period ca. 1704. It seems unlikely that Bach would have written this work, with its modest proportions and limited harmonic scope, much after the time he composed the Capriccio.

Fantasia con Imitazione in b, BWV 563

Comment: like the Fantasia in C, this composition first appears in the *Andreas Bach Buch*. Its presence in this collection suggests an early origin.

Stylistically, the Fantasia is similar to the Fantasia in C. It displays the same type of form, melodic material, part-writing, and ad libitum pedal. This implies that it was derived from the same source, the works of Pachelbel and Fischer. The Imitazione resembles the "Fuga all'imitazione della cornetta di postiglione" of the Capriccio in B♭. Its theme is shorter, and this leads to more concise counterpoint. But the limited harmonic scope and the abruptness of the individual modulations show that this movement belongs to the same period as the Capriccio fugue. These facts imply that the Fantasia con Imitazione was written around 1704.

Four other preludes appear to predate the above works because they display compositional features that are less advanced. The first two may have been written during Bach's initial year in Arnstadt. The second two seem to date from an even earlier period; their resemblance to the free compositions of Böhm suggests they may have been written in Lüneburg.

Prelude in a, BWV 569

Comment: Manuscript evidence is of little help in dating this work. The earliest sources are copies by Johann Gottfried Walther, Johann Peter Kellner, and Johann Gottlieb Preller in Berlin, DStB: *P 801*, Berlin, SPK: *P 288*, and MBLpz: *Ms. 7*, respectively. The Walther copy probably dates from Weimar. The others were written during Bach's Leipzig years or sometime thereafter. In all cases the Prelude is notated in the soprano clef.

The highly derivative nature of the work points to a very early origin. The ostinato-variation form reflects the chaconnes and passacaglias of Buxtehude and Pachelbel. Certain sections of the Prelude, in fact, are patterned directly after conventional types of variations appearing in the works of these composers. The overall plan of the Prelude, however, falls far short of contemporary models. The abruptness of the individual modulations and the awkward nature of the harmonic design suggest that the piece antedates the Capriccio in B♭.

The Prelude in a may be a written-down improvisation. Other early works such as the Prelude & Fugue in e or the Toccata in E display a calculated structure despite technical shortcomings. By comparison, the Prelude in a, with its erratically ordered variations, is strikingly anomalous. The Passacaglia in c illustrates the extent to which Bach refined the ostinato-variation form at a later date (see under 1706-ca. 1712, below).

Prelude in a, BWV 551

Comment: Manuscript evidence is of no help in dating this work. The earliest sources are copies by Johann Ringk and J.N. Mempell in

Berlin, SPK: *P 595* and MBLpz: *Ms. 7*, respectively. Both of these appear to have been written no earlier than 1725, that is, undoubtedly long after the Prelude was composed.

Stylistic features such as the north-German form, the Buxtehude-like melodic material, and the extremely restricted harmonic plan suggest a very early origin. The five-part multisectional design — introduction, fugue, interlude, fugue, conclusion — is much more rudimentary than that of the Toccata in E, BWV 566 (see below). More telling is the part-writing in the two fugues, which is similar, though slightly inferior to that of the Fugue in g, BWV 535a, and the "Fuga all'imitazione della cornetta di postiglione" of the Capriccio in B♭. This implies that the Prelude in a was written before 1704.

Prelude & Fugue in C, BWV 531

Comment: The earliest source of this composition is a manuscript copy contained in the *Möller Handschrift*, where both Prelude and Fugue are notated in the soprano clef.

Stylistically the work is remarkably like Böhm's Prelude & Fugue in C. The composition as a whole displays the same distinct pairing of prelude and fugue. The Prelude has a similar sectional form and opening pedal solo, and the fugue has an equally restricted harmonic design. The melodic material with its conspicuous absence of the *trillo longo* and other Buxtehudian characteristics also points to Böhm's influence. These factors indicate that the work may have been written in Lüneburg, where Bach appears to have studied with Böhm.

In addition, several compositional features suggest that the Prelude & Fugue in C was written before the works discussed up to this point. The first is the diffuse nature of the Prelude. The preludes assigned to ca. 1704 are more carefully organized and contain less extraneous material. The second factor is the part-writing in the Fugue. Little effort is made to separate the individual voices by tessitura. Parts are added and subtracted so indiscriminately (m. 23, m. 29, et passim) that it is difficult to tell whether this is a three-, a four-, or a five-voice composition.[15] By contrast, Bach's works dated ca. 1704 already show indications of real part-writing. The third distinguishing characteristic is the cursory treatment of the pedal in the Fugue: the pedal does not even enter into the initial exposition. When it does appear later, it is accompanied awkwardly in the manuals. This type of writing must certainly reflect Bach's initial efforts at *pedaliter* composition.

Prelude & Fugue in d, BWV 549a

Comment: This work also appears in the *Möller Handschrift*. In this source it is notated in the soprano clef and dorian notation and bears the title "Praeludium ô Fantasia Pedaliter."

Stylistically the work is very similar to the Prelude & Fugue in C, BWV 531. The Prelude has a through-composed, sectional form beginning with a pedal solo. The Fugue has a very limited harmonic plan that calls for no modulations outside the tonic and dominant. The melodic material resembles that of Böhm rather than Buxtehude. In addition, the work suffers from the same technical shortcomings: superfluous material in the Prelude, ambiguous part-writing and cursory treatment of the pedal in the Fugue. All these factors suggest that it originates from the same period as the Prelude & Fugue in C, Lüneburg.

At a later date Bach revised this work and transposed it to C minor. He may have made these changes in connection with his teaching activities in Cöthen or Leipzig (see under Revised Versions, below).

One final work can be placed at the very end of the 1700-1706 period. Its compositional level indicates it was written after the pieces assigned to ca. 1704; its style specifically links it to Bach's visit with Buxtehude in the winter of 1705-1706.

Toccata in E, BWV 566

Comment: The earliest sources of this work are the copies written by Johann Tobias Krebs and Johann Peter Kellner in Berlin, DStB: *P 803* and Berlin, SPK: *P 286*, respectively. In both cases the Toccata is in C major. The Kellner copy dates from Bach's Weimar tenure at the earliest. Whether in C major or E major, the Toccata is notated in the soprano clef in all eighteenth-century sources.

The style of the work suggests that it was written while Bach was working under the direct influence of Buxtehude. The overall design—free introduction, fugue (in duple meter) based on the introduction, free interlude, fugue (in triple meter) based on the introduction, free conclusion—reflects Buxtehude's writing, as does the melodic material, especially the *repercussio* theme of the initial fugue. The Toccata in E is not merely derivative. It is an exact model of a Buxtehude multisectional Praeludium Pedaliter. It is hard to imagine when Bach would have attempted to imitate Buxtehude in such an exacting and ambitious manner other than during his period of study in Lübeck in the winter of 1705-1706.

A comparison with the works assigned to ca. 1704 supports this hypothesis, for stylistically the Toccata appears to stem from a slightly later date than these compositions. The part-writing in the initial fugue is somewhat better than that of the Fugues in g, A, or e; the introductory material (mm. 1-33) is organized more carefully than that of the Toccata in d; and the overall proportions of the work exceed by far those of any of the compositions in question. The careless doublings in the free introduction and the additional voices that appear unpredictably in the second fugue indicate that the Toccata is still an early piece, however.

All these factors imply that the Toccata in E dates from ca. 1706.

1706-ca. 1712

This period includes Bach's remaining year in Arnstadt, his stay in Mühlhausen, and his Weimar tenure up to ca. 1712. It seems safe to assume that within a short time after his return from Lübeck Bach must have fully assimilated Buxtehude's compositional style amd must have begun to adapt it for his own purposes. In June, 1707, he left Arnstadt to become the organist of the Blasiuskirche in Mühlhausen. This new post offered him several advantages: a higher salary, a more stimulating atmosphere in which to work, and the opportunity to compose church cantatas. Of his accomplishments as an organist during this time, nothing is documented except his well-known recommendations for improving the instrument in the Blasiuskirche.[16] These recommendations were submitted in February, 1708, but were not carried out until after Bach departed for Weimar.

The lack of biographical information makes it difficult to ascertain precisely what changes, if any, took place in Bach's prelude writing in Mühlhausen. No datable keyboard work from that time is available for comparison, as the Capriccio in B$\flat$ is for the period 1704. The only compositions that can be assigned with certainty to Mühlhausen are Cantata #131, *Aus der Tiefe rufe ich, Herr, zu dir*, and Cantata #71, *Gott ist mein König*. Although these two vocal works are not directly analogous to the organ preludes, they demonstrate that Bach's vision at this point still did not extend beyond traditional, late-seventeenth-century German models. The structure, the melodic material, and the harmonic scope of these cantatas reflect the works of Bach's predecessors and do not show the influence of the newer Italian style. The fugue writing demonstrates his increasing ability to handle four-part contrapuntal texture (cf. Cantata #71 and the Capriccio in B$\flat$) and his early use of the permutation technique that appears more skillfully developed in the datable Weimar cantatas of 1713.

In June, 1708, Bach assumed the post of Court Organist in Weimar. Here his talents were ardently appreciated, for both Duke Ernst August, his employer, and Prince Johann Ernst, the Duke's brother, were dedicated amateur musicians. They vigorously promoted musical activities at the court and enthusiastically fostered Bach's organ playing. According to the *Nekrolog* of 1754, the pleasure the Duke took in organ music filled Bach "with the desire to try every possible artistry in his treatment of the organ."[17] This statement is supported by the remark of Philipp David Kräuter, a student of Bach's in Weimar, who wrote in the spring of 1713 that his teacher was planning to play "incomparable things" on the newly renovated organ of the "Himmelsburg" Kapelle.[18]

During the Weimar years Bach's reputation as an organist of unusual talent grew rapidly. In 1710 and 1716 he served as an examiner for new instruments. In 1713 he competed for and was offered the position of Organist at the Frauenkirche in Halle. In 1717 he achieved his well-publicized victory over the French organist Louis Marchand in Dresden. These events, combined with the lively activity at the Weimar court, led to a phase of fruitful composition and experimentation, causing Spitta to term the Weimar years "die goldene Zeit" of Bach's career as an organist. Indeed, the *Nekrolog* states that it was in Weimar that Bach wrote "most of his organ works." With regard to the organ preludes, this productive period can be divided into two distinct phases: 1708-ca. 1712, the years leading up to Bach's discovery of Vivaldi's works, and ca. 1712-1717, the years during which he assimilated Vivaldi's instrumental style.

Although very little about Bach's compositional activities during the period 1708-ca. 1712 can be documented, certain inferences can be drawn from external evidence. First, Bach had access for the first time to two sources of music, the court library and Johann Gottfried Walther's private collection.[19] Both were substantial in size and must have provided Bach with new compositional models, including the works of the pre-Vivaldi generation of Italians: Corelli, Torelli, and others. Second, encouraged by Duke Ernst August and Prince Johann Ernst and given many opportunities to perform, he must have endeavored to improve his style and to try "every possible artistry" in his organ works.

To judge from the pieces written before and afterwards, during the period 1706-ca. 1712 Bach must have altered his prelude writing in the following ways. It seems likely that he modified and expanded traditional forms as far as possible and turned to unusual composite structures in an effort to find new ways to organize the prelude. Moreover, he apparently refined further north-German keyboard figures and began to use instrumental motives drawn from the French repertoire and from the works of the pre-Vivaldi generation of Italian composers.

A Proposed Outline

One would also expect the part-writing in the preludes written during this time to be better than that of the works assigned to 1700-1706. This could be attributed both to Bach's experience writing cantatas in Mühlhausen and to his exposure to the contrapuntal style of the "Bologna School."[20] Without a doubt, the harmonic structure of the preludes also benefited from these events. Through the use of more extended modulatory patterns (circle of fifth progressions, etc.) Bach would have been able to expand the size of traditional forms. These advances, together with the notable absence of Vivaldian features, can be observed in eight works which consequently can be assigned to the years 1706-ca. 1712. These works are discussed in the order in which they seem to have been composed.

Prelude & Fugue in G, BWV 550

Comment: The Prelude & Fugue in G appears to be an early work because it is always written in the soprano clef, but the sources provide no precise indication of its date. Several stylistic features show a close connection with pieces assigned to 1700-1706: the through-composed, sectional form of the Prelude, the *repercussio* theme of the Fugue, and the somewhat digressive and redundant harmonic progressions found in the entire piece. The 4/4 bridge between the Prelude and the Fugue, labeled "Grave" in several sources, reflects north-German practice (Bruhns and Buxtehude in particular) and shows that Bach was still writing under the direct influence of that school.

However, other factors imply the Prelude & Fugue was composed at a slightly later date than the works assigned to 1700-1706. The first indication is the cohesiveness of the Prelude, which is highly unified—almost to the point of monotony—by the constant reiteration of a single motive and by the maintenance of eighth-note motion. The second clue is the part-writing in the Fugue: the voices are clearly distinguished from one another by range, the pedal is given a completely independent line, and four-part texture is maintained without difficulty (cf. the initial exposition).

In short, the Prelude & Fugue in G seems to have been written after the works assigned to 1700-1706. Its uninnovative style and its ties with north-German practice suggest that it was composed towards the beginning of the period 1706-ca. 1712, perhaps between 1706 and 1708.

Prelude & Fugue in a, BWV 543a

Comment: The sources are of no help in dating this work. The Prelude's through-composed, sectional design and north-German melodic material (cf. the *trillo longo*, m. 14) imply that it was written while Bach was still working in the north-German idiom. What distinguishes this Prelude from those of the period 1700-1706 is the refined treatment of form. The *passaggio* introduction, typical of Bach's early works, has been greatly enlarged. At the same time it has been unified to an unprecedented degree through the use of recurring motives. A carefully-worked-out accelerando connects this *passaggio* with the Prelude's principal section, which is remarkably concise.

The Fugue also shows advances not encountered in the works dated 1700-1706. The part-writing is excellent (four-part texture is handled without difficulty), and the fugue theme is modified to accommodate the pedals when it appears in the bass. The free conclusion has been carefully incorporated into the Fugue rather than simply tacked into it (cf. the Prelude in a, BWV 551).

These factors suggest that the Prelude & Fugue in a was written towards the beginning of the period 1706-ca. 1712, probably around the time the Prelude & Fugue in G, BWV 550, was composed (1706-1708?). Bach revised the Prelude & Fugue in a at a later date, producing the version of the work which is regularly used today, BWV 543. To judge from the sources, this revision was carried out in Leipzig (see under Revised Versions, below).

Fantasia & Fugue in c, BWV 562/1a & BWV 546/2a[21]

Comment: The Fantasia & Fugue in c appears to be an early composition because it is notated in the soprano clef in the sources. Aside from this, manuscript evidence is of little help in determining when the work was written.

The Fantasia's style points to the period 1706-ca. 1712. The through-composed, continuous form is like that used in the Fantasia in C, BWV 570, and the Fantasia con Imitazione in b, BWV 563, two works that appear to date from ca. 1704. In the Fantasia in c this design is treated in a more sophisticated manner. Instead of four-part *Fortspinnung*, the work is composed of five-part imitation. The shape of the melodic material and the manner of imitation reflect French practice. The harmonic plan with its clearly established tonal stations is Italian. The fact that the Fantasia is an amalgamation of French and Italian styles implies that it was composed after the Prelude & Fugue in a, which are still north-German oriented. The redundancy of certain progressions shows that Bach had not yet mastered fully the harmonic practices of the Bologna School. These tendencies suggest the Fantasia may have been written during the earliest Weimar years, 1708-1710. The

Fugue, which has a matching five-part texture, appears to stem from the same period.

At a later date, undoubtedly during the Leipzig years (see under Revised Versions, below), Bach altered the Fantasia & Fugue in c. First, he revised the Fugue and paired it with the Prelude in c, BWV 546/1, probably in the late 1720's. Later, apparently around 1730, he revised the Fantasia as an independent piece (=BWV 562/1). Finally, around 1740, he wrote, or started to write, a new fugue (=BWV 562/2) for the revised Fantasia.[22] The following *stemma* summarizes the hypothetical history of the Fantasia & Fugue:

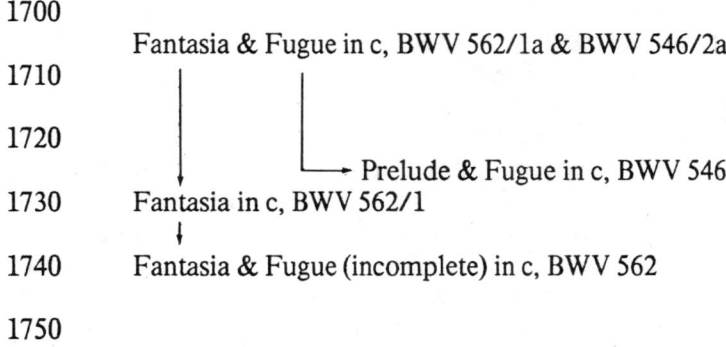

```
1700
            Fantasia & Fugue in c, BWV 562/1a & BWV 546/2a
1710        │           │
1720        │           └─→ Prelude & Fugue in c, BWV 546
            ↓
1730        Fantasia in c, BWV 562/1
            ↓
1740        Fantasia & Fugue (incomplete) in c, BWV 562

1750
```

Passacaglia in c, BWV 582

Comment: The Passacaglia appears in the *Andreas Bach Buch*, where it is written in the soprano clef and dorian notation. This implies a rather early date of composition.

Several stylistic features point to the period 1706-ca. 1712. The ostinato-variation form, the grouping of variations, and the melodic material reflect the chaconnes and passacaglias of Buxtehude and Pachelbel. This suggests that Bach was still working within the bounds of north- and middle-German practice. However, the extraordinary extension and refinement of the ostinato design and the addition of a fugue to it represent innovations that go beyond conventional prototypes. This implies that the Passacaglia was written after the Toccata in E, which is still highly derivative and appears to stem from ca. 1706.

To judge from the part-writing and harmonic design of its fugue, the Passacaglia was composed during the initial Weimar years. The four-part texture is handled with considerably more skill than in compositions assigned to the period 1700-1706. Of greater significance, the double invertible counterpoint reflects the permutation technique that Bach developed in Mühlhausen (cf. Cantata #71, *Gott ist mein König*) and used in early Weimar works (cf. Cantata #21, *Ich hatte viel Bekümmernis*).[23] The harmonic plan, with its well-designed tonal areas, is much like that of the Fantasia in c, BWV 562/1a, and similarly shows the growing influence of Italian style on Bach's handling of modulation. These facts link the Passacaglia with the Fantasia & Fugue in c and place it after the Preludes & Fugues in G and a.

Prelude & Fugue in D, BWV 532

Comment: The sources indicate that the Prelude and the Fugue of this work were not written at the same time.[24] Both appear to be early compositions because they are handed down in the soprano clef.

Several stylistic features of the Prelude reflect north-German practice: the sectional, through-composed form, the melodic material of the introduction (cf. the *trillo longo*, mm. 12-14), and the double-pedal writing in the conclusion. Other factors indicate that the piece goes far beyond its models. The first is the extreme formalization of the overall design, in which *passaggio* introduction, principal section, and conclusion are set off from each other by abrupt changes in tempo. The second is the juxtaposition of styles: a north-German introduction and conclusion frame an Italian, Corelli-derived principal section ("alla breve"). It is unlikely that Bach could have achieved such a stylistic synthesis before the early Weimar years, 1708-ca. 1712, and thus it seems reasonable to assume that the Prelude stems from that time.

The independent treatment of the pedal and the consistent four-part texture imply that the Fugue was written after 1706. The redundant harmonic progressions, the digressive episodes, and the free conclusion point to a fairly early period, however. There is no reason to doubt that the Fugue, like the Prelude, dates from between 1706 and ca. 1712, though the two may not have been paired together until a later time.

Fantasia in G, BWV 572

Comment: A manuscript copy written by Johann Gottfried Walther (in Berlin, DStB: *P 801*) confirms that the Fantasia was written before or during Bach's Weimar years.

To judge from its style, the work stems from the first half of the Weimar period, 1708-ca. 1712. The form, like that of the Prelude in D, BWV 532/1, represents a late expansion of the through-composed, sectional design found in earlier preludes. The three sections — *passaggio* introduction ("Très vitement"), principal section ("Gravement"), and conclusion ("Lentement") – have been formalized to an even greater degree than in the Prelude in D. It is highly improbable that this development took place before the initial years of Bach's Weimar tenure. Moreover, the melodic material can be linked to compositions that appear to date from between 1708 and ca. 1712. The *passaggio* of the "Très vitement" resembles the introduction of the Toccata in C, BWV 564/1 (see below), and the homophony of the "Gravement" is similar to the five-part French scoring that appears in the earliest Weimar cantatas. These factors suggest an origin of 1708-ca. 1712.

Toccata, Adagio, & Fugue in C, BWV 564

Comment: The earliest source of this work, a manuscript copy written by Johann Peter Kellner (in Berlin, SPK: P 286), dates from Bach's Leipzig years. That the Toccata, Adagio, & Fugue was composed before that time is implied by the soprano clef notation used in Kellner's score and other sources.

Stylistic considerations place the work in the early Weimar years, 1708-ca. 1712. The three-movement sequence – prelude, adagio, fugue – obviously reflects Bach's initial preoccupation with the Italian concerto in Weimar. Also suggestive of the early Weimar period are the Grave bridge between the Adagio and the Fugue (characteristic of Corelli or Albinoni rather than Vivaldi) and the unusual quiet ending of the Fugue (characteristic of certain early-Weimar cantatas).[25] The Toccata is made up of a north-German-derived free introduction and an Italian-derived concerto movement. This amalgamative plan links the piece with the Fantasia in G, BWV 572, and the Prelude in D, BWV 532/1, which display equally eclectic sectional designs. The melodic material of the concerto shows no trace of Vivaldi's writing.

All the above factors indicate that the Toccata, Adagio, and Fugue was probably written in the Weimar years preceding ca. 1712.

Fantasia & Fugue in g, BWV 542

Comment: the Fantasia and the Fugue of this work must be considered separately since they did not originate as a prelude-fugue pair.[26]

To judge from its style, the Fantasia dates from the last years of the period 1706-ca. 1712. Its form, consisting of alternating free and strict sections, represents a sophisticated distillation of the north-German multisectional *Praeludium Pedaliter*. While the free material shows certain north-German characteristics (cf. mm. 4-8 and the *passaggio* of the

Prelude in a, BWV 543a/1, or the Toccata in C, BWV 564/1), the strict material with its treble/basso continuo texture reflects the Italian instrumental writing of Corelli or Torelli. The amalgamation of such diverse styles in a composite structure links the Fantasia with the Prelude in D, BWV 532/1, the Fantasia in G, BWV 572, and the Toccata in C, BWV 564/1, which display similarly experimental designs. In addition, chordal passages in the Fantasia mirror perfectly sections of the Prelude and the Toccata in terms of harmony and part-writing (cf. mm. 35-39 of the Fantasia, the Adagio of the Prelude, and the Grave of the Adagio movement of the Toccata). Since the Prelude in D, the Fantasia in G, and the Toccata in C appear to have been written in Weimar between 1798 and ca. 1712, it is probable that the Fantasia in g stems from this time as well.

Other factors distinguish the Fantasia in g as a slightly more mature work. The use of recitative-like melodic material ties the Fantasia to later Weimar pieces such as the Adagio of the Concerto in C, BWV 594, and the Sinfonia of Cantata 21, *Ich hatte viel Bekümmernis* (1714).[27] The use of corresponding sections, a feature not found in the Prelude in D or the Fantasia in G, foreshadows the procedure that is employed on a more extensive basis in the Toccata in d, BWV 538/1. Hence it is possible that the Fantasia was written in Weimar sometime after ca. 1712. The treatment of form and part-writing argues against this alternative, however.

The Fantasia is handed down in six sources, all post-1750 copies. In these manuscripts it is notated in the soprano clef and modern key signature (G minor = 2 flats). This suggests that Bach revised the work sometime after the Weimar period, retaining the soprano clef while updating the dorian notation.

The Fugue seems to have been written in Weimar between ca. 1712 and 1717. The fact that it is consistently transmitted in the soprano clef and dorian notation implies that it was composed before Bach's Cöthen tenure. The well-defined harmonic scheme and the extensive use of verbatim repetition in the manual episodes point to the later Weimar years (cf. the Toccata in d, BWV 538/1). One of the oldest sources of the Fugue, the manuscript copy of Johann Tobias Krebs (in Berlin, DStB: *P 803*) may date from that time.

To summarize: both the Fantasia in g and the Fugue in g appear to have been composed in Weimar, the former between 1708 and ca. 1712 and the latter between ca. 1712 and 1717. The two pieces do not seem to have been paired together until a fairly late date, possibly not until after Bach's death.[28]

Ca. 1712-1723

This period includes the second half of Bach's Weimar tenure as well as his stay in Cöthen. The years surrounding 1712 represent one of the most important turning points in Bach's development as a composer, for it was then that he encountered for the first time Vivaldi's instrumental works: Op. III, *L'Estro armonico*, published in 1711,[29] and other concertos that were circulating in manuscript form. The result of this experience is well-known. Bach arranged many of the concertos for keyboard and at the same time began to incorporate Vivaldi's techniques into his own compositions. The cantatas and *Orgelbüchlein* chorales that date from 1713 and 1714 attest to the alacrity and thoroughness with which he adopted the new Italian idiom.

Encouraged by Duke Ernst August and Prince Johann Ernst, Bach must have endeavored during his remaining years to incorporate Vivaldi's ingenious techniques into his prelude writing. It is safe to assume that decisive changes took place as he assimilated the Vivaldi concerto style. The concerto form and the A B A B form supplanted more conventional, derivative designs. Triadic, motoric melodic material replaced north-German and Corellian idioms. Harmonic plans began to display increasing polarization of modulatory and non-modulatory sections. The modulatory sections, in turn, grew in length through the use of extended sequential patterns, frequently repeated note for note at a different pitch level at a different place in the piece. The result was a new type of prelude, distinctly different from the works written before Bach's espousal of Vivaldi's style.

In December, 1717, Bach left Weimar to accept the post of Capellmeister for Prince Leopold of Anhalt-Cöthen. The Prince was an able and enthusiastic musician, and consequently Bach's talents were highly esteemed. Since the Cöthen court was Reformed, however, Bach's duties involved the composition and performance of chamber music only.[30] The unaccompanied violin and cello sonatas, most of the orchestral suites and Brandenburg concertos, and host of other chamber works date from this period.

As far as prelude writing is concerned, the move to Cöthen brought to an end the steady production of the Weimar years. In Cöthen Bach needed organ works only occasionally — for performance out of town[31] or for the education of young Wilhelm Friedemann. There is no reason to suspect that the preludes which he did write during this time differed substantially from those composed during the later Weimar years. Bach's refinement and modification of Vivaldi-oriented procedures seems to have continued until the Leipzig period, when the weekly production of cantatas thrust his writing in a different direction. The Fantasia in C (incomplete), BWV 573, can be assigned by reliable manuscript evidence to the years 1722-1723 (See below). The fact that it is still clearly Vivaldian in nature is indicative of the relative stylistic continuity of the late-Weimar—Cöthen works.

Seven compositions can be assigned to the period ca. 1712-1723. The first five appear to stem from Weimar; the last two seem to have been written in Cöthen:

Prelude & Fugue in C, BWV 545a

Comment: The *terminus ante quem non* for this work is established by the style of the Prelude. The A B A B form, the instrumental-derived melodic material, the sixteenth-note motoric pulse, and the sequential patterns all reflect Vivaldi's influence. This suggests that the Prelude & Fugue in C dates from after ca. 1712.

A reliable *terminus post quem non* is provided by manuscript evidence. The sources of BWV 545a are of no avail since they all date from after 1750. However, Johann Gottfried Walther's copy (Yale: *LM 4718*) of the revised version of BWV 545a, BWV 545 (see below), can be assigned to Bach's Weimar years. This means that BWV 545a must have been completed while Bach was still in Weimar, i.e., before December, 1717.

Prelude & Fugue in f, BWV 534

Comment: The only source for the Prelude & Fugue in f is an early nineteenth-century copy (in MBLpz: *III.8.21*) written by Johann Andreas Dröbs. Dröbs was a student of Johann Christian Kittel, who in turn had studied with Bach. Hence *III.8.21* can be deemed reliable despite its late date. In this source the Prelude is written in the soprano clef and dorian notation, a fact which points to a pre-Cöthen origin.

Several stylistic features of the Prelude suggest that the work was written in Weimar between ca. 1712 and 1717. The first is the A B A B structure, which reflects Bach's experience with Vivaldi's ritornello forms. The second is the instrumental-derived melodic material, which shows the direct influence of violin writing (cf. mm. 9-11 and the closing cadenza). The third is the motoric pulse that is maintained almost throughout the entire piece. This, too, can be traced to Vivaldi.

Toccata & Fugue in d ("Dorian"), BWV 538

Comment: The style of the Toccata suggests that this work originated in Weimar between ca. 1712 and 1717. The concerto form, the instrumental-derived melodic figures, the sixteenth-note motoric pulse, and the extended circle-of-fifth sequences all reflect the direct influence of Vivaldi. Moreover, the Toccata shows a very close chronological relationship with Bach's concerto arrangements for organ. These arrangements undoubtedly date from late Weimar and, like the Toccata, are written for an Oberwerk-Positiv setting.

Manuscript evidence supports the above conclusions. The earliest source of the Toccata & Fugue is a manuscript copy (in Berlin, DStB: *P 803*) written by Johann Gottfried Walther during Bach's stay in Weimar. This source provides a *terminus post quem non* of December, 1717, for the work.

Toccata & Fugue in F, BWV 540

Comment: As far as chronology is concerned the Toccata and the Fugue of this work must be treated separately since they were not originally paired together.[32] The earliest source of the Toccata is Johann Tobias Krebs' copy in Berlin, DStB: *P 803*. Since this manuscript could have been written during Bach's tenure in either Weimar or Leipzig, it offers no conclusive evidence for chronology. However, the soprano clef notation suggests that the Toccata dates from ca. 1723. The style of the piece points to the Weimar years ca. 1712-1717. The instrumental-derived melodic material, the sixteenth-note motoric pulse, and the extended circle-of-fifth sequences reflect the direct influence of Vivaldi and link the work chronologically with the Toccata in d ("Dorian"). The hybrid form, which combines a *passaggio* introduction with a concerto movement, is a refined version of the design used earlier in the Toccata in C, BWV 564/1.

The earliest source of the Fugue is Johann Ludwig Krebs' copy in *P 803*. Although this copy was probably written between 1726 and 1735, the years Krebs was a *Thomaner*, the use of soprano clef-notation suggests that the piece dates from an earlier period. Stylistically the Fugue displays features appearing in Bach's works between the years ca. 1712 and 1723. The melodic material is very similar to that of the Fugue in d, BWV 538/2. The extended harmonic plan, which includes the use of parallel tonalities (C major and C minor), connects the piece with the Toccata in F, the Toccata in d ("Dorian"), and the Prelude in C, BWV 547/1 (see below). The combining of two subjects reflects the same interest devices seen in the Fugue in C, BWV 547/2, and the fugues of the solo violin sonatas in a and C, BWV 1003 and 1005, of 1720. Hence it is possible that the Fugue in F was written either in Weimar after ca. 1712 or in Cöthen.

In summary, to judge from the evidence available, the Toccata in F was written in Weimar, between ca. 1712 and 1717. The Fugue in F originated either in Weimar, after ca. 1712 or in Cöthen. The two pieces were paired together sometime before 1735 (the *terminus post quem non* of the *P 803* copy).

Prelude & Fugue in G, BWV 541

Comment: The style of the Prelude suggests that this work was written in Weimar, between ca. 1712 and 1717. The instrumental-derived melodic material, the motoric sixteenth-note pulse, and the direct, well-defined harmonic plan all reflect Vivaldi's immediate influence. The form is the same hybrid design (introductory *passaggio* plus concerto movement) used in the Toccata in C, BWV 654/1, and the Toccata in F, BWV 540/1. The extremely refined, concise treatment of this plan implies that the Prelude postdates both of these works. The close motivic relationship between the Fugue and initial chorus of Cantata 21, *Ich hatte viel Bekümmernis* (1714), suggests that the Prelude & Fugue may have been written in 1714 or sometime soon thereafter.

The sources show that Bach revised the Prelude & Fugue in G several times. The latest version, handed down in Bach's own *Reinschrift* (New York: Hinrichsen Collection) appears to have been made after 1733.[33] Although the work is generally transmitted in the treble clef, a copy of the earliest surviving version of the Prelude (in Berlin, SPK: *P 595*) written in the soprano clef supports the hypothesis that the Prelude & Fugue stems from Weimar.

Prelude & Fugue in C, BWV 547

Comment: Two factors indicate that the Prelude & Fugue in C was written in Cöthen. The first is the way the work is notated in the sources; the second is the manner in which the ritornello of the Prelude is constructed.

The earliest source of the Prelude & Fugue is Kellner's apograph[34] in Berlin, SPK: *P 274*, a *Konvolut* dating from about 1725-1735. In *P 274* and in all other sources the work is notated in the treble clef. This suggests that it was written sometime after Bach's Weimar years, But the general style of the Prelude is not unlike that of compositions that appear to stem from late Weimar. The concerto form, the instrumental-derived melodic material, and the clearly defined harmonic plan all reflect Vivaldi's influence. The concise, sophisticated construction of the ritornello, however, distinguishes the Prelude in C as a later work. The ritornello is made up of a short series of interrelated motives that are presented in double counterpoint. Since this same technique is used in the first movement of Brandenburg Concerto No. 2 in F, it is possible that the Prelude stems from Cöthen, ca. 1719, the period when the Concerto appears to have been written.[35] In addition, the fugue of the Prelude & Fugue in C shows a close relationship to the fugues of the solo violin sonatas in a and C, BWV 1003 and 1005, which bear the date 1720.

Fantasia in C (incomplete), BWV 573

Comment: This is one of the few preludes that can be dated reliably on the basis of manuscript evidence alone. The unfinished composing score is contained in the *Klavierbüchlein für Anna Magdalena Bach* of 1722 (Berlin, SPK: *P 224*). To judge from Bach's handwriting, this score was entered into the collection between 1722 and 1723.

1723-1750

In May, 1723, Bach resigned as Capellmeister in Cöthen in order to accept the post of Thomaskantor in Leipzig. In assuming this new position he returned to the realm of sacred music, for as Thomaskantor he was responsible for the musical direction of all of Leipzig's principal churches. Initially he approached this task with enthusiasm. Between 1723 and 1728 he composed an immense number of vocal works for services at the Thomaskirche and the Nikolaikirche: the St. John and the St. Matthew Passions, the motets, and the bulk of the cantata repertoire. Later, in 1729, when relations with the Town Council became strained, he turned his attention from the production of vocal music for the church to other endeavors: the composition of chamber pieces for the Collegium Musicum, the assembling of encyclopedic keyboard collections for publication, the writing of pedagogical works for teaching, and the revision and reordering of earlier compositions.

During the entire Leipzig period Bach was not responsible for organ music in the town churches. Between 1723 and 1750 Christian Gräbner, Johann Gottlieb Görner, and Johann Schneider served as organists of the Thomaskirche and the Nikolaikirche. Bach himself was answerable for vocal music alone. As a result, he needed organ works only for occasional purposes: teaching, recitals, and the publication of *Clavierübung* III in 1739. Thus the low productivity of Cöthen continued in Leipzig, and Bach apparently relied for the most part on his store of pieces from earlier years.

One can assume, however, that he did write a few preludes during this time,[36] for several works display stylistic features that do not appear in his oeuvre before the cantatas of 1723-1728. At no other time was Bach so completely immersed in the compositional challenges posed by one genre. Hence it was undoubtedly at this point that his own vocal works began to eclipse Vivaldi's concertos as the principal model for his prelude writing. The concerto form and the A B A B form were reinterpreted in light of the experience writing cantatas. The motoric instrumental figures of Vivaldi were replaced by more flexible melodic material. Harmonic schemes were formalized to an even greater degree than before, with even clearer distinction between modulatory and nonmodulatory areas. Five works show these types of changes and thus appear to date from the Leipzig period.

Prelude & Fugue in e, BWV 548

Comment: The earliest source of the Prelude & Fugue in e is the partially autograph manuscript contained in Berlin, SPK: *P 274*. This manuscript can be assigned to the years 1727-1731 on the basis of watermarks. The fact that it is only part autograph implies the existence of an earlier, now-lost source. This means the Prelude & Fugue may have been composed sometime before the period from which *P 274* stems. A *terminus ante quem non* of ca. 1723 is suggested by the treble clef notation found in all surviving sources.

The style of the Prelude points to the period 1725-1728. The piece displays a concerto form, but a type different from that which Bach used in Weimar and Cöthen. The ritornello shows a highly formalized, segmented construction that first appears in the opening choruses of the chorale cantatas of the second Leipzig *Jahrgang* (1724-1725). The episodes, too, display a segmented design derived from the same source. The melodic material does not reflect Vivaldi's concerto style. It mirrors, rather, an unusual type of cantilena writing found in the instrumental parts of certain cantata arias composed between 1725 and 1728. A motoric pulse is present in the Prelude, but it is handled with much more flexibility than in the late-Weimar and Cöthen works.

All these factors indicate that the Prelude & Fugue in e was written during the period 1725-1728.

Prelude & Fugue in b, BWV 544

Comment: Almost all the arguments used to date the Prelude & Fugue in e can be applied to the Prelude & Fugue in b. The earliest source of the work is an autograph (Oxford: Rosenthal Collection) from the period 1727-1731. Since this autograph is a *Reinschrift*, it is possible that the Prelude & Fugue was composed at an earlier time. The treble clef notation used in all sources implies a *terminus ante quem non* of ca. 1723.

The nature of the Prelude suggests an origin of 1725-1728. Stylistically, the piece resembles the Prelude in e to a remarkable degree. The segmented construction of the ritornello and the episodes reflect the technique Bach developed in the second Leipzig cantata *Jahrgang*. The cantilena melodic material points to cantata movements written between 1725 and 1728. In light of this, the Prelude & Fugue in b can be assigned to the same period as the Prelude & Fugue in e, 1725-1728.

Prelude & Fugue in c, BWV 546

Comment: The Prelude and the Fugue of this work originated at different times. The Prelude appears to have been composed in Leipzig. The Fugue, on the other hand, is the revised version of a piece which seems to date from between 1706 and ca. 1712 (see above).

The oldest source of the Prelude & Fugue in c is an apograph (in Berlin, SPK: *P 286*) written by Johann Peter Kellner during Bach's Leipzig years. In this manuscript both the Prelude and the Fugue are notated in the treble clef. However, a later source, a copy in Berlin, SPK: *P 290*, seems to reflect an earlier state of the work: the Prelude is notated in treble clef while the Fugue is still written in pre-ca. 1723 notation, the soprano clef.

Stylistic considerations suggest the Prelude was composed in Leipzig between 1725 and 1729. The form is a concerto design modified by the influence of Bach's chorale cantatas. The melodic material resembles that used in the double chorus motets (written between 1723 and 1729) and the opening chorus of Cantata #47, *Wer sich selbst erhöhet* (1726). These features link the Prelude with the Prelude in e and the Prelude in b above. What separates the Prelude in c from these works is the subtle treatment of rhythmic pulse. In the Prelude in c an extraordinary number of fundamental rhythmic units are used: the half note, the quarter note, the eighth note, the triplet, and the sixteenth note. The graduated accelerando created through the manipulation of these values contrasts greatly with the technique used in the Preludes in e and b, which are each dominated by a single atomic unit. The handling of rhythmic pulse suggests that the Prelude in c was composed at a slightly later date than the other two works.

An additional piece of chronological evidence for dating the Prelude & Fugue in c can be gleaned from the Fantasia in c, BWV 562/1a, which appears to have been written between 1706 and ca. 1712 and was originally paired with an early version of the C-minor Fugue, BWV 546/2a (see above). In Leipzig Bach detached the C-minor Fugue from the Fantasia, revised it, and paired it with the newly composed C-minor Prelude. He subsequently reworked the Fantasia as an independent piece. To judge from the extant autograph (Berlin, SPK: *P 490*), these revisions took place around 1730. This would indicate that the C-minor Fugue had been separated from the Fantasia and paired with the C-minor Prelude sometime before that date.[37]

Prelude & Fugue in E♭, BWV 552

Comment: This work was originally printed as part of *Clavierübung* III. For this reason it can be assigned to 1739, the year *Clavierübung* III was issued. No evidence suggests the Prelude & Fugue was written before that time.

Fantasia & Fugue in c, BWV 537

Comment: This work has traditionally been assigned to Weimar.[38] Both manuscript and stylistic evidence point to a Leipzig origin, however.

The only source of the Fantasia & Fugue is the copy contained in Berlin, DStB: *P 803*. This copy was written by Johann Tobias and Johann Ludwig Krebs[39] and carries the date Jan. 10, 1751. In *P 803* the Fantasia & Fugue is notated in treble clef and modern key signature (C minor = three flats). This fact suggests the work was composed after ca. 1723.

The style of the Fantasia supports this conjecture. The A B A B form is treated in a much more sophisticated manner than in the Prelude & Fugue in C, BWV 545, and the Prelude & Fugue in f, BWV 534. The melodic material, based on two rhetorical figures, the *exclamatio* and the *suspiratio*, is vocal-derived and characteristic of Bach's Leipzig prelude writing. The treatment of rhythmic pulse is also typical of his later style. The motoric pulse of Vivaldi's concerto is consciously avoided. It is replaced by a more flexible plan in which the fundamental rhythmic unit changes from the quarter note to the eighth note to the sixteenth note.

The extremely refined connection between the Fantasia and the Fugue points to a late date: the Fantasia leads directly into the Fugue by concluding on the dominant; the Fantasia contains, in diminution, the theme which becomes the second subject of the Fugue. Also to be considered is the close stylistic tie between the Fugue and the da capo lute fugues from the Partita in c, BWV 997, and the Prelude, Fugue, and Allegro in E♭, BWV 998. The latter appear to stem from the last decade of Bach's life.[40] It is quite possible that the Fantasia & Fugue in c dates from this period as well.

Revised Versions of Earlier Works

In the process of teaching and performing Bach often emended or rewrote pre-existing compositions. The following six works, revisions of earlier pieces, reflect this procedure:[41]

Prelude & Fugue in g, BWV 535

Comment: This work is a revision of BWV 535a, which appears to date from before 1706 (see under 1700-1706, above). The Prelude is a complete reworking of the earlier piece. The Fugue displays improved part-writing. When he transformed BWV 535a into BWV 535, Bach retained the soprano clef of the original but changed the key signature from dorian notation (G minor = 1 flat) to modern notation (G minor = 2 flats). This suggests the revision took place sometime after the Weimar years, that is, after 1717.

Prelude & Fugue in A, BWV 536

Comment: It is quite difficult to establish the date of this work, a revision of the early composition BWV 536a (see under 1700-1706, above). Bach's alterations in BWV 536 are limited to matters of detail. Since BWV 536 appears in Berlin, SPK: *P 804*, among pieces dated 1725 and 1726, one can postulate that it was completed by the first decade of Bach's Leipzig tenure. Thus the work would stem from between ca. 1704 and ca. 1725.

The similarity between the Fugue and the Sinfonia of Cantata #152, *Tritt auf die Glaubensbahn* also provides a clue, albeit a highly hypothetical one, for chronology. It suggests Bach may have been revising the Prelude & Fugue in A around 1714, the time he wrote the Cantata.

Prelude & Fugue in a, BWV 543

Comment: This work is a revision of the early composition BWV 543a (see under 1706-ca. 1712, above). The surviving source material suggests that BWV 543 dates from the Leipzig period. Only two pre-1750 manuscripts transmit the Prelude & Fugue in a: Berlin, SPK: *P 288*, which contains a copy by Johann Peter Kellner, and Berlin, DStB: *P 803*, which contains a copy by a Krebs-circle scribe. Both manuscripts stem from the Leipzig years, and both exhibit BWV 543a. Kellner and the Krebs family were in direct contact with Bach, and they probably would have had access to BWV 543 if it existed at the time they were copying. In light of this, it appears that Bach did not revise the Prelude & Fugue in a until a fairly late date, perhaps after ca. 1730.

Prelude & Fugue in C, BWV 545

Comment: This Prelude & Fugue is a revision of BWV 545a, which appears to have been written between ca. 1712 and 1717 (see under ca. 1712-1723, above). Since BWV 545 is contained in a manuscript dating from the Weimar period (Yale: *LM 4718*), one can assume that it was completed before 1717. Therefore BWV 545, like BWV 545a, can be assigned to the years ca. 1712-1717.

Prelude & Fugue in c, BWV 549

Comment: This work is a revised and transposed version of the Prelude & Fugue in d, BWV 549a (see under 1700-1706, above). The modern key signature (C minor = three flats) found in all surviving sources suggests that BWV 549 dates from the Cöthen or Leipzig years, that is, after 1717.

Fantasia & Fugue (incomplete) in c, BWV 562

Comment: The source material reveals that the Fantasia & Fugue were written at different times. The Fantasia is a revised version of the early composition BWV 562/1a (see under 1706-ca. 1712, above). To judge from Bach's autograph (Berlin, SPK: *P 490*), it was written around 1730. The Fugue—in accordance with this same source—was not begun until the 1740's.[42]

Special Cases

Finally, substantial evidence suggests that two works should not be counted among Bach's authentic organ preludes. The first appears to be spurious, the second seems to be a clavier piece.

Prelude in G, BWV 568

Comment: Incongruous stylistic elements suggest that the Prelude in G was not written by Bach. The north-German keyboard and pedal figurations, the awkward part-writing, and the careless doubling reflect Bach's style between 1700 and 1706. The work's concerto design, however, cannot be reconciled with this early date, for nothing indicates Bach used ritornello forms before Weimar. But if the Prelude in G was written in Weimar, it surely would not display such pronounced compositional shortcomings. It is probable that the piece was indeed written after 1706, but by someone other than Bach.

The provenance of the Prelude casts further doubt on its authenticity. The earliest source of the work, Berlin, SPK: *P 1107*, was written in the second half of the eighteenth century by an anonymous scribe. All other sources of the piece date from the nineteenth century. In *P 1107* the author of the Prelude is not named. The other composition in the manuscript, the Little Harmonic Labyrinth, BWV 591, is ascribed to Bach. This might have led later scribes to assume that the Prelude stemmed from Bach's pen as well. But since the Little Harmonic Labyrinth has been discredited,[43] the connection between Bach and the Prelude in G established in *P 1107* is doubly suspect.

Prelude in d, BWV 539/1

Comment: Stylistic and manuscript evidence indicates that the Prelude in d is a clavier piece which was appropriated for pairing with the Fugue in d, BWV 539/2 (a transcription of the second movement of the Sonata in g for unaccompanied violin, BWV 1001). The purely *manualiter* nature of the Prelude reflects Bach's clavier compositions rather than his organ works.

It is unlikely that Bach would have joined such a modest *manualiter* prelude with such a lengthy *pedaliter* fugue. Indeed, the sources indicate he probably was not responsible for the pairing. The Prelude is handed down in only one source, an early nineteenth-century manuscript (Berlin, SPK: *P 517*) in which it appears together with the Fugue in d. In this source the Prelude is notated in the treble clef while the Fugue is notated in the soprano clef. To judge from this, the Prelude was added to the Fugue sometime after the two were written.

Taking into account its provenance, Dietrich Kilian suggested that the Prelude & Fugue is an arrangement stemming from the nineteenth century.[44] Forkel knew of the pairing, however, so it may date from a slightly earlier period.[45] Bach's followers in the second half of the eighteenth century must have been tempted to create new organ preludes and fugues out of single compositions if pieces in the same key could be found. The Prelude & Fugue in d seems to be the result of such a posthumous pairing.

The present discussion of chronology can be summarized in the following table, which compares the dates proposed for each work with those given by Spitta, Schmieder, and Keller.

Work	Date Proposed General Period	Specific Period	Date Given By Spitta[46]	Date Given By Schmieder[47]	Date Given By Keller[48]
Prelude & Fugue in C, BWV 531	1700-1706	Lüneburg (1700-1703)	Weimar, ca. 1709	Weimar, ca. 1709 (or: Lüneberg?)	1700-1705
Prelude & Fugue in D, BWV 532	1706-ca. 1712	Weimar, 1708-ca. 1712	Weimar, ca. 1709	Weimar, ca. 1709 (or: Arnstadt?)	1706-1708
Prelude & Fugue in e, BWV 533	1700-1706	Arnstadt, ca. 1704	Weimar, ca. 1709	Weimar, ca. 1709 (or: Arnstadt?)	1706-1708
Prelude & Fugue in f, BWV 534	ca. 1712-1723	Weimar, ca. 1712-1717	Weimar, ca. 1716	Weimar, ca. 1717	Weimar
Prelude & Fugue in g, BWV 535	After 1717	–	Weimar, ca. 1709	Weimar, ca. 1709 (or: Arnstadt?)	1706-1708
–, BWV 535a	1700-1706	Arnstadt, ca. 1704	–	–	–
Prelude & Fugue in A, BWV 536	Between ca. 1704 and ca. 1725	–	Weimar, ca. 1716	Weimar, ca. 1716	Weimar
–, BWV 536a	1700-1706	Arnstadt, ca. 1704	–	–	–
Fantasia & Fugue in c, BWV 537	Leipzig, (1723-1750)	Leipzig, 1729-1750	Weimar, ca. 1716	Weimar, ca. 1716	Weimar
Toccata & Fugue in d, BWV 538	ca. 1712-1723	Weimar, ca. 1712-1717	Leipzig, 1727-1736	Leipzig, 1727-1736 (or: Cöthen?)	Late Weimar-Cöthen

A Proposed Outline

Work	Date Proposed General Period	Date Proposed Specific Period	Date Given By Spitta	Date Given By Schmieder	Date Given By Keller
Prelude & Fugue in d, BWV 539	Prelude; not intended for organ Fugue: late Cöthen or Leipzig (before 1725?)	Prelude: — Fugue: ?	Leipzig, 1724-1725	Leipzig, 1724-1725	Cöthen
Toccata & Fugue in F, BWV 540	Toccata: ca. 1712-1723 Fugue: ca. 1712-1723	Toccata: Weimar, ca. 1712-1717 Fugue: ?	Toccata: Cöthen Fugue: Weimar	Toccata: Cöthen Fugue: Weimar	Late Weimar-Cöthen
Prelude & Fugue in G, BWV 541	ca. 1712-1723	Weimar, ca. 1712-1717	Leipzig, 1724-1725	Leipzig, 1724-1725	Leipzig, 1723-1730
Fantasia & Fugue in g, BWV 542	Fantasia: 1706-ca. 1712 Fugue: ca. 1712-1723	Fantasia: Weimar, 1708- ca. 1712 Fugue: Weimar, ca. 1712-1717	Cöthen, ca. 1720	Cöthen, ca. 1720	Late Weimar-Cöthen
Prelude & Fugue in a, BWV 543	Leipzig, after ca. 1730	–	Weimar, ca. 1709	Weimar, ca. 1709	Late Weimar-Cöthen
–, BWV 543a	1706-ca. 1712	1706-1708	–	–	–
Prelude & Fugue in b, BWV 544	Leipzig (1723-1750)	Leipzig, 1725-1728	Leipzig, 1727-1736	Leipzig, 1727-1736	Leipzig, ca. 1730-1740
Prelude & Fugue in C, BWV 545	ca. 1712-1717	–	Leipzig, ca. 1730	Leipzig, ca. 1730	Leipzig, 1723-1730
BWV 545a	ca. 1712-1723	Weimar, ca. 1712-1717	–	–	–
Prelude & Fugue in c, BWV 546	Prelude: Leipzig (1723-1750) Fugue (revision of BWV 562/2a): Leipzig	Prelude: Leipzig, 1725-1729 Fugue (revision of BWV 562/2a): Leipzig, 1725-1729	Prelude: Leipzig, ca. 1730 Fugue: Weimar, ca. 1716	Prelude: Leipzig, ca. 1730 Fugue: Weimar, ca. 1716	Leipzig, ca. 1730-1740

Work	Date Proposed General Period	Date Proposed Specific Period	Date Given By Spitta	Date Given By Schmieder	Date Given By Keller
Prelude & Fugue in C, BWV 547	ca. 1712-1723	Cöthen, ca. 1719	Leipzig, ca. 1744	Leipzig, ca. 1744	Leipzig, ca. 1730-1740
Prelude & Fugue in e, BWV 548	Leipzig (1723-1750)	Leipzig, 1725-1728	Leipzig, 1727-1736	Leipzig, 1727-1736	Leipzig, ca. 1730-1740
Prelude & Fugue in c, BWV 549	After 1717	–	Arnstadt, ca. 1703-1704	Arnstadt, ca. 1703-1704 (or: Lüneburg?)	1700-1705
Prelude & Fugue in d, BWV 549a	1700-1706	Lüneburg (1700-1703)	–	–	–
Prelude & Fugue in G, BWV 550	1706-ca. 1712	1706-1708	Weimar, ca. 1709	Weimar, ca. 1709 (or: Arnstadt?)	Weimar
Prelude in a, BWV 551	1700-1706	Arnstadt, 1703-ca. 1704	Arnstadt, before 1706	Arnstadt, before 1706 (or: Lüneburg?)	1700-1705
Prelude & Fugue in E♭, BWV 552	Leipzig (1723-1750)	Leipzig, 1739	Leipzig, 1739	Leipzig, 1739	Leipzig, 1739
Fantasia & Fugue in c, BWV 562	Fantasia (revision of BWV 562/1a): Leipzig (1723-1750) Fugue: Leipzig (1723-1750)	Fantasia (revision of BWV 562/1a): Leipzig, ca. 1730 Fugue: Leipzig, ca. 1740	Weimar, 1712-1716	Weimar, 1712-1716 (or: Cöthen?)	Late Weimar-Cöthen
Fantasia & Fugue in c, BWV 562/1a & BWV 546/2a	1706-ca. 1712	Weimar, 1708-1710	–	–	–
Fantasia con Imitazione in b, BWV 563	1700-1706	Arnstadt, ca. 1704	Weimar, ca. 1710	Weimar, ca. 1710 (or: Arnstadt?)	1700-1705
Toccata, Adagio, & Fugue in C, BWV 564	1706-ca. 1712	Weimar, 1708-ca. 1712	Weimar, ca. 1709	Weimar, ca. 1709	Weimar
Toccata in d, BWV 565	1700-1706	Arnstadt, ca. 1704	Weimar, ca. 1709	Weimar, ca. 1709 (or: Arnstadt?)	1706-1708

A Proposed Outline

Work	Date Proposed General Period	Date Proposed Specific Period	Date Given By Spitta	Date Given By Schmieder	Date Given By Keller
Toccata in E, BWV 566	1700-1706	Arnstadt, ca. 1706	Arnstadt, ca. 1707	Arnstadt, ca. 1707	1706-1608
Prelude in G, BWV 568	Spurious	–	Mühlhausen ca. 1708	Mühlhausen ca. 1708 (or: Lüneburg?)	1700-1705
Prelude in a, BWV 569	1700-1706	Arnstadt, 1703-ca. 1704	Weimar, ca. 1709	Weimar, ca. 1709 (or: Arnstadt?)	1700-1705
Fantasia in C, BWV 570	1700-1706	Arnstadt, ca. 1704	Weimar, ca. 1709	Weimar, ca. 1709 (or: Arnstadt?)	1700-1705
Fantasia in G, BWV 572	1706-ca. 1712	Weimar, 1708-ca. 1712	Arnstadt, 1705-1706	Arnstadt 1705-1706 (or: Weimar?)	Weimar
Fantasia in C (incomplete), BWV 573	ca. 1712-1723	Cöthen, 1722-1723	Cöthen, 1722	Cöthen, 1722	Cöthen, 1722
Passacaglia in c, BWV 582	1706-ca. 1712	Weimar, 1708-1710	Weimar, ca. 1716-1717	Weimar, ca. 1716-1717 (or: Cöthen?)	Late Weimar-Cöthen

V
The Pairing of Prelude and Fugue

The extended discussions of style and chronology help to explain how and when Bach developed the organ prelude. What remains to be investigated is the motivating force behind this development: What compelled Bach to expand and refine this type of piece to such an extraordinary degree? The answer to this question seems to lie not in the prelude itself but rather in Bach's establishment of the prelude-fugue pair as an aesthetic ideal.

The fundamental principle behind the prelude and fugue—the juxtaposition of free and contrapuntal styles—was current in Germany in the seventeenth century. In North Germany the pattern of free introduction, fugue, free conclusion can already be observed by 1650 in the short *Praeludia Pedaliter* of Scheidemann, Tunder, and others. The next generation, represented chiefly by Buxtehude, enlarged this plan by expanding the individual sections of the *Praeludium* and by stringing more of these sections together.[1] The extent to which this procedure could be carried out is illustrated by Buxtehude's *Praeludium* in e (BuxWV 142), which displays a seven-part plan: free introduction, fugue (in 4/4), free interlude, fugue (in 3/2), free interlude, fugue (in 12/8), and free conclusion. The chief unifying factor in compositions of this type is the thematic connection between the free and contrapuntal material: the fugues are usually based on the concise, imitative treatment of motives presented in a more expansive manner in the free introduction. In Buxtehude's *Praeludium* in e the *soggetti* of the three fugues are all derived from the opening motive:

Free introduction:

First fugue:

Second fugue:

Third fugue:

In South Germany the trend towards combining free and contrapuntal forms can be seen even more clearly. J.K.F. Fischer's *Blumen-Strauss* and *Ariadne Musica*,[2] for example, both display the unambiguous joining of prelude and fugue. *Blumen-Strauss* contains a cycle of prelude, six fugues, and finale for each of the eight ecclesiastical modes. *Ariadne Musica* contains twenty prelude-fugue pairs, each in a different key. Although the preludes in both collections are extremely small (they average about ten measures in length), the fact that they are often thematically independent from the fugues with which they are paired is quite significant. It implies that south-German composers considered the juxtaposition of prelude and fugue more important than the thematic unification of the two forms.

Clearly Bach was aware of both north- and south-German practice. The Prelude in a, BWV 551, the Toccata in d, BWV 565, and the Toccata in E, BWV 566, reflect the north-German multisectional *Praeludium Pedaliter*, whereas the Fantasia con Imitazione in b, BWV 563, mirrors the south-German *manualiter* prelude and fugue. Either of these genres could have served as a point of departure for his development of the large-scale prelude-fugue pair. If Bach began with the north-German *Praeludium*, he could have selectively eliminated sections until only two remained: free introduction (=prelude) and fugue. If he started with the south-German prelude and fugue, he could have expanded the entire structure, making it *pedaliter* in the process. In both cases he would have faced the same problem: How could the prelude material be organized effectively? A series of improvisatory gestures had sufficed for the introductory section of a north-German Praeludium or for the diminutive south-German prelude, but more sophisticated techniques were necessary for a large independent prelude.

To judge from the style and the *pedaliter* setting of his earliest free works, Bach leaned towards the north-German school. It is generally assumed that he first copied contemporary multisectional prototypes and then evolved his own prelude and fugue plan out of this experience.[3] What stands against this theory is the fact that several works of a distinct prelude and fugue character clearly predate the pieces with a north-German multisectional structure. The Prelude & Fugue in d, BWV 549a, and the Prelude & Fugue in C, BWV 531, probably Bach's earliest surviving free organ compositions,[4] already show a pronounced prelude and fugue design. The preludes of both works display a well-rounded form: *passaggio* introduction, principal section, free conclusion (in the Prelude in C). This kind of calculated organizational scheme is lacking in the introductory material of the Prelude in a or the Toccata in d. Certain features of the Prelude & Fugue in d and the Prelude & Fugue in C reflect north-German convention: the thematic tie between prelude and fugue and the free conclusion which brings the fugue to a close. The conscious attempt to balance prelude and fugue does not, however. Buxtehude's *Praeludia* do not show the same marked tendency towards a bipartite plan in which prelude and fugue are separated by a double bar.

Other early works, undoubtedly written in Arnstadt, show an even clearer formalization of the prelude-fugue relationship. In the Prelude & Fugue in A, BWV 536a, and the Prelude & Fugue in e, BWV 533, prelude and fugue remain related motivically. But in both compositions the free conclusion at the end of the fugue is dropped completely, producing an unequivocal two-part prelude and fugue design. The prelude, with a fully developed form of its own, is treated with as much deliberation as the fugue.

What caused Bach to enlarge the prelude and to give it a prominent role at such an early date? The pairing of prelude and fugue in the Preludes & Fugues in d, C, A, and e may not have resulted simply from his desire to refine existing models. It may have stemmed, rather, from his early propensity for fugue writing. If contemporary accounts agree on anything, it is on Bach's life-long interest in fugues. This interest can be traced from the earliest surviving keyboard works to the unfinished compendium, the Art of Fugue. C.P.E. Bach, in a letter for Forkel, stated that even in his youth his father became a "pure and strong fugue writer" through his own energies and through his desire to master the techniques of other composers.[5] Several works attest to this statement. The Fugue in c on a theme by Legrenzi, BWV 574, the Fugue in b on a theme by Corelli, BWV 579, and the Fugue in c, BWV 575, show that Bach could write a lengthy—if unrefined—fugue at a very early date. However, to judge from the aesthetic principles prevailing at that time in both North and South Germany, such fugues could not stand alone. One had to preface them with a free introduction.[6] If it was modest in size, an introduction of this type could easily be improvised on the spur of the moment. There was no reason to write it down, beforehand or afterwards. This might explain why far fewer preludes than fugues have been transmitted in late seventeenth- and early eighteenth-century sources.[7]

Among Bach's compositions the Prelude & Fugue in g, BWV 535a, appears to reflect the process of prefacing a predeliberated fugue with an improvised prelude. In this work Bach introduced a carefully planned fugue with a cursory prelude that he apparently dashed off at the last minute.[8] He seems to have been dissatisfied with the unbalanced pairing which resulted from this procedure, however, for he later enlarged the Prelude to produce a more symmetrical plan.

Bach's ambitious fugue writing, then, produced an imbalance between prelude and fugue which could be resolved in only one way, namely, by expanding substantially the scope of the prelude. This could not be achieved through a series of improvisatory gestures, but through the use of forms which would serve as an organizational framework for the musical material. Bach did not invent the prelude. What he succeeded in doing was to organize it in a new manner.

Working within the general context of north-German practice which called for the thematic unification of prelude and fugue, Bach must have realized that the primary structural problem with the prelude was the treatment of the opening melodic material. How could this material be developed in a manner which would give a cohesive shape to the prelude and yet at the same time not impinge on the contrapuntal nature of the fugue? The answer initially was the through-composed, sectional form in which the opening material was first treated freely (*passaggio* introduction) and then more concisely (principal section). This procedure can be observed in many of Bach's early works. In the Prelude & Fugue in a, BWV 543, for example, the initial theme is developed in a free manner, in an imitative manner, and finally, in a fugal manner:

Prelude, free introduction:

Prelude, principal section:

Fugue:

The metamorphosis of the melodic material in the Prelude & Fugue in a reflects the technique used in the north-German multisectional *Praeludium Pedaliter*. What is different is the fact that the principal theme is manipulated within the bounds of such a carefully delineated and calculated form.

As Bach continued to expand and formalize the structure of the prelude, it eventually became unnecessary to continue the thematic relationship between prelude and fugue. The prelude at this point of development could stand alone by virtue of its form. This can be seen in the Prelude in D, BWV 532/1, and the Fantasia in G, BWV 572. These works represent the last stage in Bach's evolution of the through-composed, sectional design. Both pieces were written independently of fugues.[9]

This decisive change in Bach's approach to the prelude appears to have taken place during the initial Weimar years, the period from which the Prelude in D and the Fantasia in G seem to date. In Weimar Bach systematically assimilated Italian practice, and it is quite possible that this experience influenced his decision to pair together fully developed but thematically autonomous preludes and fugues. In the typical Italian concerto, for example, the first movement is usually independent melodically from the last. This type of dissociation appears in Bach's earliest organ adaptation of the concerto, the Toccata, Adagio, & Fugue in C, BWV 564. In this work the Toccata and the Fugue are not related thematically, a feature of great moment for Bach's later writing.

Bach's subsequent embracement of concerto-derived forms allowed him to endow the prelude with an unprecedented degree of independence. At the same time it enabled him to experiment with new ways of uniting prelude and fugue. In the Prelude & Fugue in f, BWV 534, the Prelude & Fugue in C, BWV 545, and the Prelude & Fugue in d ("Dorian"), BWV 538, prelude and fugue reflect one another chiefly by virtue of motivic patterns which appear as opening material in the prelude and as passagework in the fugue:

Prelude & Fugue in f

Prelude:

Fugue:

Prelude & Fugue in C

Prelude:

Fugue:

Toccata & Fugue in d

Toccata:

Fugue:

In all three works Bach clearly intended the ¢ time signatures to be interpreted proportionally. This type of sophisticated motivic, rhythmic, and metrical connection between prelude and fugue is quite different from the north-German method of unification used in earlier compositions. In the Prelude & Fugue in G, BWV 541, and the Fantasia & Fugue in c, BWV 562/1a & BWV 546/2a, the link between prelude and fugue is even more abstract. In the former, prelude and fugue are bound together by short, incisive rhythmic motives (♪ ♫♩ and ♫♩). In the latter, prelude and fugue are related by means of texture, which is five-part in both pieces.

In several cases Bach completely abandoned the principle of conceptual unification and joined together independent compositions. This can be observed in the Prelude & Fugue in D, BWV 532,[10] the

Toccata & Fugue in F, BWV 540,[11] and the Fantasia & Fugue in g, BWV 542.[12] In these works it is the complementary effect of opposite styles that binds prelude and fugue together. Bach later canonized this ideal in the Well-Tempered Clavier. But such a step could not be taken before he had developed the prelude as a self-sufficient form in works such as the Fantasia in G, BWV 572, the Toccata in C, BWV 564/1, and the Toccata in d, BWV 538/1.

The formalization of the prelude-fugue pair in Weimar is also mirrored in Bach's experiments with the three-movement concerto sequence. In the Toccata, Adagio, & Fugue in C he transferred this plan to the organ *in toto*. In two other cases, the Prelude & Fugue in C, BWV 545, and the Prelude & Fugue in G, BWV 541, he apparently inserted a middle movement between prelude and fugue but later changed his mind and removed it.[13] It seems likely he would have manipulated material in this manner only after he came to view the prelude and the fugue as separable forms.

During the Cöthen and Leipzig years Bach did not settle on a standard formula for pairing prelude and fugue. He continued, rather, to exercise methods that he used in earlier works. The Prelude & Fugue in b, BWV 544, and the Fantasia & Fugue in c, BWV 537, reflect the north-German approach. In the first work cadential material appearing in the Prelude is transformed into the subject of the Fugue:[14]

Prelude:

Fugue:

In the second work a chromatic line appearing at the end of the Fantasia serves as the "B" theme of the da capo Fugue:

Fantasia:

Fugue:

By contrast, the Prelude & Fugue in C, BWV 547, and the Prelude & Fugue in e, BWV 548, reflect the structural approach. In the former the prelude and the fugue have similar chordal sections before the final return to the tonic (Prelude, mm. 77-80; Fugue, mm. 64-66). In the latter the prelude and the fugue are both based on concerto forms. Finally, the Prelude & Fugue in c, BWV 546, reflects the practice of joining together two independent pieces: the Prelude was newly composed in Leipzig while the Fugue was drawn from an earlier composition. In these five mature works, the Prelude & Fugue in b, the Fantasia & Fugue in c, the Prelude & Fugue in C, the Prelude & Fugue in e, and the Prelude & Fugue in c, Bach seemed to be reviewing the different possible ways to form a prelude-fugue pair.

In what appears to have been his last free organ work, the Prelude & Fugue in E♭, BWV 552, he separated prelude and fugue completely and used them as framing elements in *Clavierübung* III. It is reasonable to assume that he meant the Prelude in E♭ and the Fugue in E♭ to be performed as a pair.[15] Nevertheless, their thematic independence and spatial segregation in *Clavierübung* III symbolize the final phase of a long development. By the end of Bach's life prelude and fugue consisted of two entirely equal — and therefore separable — halves.

In summary, it can be said that the trend towards the prelude-fugue pair can be observed at a very early stage in Bach's writing, in works probably dating from the Lüneburg and Arnstadt periods. In Weimar he established the prelude as a form in its own right and gradually settled upon the prelude and fugue as an aesthetic ideal. This led to the pairing together of separate pieces and to the eventual abandonment of the three-movement sequence: prelude, middle movement, fugue. In Cöthen and Leipzig Bach employed the prelude and fugue design as the standard scheme for free organ compositions. Aside from the Trio Sonatas, he apparently wrote no free organ works other than prelude-fugue pairs during the last thirty-two years of his life.

Bach's championing of the prelude and fugue had several curious side effects. It induced many scribes to entitle "prelude and fugue" works which did not have a prelude-fugue structure. For example, the tradition of calling Buxtehude's multisectional *Praeludia* "preludes and fugues" was initiated only in the second half of the eighteenth century, after Bach had written his works in that form.[16] The desire to create preludes and fugues *ex post facto* also led to the corruption of existing works. In one instance Kittel, or someone in his circle, attempted to transform the Toccata in E, BWV 566, into two preludes and fugues by cutting it in half.[17] In another case a zealous prelude and fugue advocate apparently joined Bach's transcription of the Fugue from the Sonata in g for solo violin with a short harpsichord prelude.[18] The result was the Prelude & Fugue in d, BWV 539, a makeshift arrangement that undoubtedly does not reflect the intentions of Bach, who had successfully established the standard of a more balanced prelude-fugue pair.

VI
The Function of the Preludes

Like most baroque musicians, Bach took a pragmatic approach towards composition. When he wrote a piece, he considered carefully the practical exigencies of the situation at hand. As a result, the very nature of a Bach work—its genre, its form, its musical content, its technical difficulty—reflects the circumstances of its origin. It is for this reason that the function of the organ preludes is so important. Might not the original purpose of the repertory help to explain the unusual style of the pieces?

Early Bach scholars remained steadfastly noncommital on the subject of function. In his Bach biography of 1802 Forkel alluded to the use of the free organ works in the worship service, but he also connected the pieces with Bach's informal extemporizations.[1] Griepenkerl was more probing in the foreword to Volume IV of the Peters Edition. He listed quite systematically the various occasions for which Bach might have written organ compositions. Unfortunately, he did not carry the investigation further, and he did not come to any conclusions about the purpose of the free works.[2] Spitta discussed two possibilities in his influential biography of 1873-1879. At one point he examined the role of preludes and fugues in the worship service.[3] Elsewhere, he suggested certain works might have been written for concertizing.[4] But with uncharacteristic inconclusiveness, Spitta dropped the issue. Recent scholars have added nothing to the debate.

Clearly the time has arrived to open the discussion again and to see if the primary materials shed any new light on the matter. Bach could have employed his free preludes for three general purposes: for the Lutheran worship service, for organ examinations and recitals, and for teaching. Each of these must be considered in turn.

The Preludes
and the Lutheran Worship Service

Hauptgottesdienst, the principal Lutheran worship service, afforded only two opportunities for the performance of free organ works: 1) the preluding before and after the service proper, and 2) the preluding before the concerted music (i.e., the cantata) that was presented in the first half of the service and during Communion.[5] This can be observed from Bach's own outline of *Hauptgottesdienst* in Leipzig, where the liturgy reflected conventional Lutheran practice:

1. Preluding
2. Motet
3. Preluding on the Kyrie, which is concerted throughout
4. Intoning before the altar
5. Reading of the Epistle
6. Singing of the Litany
7. Preluding on the chorale
8. Reading of the Gospel
9. Preluding on the principal composition
10. Singing of the Creed
11. The sermon
12. After the sermon, as usual, singing of several verses of a chorale
13. Words of Institution
14. Preluding on the composition. Afterwards, alternate preluding and singing of chorales until the end of the Communion, and so forth.[6]

In Bach's order of service, numbers three, seven, and fourteen (second part) refer to chorale preludes, that is, preludes based on the melody of the pieces they precede. Numbers one, nine, and fourteen (first part), on the other hand, refer to free preludes, preludes not restricted by the music which follows them. The fact that the postlude is not included on this list can be interpreted in two ways. Either postludes were not played in Leipzig, or they were performed so customarily that Bach felt it unnecessary to mention the practice.[7] That they were performed in some German cities is affirmed by several eighteenth-century theorists (see below).

Vespergottesdienst, special *Festtag* services, and certain occasional ceremonies—weddings (*Trauungen*), commemorations (*Trauerfeier*), and others—also afforded an organist an opportunity to play free organ works. In these events free pieces fulfilled the same role they served in *Hauptgottesdienst*: they functioned as preludes and postludes to the service proper and as preludes to concerted music when it was performed.[8]

Specific descriptions of these free-preluding practices can be found in contemporary treatises. The preluding that took place before and after the worship service is discussed by several theorists. In *Der Vollkommene Capellmeister*, Johann Mattheson states that the execution of a prelude or a postlude for a service is closely allied to the art of *fantasieren*, or free improvisation:

> Under the rubric of free improvisation we also include the prelude. Even more important, however, is the postlude, for during the postlude one has more time and liberty than during the prelude (this is especially true on the organ). Since free improvisation can prove to be a helpful expedient in both instances, we will want to deal with it in considerable detail.[9]

Although Mattheson implies that playing after the service afforded an organist the best opportunity to display his skills, he also decries the abuse of the custom:

> In general the Church suffers less from digressive and long-winded playing during the prelude than during the postlude. This is true even when the most talented organists in the area cultivate their best ideas at the so-called "Ausgang." Such postludes are customary only in church.[10]

What types of pieces were performed as preludes and postludes? Mattheson presents a long list: "Intonazioni, Arpeggi (senza e con battuta), Arioso, Adagio, Passaggi, Fughe, Fantasie, and Ciacona." Of these, "Intonazioni," "Arpeggi," "Arioso," "Adagio," "Passaggi," and "Fantasie," represent different kinds of free preludes. "Fughe," of course, refers to fugues. Elsewhere, in his discussion of fugue writing, Mattheson adds that the prelude-fugue pair (for which a fugue served as "a conclusion") and the north-German multisectional *Praeludium Pedaliter* (for which a fugue served as "a part") were also used as prelude and postlude material:

> As for fugue-playing, there are two types. The first concerns the execution of chorale preludes. In this case the fugue material is derived directly from the melody of the chorale. The second has to do with the prelude and postlude, as a part or conclusion of the same. In this instance one can choose or invent whatever themes one wishes.[11]

In *Der Critische Musicus*, Johann Adolph Scheibe, a Bach student, judges the prelude and fugue the ideal genre for a prelude or postlude. He describes in much greater detail than Mattheson the process of improvising such a piece:

> I have yet to talk about the second manner of preluding – that is, when one improvises freely, without being bound to a chorale. It must be remembered that this generally takes place with the full organ. One should employ good and lively

invention and should crown such a prelude or postlude with a fine and magnificent fugue. Moreover, when an organist plays at the beginning or end of the worship service and, as it often happens, has plenty of time to execute something ambitious, then he can truly demonstrate the extent of his inventiveness and show how skillful a performer he is.[12]

To judge from the accounts of later theorists such as Johann Samuel Petri and Daniel Gottlob Türk, the practice of performing preludes and fugues before and after the worship service continued in the second half of the eighteenth century. In his *Anleitung zur praktischen Musik* of 1782, Petri remarks:

With regard to the enlivenment and amusement of an audience, it is certainly permitted for an organist in a prelude before a wedding, during (as is customary in some cities) the exiting of the congregation from church, before the Te Deum, and in various similar situations to display all of his ingenuity, and to allow himself to be heard with the full organ in brilliant thematic or fugal preludes, pedal solos, and similar things.[13]

Türk, writing five years later, also mentions the use of pedal solos in the postlude. Like Mattheson, he considers the postlude the most ideal spot for an extended improvisation. (It is equally clear from his comments that eighteenth-century congregations were sometimes no less indifferent to organ postludes than their twentieth-century counterparts!)

Under the heading of postlude . . . I group the free fantasia, which in many places is customarily performed at the end of the worship service. For the most part, these fantasias are nothing more than simple preludes, though a fugue would also fit in most appropriately. Perhaps the postlude is the most suitable spot for an organist to display his complete dexterity. He may weave in a pedal solo and may make use of everything that demonstrates his ingenuity. If he yields to excess in the process, the disturbance which he produces is not very considerable, for most of the congregation – isn't listening any more![14]

Precisely how wide-spread the custom of preluding and postluding in the worship service was during Bach's lifetime is difficult to determine. Both Türk and Petri, writing after Bach's death, specifically mention it took place in "some" cities. One can assume, therefore, that it was not a universal practice in the Lutheran church in the eighteenth century. The theorists who cite the improvisation of preludes and postludes are predominantly north German. This suggests the custom may have emanated from North Germany, where a special interest in organ music was traditionally nurtured in commercial cities. In Lübeck and Hamburg, the original *Hansestädte*, organ concerts were presented for the entertainment of townspeople as early as 1650 (see below). It is not improbable that this practice eventually resulted in the adoption of extended organ preludes and postludes as captious appendages to the worship service in many north- and middle-German towns.

How would the Bach preludes fit into this picture? One can postulate that they originated from Bach's own service playing and were written down afterwards for the benefit of colleagues and students. This hypothesis gains credence when one considers that most of the free works were composed during the Arnstadt, Mühlhausen, and Weimar years, the period when Bach was employed as a church or court organist rather than as Capellmeister or Kantor. The ambitious nature of many of the pre-Cöthen preludes could reflect the tradition described by Mattheson, Scheibe, Petri, and Turk.

Additional support for this theory can be derived from *Clavierübung* III. If one views this collection as a paradigm of liturgical practice, the Prelude in E♭ would be performed before, the chorale preludes during, and the Fugue in E♭ after the worship service. Where the duets are to be played is unclear.[15]

Several factors raise doubts as to whether Bach actually intended his free works for this purpose, however. First, contemporary accounts make no mention of his playing preludes or fugues before or after worship services, whereas they do connect the pieces with other functions (see below). Second, the transmission of the preludes in the sources casts doubt on their use as sacred works. Two distinctly different manuscript traditions can be observed: one encompasses the chorale preludes, and the other the free organ and clavier compositions. When chorale preludes appear together with free organ and clavier works in a manuscript, it is often the result of a binding which took place some time after the pieces were copied. The general segregation of these genres in the sources suggest that they may have been intended for different spheres of musical activity, sacred and secular.

The organization of the free works within collections also raises questions about their possible liturgical use. None of the extant manuscripts give any indication that Bach attempted to compile preludes and fugues in the same way he assembled chorale preludes in *Clavierübung* III, the *Orgelbüchlein*, the "Schübler" Chorales, or the so-called "Great Eighteen" collection. If he was using the free works for the same weekly purpose as the chorale preludes, why didn't he gather them into a collection, perhaps arranging them by key for the sake of convenience?[16]

Finally, there is the modest size of the repertoire. If Bach performed a prelude and fugue every Sunday for fourteen years (1703-1717), why were so few pieces written down? Over a hundred chorale preludes survive from this period. Why should there be only thirty-odd free works? In sum, Bach could have used his preludes as preludes and postludes for the worship service, but whether or not he did so cannot be demonstrated conclusively.

Within the worship service proper, free pieces were improvised before concerted music in order to give instrumentalists an opportunity to tune. This practice is well documented throughout the baroque. The account given in Friedrich Erhardt Niedt's *Handleitung zur Variation*, a volume known to Bach, is typical:

> Musically "prelude" refers to an introduction which an organist performs on the organ before a piece of concerted music in order to enable the instrumentalists to tune properly and to allow the singers to get the pitch. In this way tuning can be accomplished without annoying the listeners. Such a prelude or preluding can be continued as long as one wishes, or until the instrumentalists have tuned and give a signal to stop.[17]

The requisites of this type of prelude are given in detail by Türk and Petri. Türk states that the piece should emphasize those keys which facilitate tuning—in normal *Chorton* ("gewöhnlicher Chorton"), C, G, F, c, and g; in high *Chorton* ("hoher Chorton"), B, F♯, E, b, and f♯:

> ... the organist must remain in these keys for some time, so that the performers can tune their string instruments properly. Only then can he pass over the principal key of the piece through a well-chosen modulation. For the sake of horns, trumpets, and timpani he must also modulate a while in the key in which these instruments stand. This may not be simply the key of the first movement of the concerted music, because horns, trumpets, and timpani might enter only in the second movement, or they might be set in another key altogether. Consequently the organist must keep these things in mind and look through the score ahead of time.[18]

Petri goes further. In his view, a "tuning" prelude should not only give the proper pitch—it should also foreshadow the music it precedes:

> A prelude before concerted music must be arranged according to the concerted music, and an experienced organist is not satisfied with simply setting his piece in the opening key. Rather, he compares his work with the first violin, or even better, he looks through the score in order to know what the tempo and the affect of the concerted music should be, and with what type of notes the first violin begins.[19]

Turning to Bach's sacred cantatas, one finds that three-quarters of them begin with an instrumental movement or chorus. For these works, a large introductory organ prelude or prelude and fugue would have

Function of the Preludes 143

been superfluous. If a piece was required for tuning purposes, a short *intonatione* would have sufficed.[20] The other fifty sacred cantatas start with an aria or a recitative, however. For these works an expansive organ prelude or prelude and fugue could have fulfilled the role of an opening sinfonia. A comparison of Cantata 52, *Falsche Welt, dir trau ich nicht*, and Cantata 183, *Sie werden euch in den Bann tun*, makes this clear. In Cantata 52 Bach used the opening movement of Brandenburg Concerto No. 1 as a sinfonia. As a result, the work has a balanced plan in which tutti outer movements frame soloistic inner movements:

> ┌→ Sinfonia (orchestra)
> │ Recitative (soprano)
> │ Aria (soprano)
> │ Recitative (soprano)
> │ Aria (soprano)
> └→ Chorale (chorus)

Cantata 183 displays a similar design but lacks an opening sinfonia:

> Recitative (bass)
> Aria (tenor)
> Recitative (alto)
> Aria (soprano)
> Chorale (chorus)

In a work such as Cantata 183 one of Bach's preludes or preludes and fugues, especially a concerto-derived piece, could have been used as an introductory movement. It would have provided the cantata with a more suitable opening and a more balanced overall plan:

> ┌→ Prelude or Prelude and Fugue (*organum plenum*)
> │ Recitative (solo)
> │ Aria (solo)
> │ Recitative (solo)
> │ Aria (solo)
> └→ Chorale (chorus)

Taking into account the less than ideal performance conditions under which he often labored, Bach might have considered a free organ work a very practical substitute for an orchestral sinfonia requiring substantial copying and rehearsal time. Perhaps it is not insignificant that many of his preludes and fugues conclude with an extended pedal point, a device especially propitious for tuning.

Also noteworthy is the thematic similarity between certain preludes and fugues and certain cantatas: the fugue of the Prelude & Fugue in G, BWV 541, is closely allied to the initial chorus of Cantata 21, *Ich hatte viel Bekümmernis*; the fugue of the Prelude & Fugue in A, BWV 536, uses a theme similar to one found in the opening sinfonia of Cantata 152, *Tritt auf die Glaubensbahn*; the prelude of the Prelude & Fugue in C, BWV 547, uses a theme quite like that found in the opening chorus of Cantata 65, *Sie werden aus Saba alle kommen.*

These thematic ties reflect the type of musical unification outlined by Petri and ostensibly suggest that these particular preludes and fugues and cantatas might have been paired at one time. Practical considerations rule against this possibility, however. Cantatas 21 and 152 originated with introductory instrumental movements and therefore would not have needed extended organ sinfonias. More importantly, when one takes into account the exigencies of *Chor-* and *Kammerton* tuning in Weimar and Leipzig, one finds that the keys of the preludes and fugues and the keys of the cantatas do not match up. In Weimar concerted music was performed in *Chorton*, the pitch of the organ. This means an organ sinfonia prefacing a cantata would have been written out in the same key as the opening movement of the cantata. In Leipzig, however, concerted music was performed in *Kammerton*, which required that the organ be played a whole step lower than the other instruments. Hence in Leipzig an organ sinfonia prefacing a cantata would have to have been written out a major second lower than the opening movement in order for the two to sound in the same key.[21] Cantata 21 begins in c. Written in 1714, it would have demanded an organ sinfonia in c (Weimar performance) or b♭ (Leipzig performance), not G. Cantata 152 begins in e. Written in 1714, it would have needed an organ sinfonia in e (Weimar performance) or d (Leipzig performance), not A. Cantata 65 begins in C. Written in 1724, it would have required an organ sinfonia in B♭, not C Thus it is quite unlikely that the Prelude & Fugue in G, the Prelude & Fugue in A, or the Prelude & Fugue in C were ever paired in performance with the cantatas in question.

What speaks more generally against the use of preludes as sinfonias? Mainly the fact that there are no remarks in the manuscripts of either the cantatas or the organ pieces that allude to the practice. Bach often marked insertions in his scores through cautionary comments. But no such *nota bene*'s linking the free works with the cantatas are to be found. In short, Bach's preludes might have been used as sinfonias, but if they were, it probably was an impromptu procedure.

The Preludes and Bach's Organ Examinations and Recitals

Bach's organ playing was not restricted to the worship service. As one of the foremost keyboard players of his day, he was frequently requested to perform at organ examinations and inaugurations, public concerts, and informal gatherings. These events were closely related to one another in terms of format, and free organ works clearly played an important role in all of them.

Best documented are the examinations and inaugurations. In Bach's time it was customary to have a new or rebuilt organ examined in order to determine whether or not the maker had met all the stipulations of the contract. Several inspectors, usually organists or organ builders, were hired to perform this task. These men were answerable to the church council and were required to submit a detailed report of their findings. The actual testing of the instrument, or *Probe*, was attended by only a few select persons, invariably members of the church council. Often one of the examiners would later present a dedicatory recital, or *Einweihung*, for the benefit of the general congregation.

Contemporary records describe eighteen examinations in which Bach took part.[22] The details of these events are summarized in the table below. It is noteworthy that in Arnstadt, Taubach, Stormtal, Gera, and Kassel Bach gave an inaugural recital in addition to examining the organ. Since the surviving reports are generally quite vague, it is possible that he presented dedicatory concerts in other instances as well.

Date	Location	Description
July 13, 1703	Arnstadt	Bach tests and "plays for the first time" the new organ (built by Johann Friedrich Wender) in the Neue Kirche.[23]
Nov. 28, 1706	Langewiesen bei Ilmenau	Bach and Johann Kister, organist in Gehren, test the new organ (built by Johann Albrecht) in the town church.[24]
Oct. 26, 1710	Taubach bei Mellingen	Bach and several officials examine the new organ (built by Heinrich Nicolaus Trebs) in the town church. Bach later inaugurates the instrument (?).[25]
April 29, 1716	Halle	Bach, Johann Kuhnau, Thomaskantor in Leipzig, and Christian Friedrich Rolle, organist in Quedlinburg, examine the new organ (built by Christoph Cuncius) in the Liebfraukirche.[26]

July 31, 1716	Erfurt	Bach and Johann Anton Weise, organ builder in Arnstadt, examine the new organ (built by Johann Georg Schröter) in the Augustinerkirche.[27]
Dec. 17, 1717	Leipzig	Bach examines the organ (repaired and rebuilt by Johann Scheibe) in the Paulinerkirche.[28]
Nov. 2, 1723	Störmtal	Bach examines the new organ (built by Zacharias Hildebrandt) in the town church. Cantata #194, *Höchsterwünschtes Freudenfest*, is performed at the inauguration of the instrument.[29]
June 25, 1724	Gera	Bach examines, certifies, and inaugurates the new organ (built by Johann Georg Finke) in the Johanniskirche.[30]
June, 1724	Gera	Bach tests and certifies the new organ (built by Johann Georg Finke) in the Salvatorkirche.[31]
Nov. 12, 1731	Stöntzsch	Bach tests the new organ (built by Johann Christoph Schmieder) in the town church. Several registers are later added to the organ, which is subsequently retested by Bach on Feb. 4, 1732.[32]
Sept. 28, 1732	Kassel	Bach and Carl Möller, organist in Kassel, examine, test, and inaugurate the organ (rebuilt by Nicolaus Becker) in the Martinskirche.[33]
June (?), 1735	Mühlhausen	Bach and his son, Johann Gottfried Bernhardt, test the organ in the Marienkirche, give advice on needed additions, and recommend a builder (Hildebrandt?).[34]
Sept. 7, 1739	Altenburg	Bach plays and judges the new organ (built by Gottfried Heinrich Trost) in the Schlosskirche.[35]
Before 1741	Görlitz	Bach and Johann Georg Silbermann (?), organ builder in Freiberg, examine (?) the organ in the Peter- und Pauluskirche.[36]
1743 (?)	Leipzig	Bach and Zacharias Hildebrandt examine the new organ (built by Johann Scheibe) in the Johanniskirche.[37]

Aug. 8, 1746	Zschortau	Bach examines the new organ (built by Johann Scheibe) in the town church.[38]
Sept. 27, 1746	Naumburg	Bach and Gottfried Silbermann, organ builder in Freiberg, examine the organ (built by Zacharias Hildebrandt) in the Wenzelskirche.[39]
Nov. (?), 1747	Leipzig	Bach and Johann Gottlieb Görner, organist of the Thomaskirche, test the organ (repaired by Johann Scheibe) in the Thomaskirche.[40]

Several reports describe Bach as a meticulous and rigorous examiner. Johann Friedrich Agricola, who studied with Bach between 1738 and 1740, states that Bach and Hildebrandt subjected the instrument in Leipzig's Johanniskirche to the "most thorough inspection ever given an organ."[41] In another account Carl Phillip Emanuel relates how his father would begin such an examination:

> The first thing he would do in trying an organ was this: he would say, in jest, "Above all I must know whether the organ has good lungs," and, to find out, he would draw out every speaking stop, and play in the fullest and richest possible texture. At this the organ builders would often grow quite pale with fright.[42]

By testing an organ's "lungs," Bach wished to determine if the bellows and wind reservoirs were sufficient to support a *plenum* combination. Since he tried it first, he obviously placed a premium on this registration. Indeed, theorists of the time state repeatedly that the *plenum* was the sound by which an organ should be judged.[43] To test this registration, Bach must have turned to genres that would exhibit it to best advantage. Chief among these was the prelude and fugue, regularly written "pro organo pleno."[44] Works such as the Toccata in d, BWV 565, or the Prelude in c, BWV 546/1, which begin with dense chordal material, would have served as ideal vehicles for determining whether or not an organ could sustain a thick *plenum* texture without a fluctuation in wind pressure.

Support in favor of this conjecture comes from the reports of Bach's examination and inauguration of the Martinskirche organ in Kassel in 1732. A few days before the event the *Casselische Zeitung* announced:

> The great and costly organ in the Collegiate Church of St. Martin's, or the so-called Great Church, on which work has been going on for almost three years, has finally been adapted to the mode of today and brought to perfection. When this organ, in accordance with the orders of High Authority, has been examined by the famous Organist and Music Director Mr. Bach of Leipzig, with the help of

the Court and Town Organist here, Mr. Carl Möller, in the hope that it will pass the desired test, it is to be played fully next Sunday (September 28, 1732), please God, in public assembly, and inaugurated with musical harmony. It is wished that the said work, chiefly intended for the Glory of God, may serve to inspirit the congregation as a whole and each person in particular.[45]

It is now known from a manuscript *marginalium* that Bach performed the Toccata & Fugue in d ("Dorian"), BWV 538, on this occasion.[46] This work would have effectively exhibited Bach's technical facility as well as the organ's *plenum* sound. Constantin Bellermann's eyewitness account of the event, though somewhat exaggerated, may actually allude to Bach's execution of the pedal passages in the Toccata:

When Bach was called from Leipzig to Kassel to pronounce an organ properly restored, he ran over the pedals with this same facility, as if his feet had wings, making the organ resound with such fullness, and so penetrate the ears of those present like a thunderbolt, that Frederick, the legitimate hereditary Prince of Kassel, admired him with such astonishment that he drew a ring with a precious stone from his finger and gave it to Bach as soon as the sound had died away. If Bach earned such a gift for the agility of his feet, what, I ask, would the Prince have given him if he had called his hands into service as well?[47]

Since it appears to have originated in Weimar,[48] the "Dorian" Toccata & Fugue was not composed especially for the Kassel instrument. Nevertheless, its performance in 1732 verifies that Bach used his preludes at organ examinations and inaugurations. It is lamentable that the dearth of documentation precludes the possibility of linking other works with other events.[49]

In addition to tests and dedications, organ recitals — both formal and informal — played a significant role in Bach's activities. The organ concert was a well-established tradition in North Germany by the time Bach set out on foot to visit Buxtehude in Lübeck in the winter of 1705-1706. Its origins can be traced back to the early seventeenth century, when organists in Holland began to present daily recitals for the townspeople in order to compensate for the Calvinistic ban on figural music in the worship service.[50] This custom appears to have been transmitted to North Germany by Dutch merchants, who wished to hear organ recitals when abroad on trading missions in the *Hansestädte*. By the mid-seventeenth century the organist of the Marienkirche in Lübeck (from 1641-1667, Tunder; from 1667-1707, Buxtehude) was being paid to play mid-day organ concerts for salesmen from the Exchange. Similar recitals can be documented in Königsberg, Stettin, Hamburg, Halle, and Wittemberg. By the eighteenth century organ concerts were a frequent and popular event in middle- and north-German commercial centers.

Function of the Preludes

Unfortunately, our knowledge of Bach's public organ recitals is sketchy, and only six concerts can be substantiated. The details concerning them are summarized in the table below. All of the recitals were large affairs that attracted considerable attention. Several appear to have been initiated by Bach's desire for advancement. Those given in the fall of 1720 were clearly intended to bolster Bach's reputation in Hamburg, where he was applying for the post of organist at the Jakobikirche. In a similar manner, the recital in 1731 paved the way for the title he formally requested from the Dresden court in 1733 and eventually received in 1736.

Date	Location	Description
Fall, 1720	Hamburg	Bach presents several organ concerts, including one in the Katharinenkirche in the presence of J.A. Reinken.[51]
Sept. 19 & 20, 1725	Dresden	Bach presents two concerts of organ and instrumental music in the Sophienkirche.[52]
Sept. 14, 1731	Dresden	Bach presents an organ concert in the Sophienkirche in the presence of the court musicians.[53]
Dec. 1, 1736	Dresden	Bach presents an organ concert in the Frauenkirche in the presence of the Russian Ambassador and other famous personages.[54]
May 8, 1747	Potsdam	Bach, while visiting Frederick the Great, plays the organ in the Heiligegeistkirche.[55]

The accounts of Bach's concertizing, though fragmentary, present certain insights into the nature of his programs. The recitals appear to have been between one and two hours long. Those in the Sophienkirche in Dresden were "more than an hour" in length. Those in the Frauenkirche in Dresden and the Katharinenkirche in Hamburg lasted two hours, the figure mentioned by Forkel in regard to Bach's performances (see below).

In the Katharinenkirche in 1720 Bach spent almost half an hour preluding extemporaneously "in various manners" on the chorale *An Wasserflüssen Babylon*. What filled the rest of the program is not known. In the Sophienkirche in 1725 Bach was heard "in preludes and divers compositions suffused with sweet instrumental music." The phrase "divers compositions suffused with sweet instrumental music" could allude to several types of organ pieces. The word "preludes" could refer to free preluding, preluding on a chorale, or both.

Forkel presents a more highly detailed picture of Bach's concert procedure:

> When Johann Sebastian Bach seated himself at the organ when there was no divine service, which he was often requested to do, he used to choose some subject and to execute it in all the various forms of organ composition so the subject constantly remained his material, even if he had played, without intermission, for two hours or more. First, he used this theme for a prelude and a fugue, with the full organ. Then he showed his art of using the stops for a trio, a quartet, etc., always upon the same subject. Afterwards followed a chorale, the melody of which was playfully surrounded in the most diversified manner by the original subject, in three or four parts. Finally, the conclusion was made by a fugue, with the full organ, in which either another treatment only of the first subject predominated, or one or, according to its nature, two others were mixed with it.[56]

Forkel's description, which mirrors that of the Sophienkirche concerts, indicates that diversity played an important part in Bach's programs. The calculated use of different genres would have been practical as well as aesthetically pleasing. It would have provided the variety necessary to sustain a one- to two-hour long program, and it would have allowed Bach to display his dexterity as an *improvisateur* and *registreur*.

Of special interest is the role of the *plenum* pieces, the preludes and fugues. According to Forkel, they appeared at the beginning and end of the recitals, where they framed less weighty genres: trios, quartets, chorale preludes, etc. The symmetrical plan resulting from this programming reflects the sonorous ideal Bach espoused in *Clavierübung* III:

Bach's organ recitals (according to Forkel):

⎡→ prelude and fugue (*organum plenum*)
⎢   trios, quartets, etc.
⎢   chorale preludes
⎣→ fugue (*organum plenum*)

Clavierübung III:

⎡→ Prelude in E♭ (*organum plenum*)
⎢   chorale preludes
⎢   duets
⎣→ Fugue in E♭ (*organum plenum*)

In *Clavierübung* III the Prelude in E♭, with its extended fugato episodes, fulfills the prefatory role of both prelude and fugue.

Which works were performed at Bach's six documented recitals? Forkel's remarks imply that the preludes formed a regular part of Bach's concert repertory, but information connecting specific compositions with specific occasions is absent. Spitta suggested Bach played the Fantasia & Fugue in g, BWV 542, at the Katharinenkirche in Hamburg in 1720.[57] Although Spitta's proposal is buoyed by sound arguments,[58] it must remain a conjecture.

Bach's informal recitals probably had a format like that of his public concerts. Several contemporary accounts provide a glimpse of these events. In the spring of 1713 an upcoming concert (or series of concerts?) on the organ of the "Himmelsburg" Kapelle in Weimar was reported by one of Bach's students, Philipp David Kräuter:

> I also know that after the new organ in Weimar is completed, Herr Bach will play certain incomparable things on it. Thus I shall be able to see, hear, and obtain copies of a great deal.[59]

What did Kräuter mean by the phrase "incomparable things"? The term could allude to the highly innovative preludes Bach wrote during the Weimar years, but this cannot be proved.

In Leipzig Bach was heard in a 1727 performance by G.H.L. Schwanenberger, who wrote the following to his father-in-law in Braunschweig:

> I wish that you should once hear Mr. Bach on the organ, for neither you nor anyone else in Braunschweig could hold your head before him: I never heard anything like it, and I must completely change my whole style of playing, for it is worth nothing. And in thoroughbass, too, I will, if God pleases and keeps me healthy, be uncommonly industrious, for I am eager to learn his style.[60]

Two years later Martin Heinrich Fuhrmann reported hearing Bach play during a recent Easter Fair:

> When I was at the Easter Fair in Leipzig recently . . . I had the good fortune to hear the world-famous Mr. Bach. I thought the Italian Frescobaldi had polished off the art of keyboard playing all by himself, and Carissimi was a most valued and cherished organist. But if one were to put the two Italians with their art on one side of the scales and the German Bach on the other, the latter would far outweigh them, and they would be lifted straight up into the air. I later heard the well-known Mr. Kirchhof play the organ in Halle, and his fingers so mastered the charms of music that I cried out: "What a shame that the hands of these two keyboard-players in Leipzig and Halle must someday turn to dust!"[61]

Since this performance did not attract attention in the local papers, one might assume it was an informal recital. Still, the fact that it took place during the Easter Fair points to the north-German *Hansestadt* tradition of providing organ music for visiting tradesmen. One wonders if Bach might not have played annually during the Leipzig Fairs even though the occurance of such events is not recorded in contemporary journals.

The accounts of Kräuter, Schwanenberger, and Fuhrmann are intriguing, for they suggest that Bach played often for friends and colleagues. But at the same time they are annoyingly vague on the matter of repertory: they fail altogether to report the types of pieces Bach performed.

The Preludes and Bach's Teaching

When questioned by Forkel about his father's teaching methods, C.P.E. Bach responded, "Since he had composed the most instructive pieces for the clavier, he brought up his students on them."[62] Bach apparently used this same approach in his organ instruction, for surviving manuscripts testify that his pupils copied and performed his chorale preludes, trios, concerto transcriptions, and free works to an extensive degree. The preludes were clearly involved in Bach's pedagogy. Handwritten copies indicate that his best organ students—J.L. Krebs, Agricola, Kirnberger, C.P.E. Bach, Kittel, and others—studied them as part of their training.

It is not surprising that Bach employed the preludes for instructional purposes. No other pieces would have provided his students with such rigorous manual and pedal training. Since Bach was an extremely systematic teacher,[63] he probably assigned the preludes in a graduated manner. The easier Lüneburg, Arnstadt, and Mühlhausen works would have been given first, followed by more difficult Weimar, Cöthen, and Leipzig compositions. Support for this theory comes from two anonymous copies of early pieces, the Prelude & Fugue in g, BWV 535, and the Prelude & Fugue in G, BWV 550. The manuscripts in question, Berlin, SPK: *P 1210* and MBLpz: *III.8.7*, date from the Leipzig years and contain corrections in Bach's hand. In Leipzig Bach undoubtedly would have been performing more mature works. The corrections in *P 1210* and *III.8.7* suggest he was using the Prelude & Fugue in g and the Prelude & Fugue in G as teaching material for two beginning students who were not yet adept at copying.

The didactic function of the preludes could well be responsible for the large number of variant readings that appear in the extant sources.

Many works exhibit changes in detail that seem to have been made over a period of years. Bach may have executed these *Verbesserungen* in connection with his instructional duties. When he went over a prelude with a pupil, he may have entered small improvements into his score. In time these accretions would have been picked up in student copies and passed down to posterity as variant readings.

It might be asked why Bach never gathered the preludes into a collection if he was using them for instruction. One can only assume that in the eighteenth century the most important improvisatory task an organist faced was the production of chorale preludes. To the practicing church musician, the performance of an extended prelude or prelude and fugue was probably of secondary concern. Bach presumably concentrated on the job of teaching his students how to improvise chorale preludes, an accomplishment he achieved through the use of the *Orgelbüchlein*, the "Schübler" Chorales, and other collections. It seems likely that he viewed larger free works as supplementary material, to be assigned on an individual basis to his more advanced pupils.

To summarize: Substantial evidence indicates Bach used the preludes for concerts, for organ examinations, and for teaching. Judging from contemporary practice, it is quite possible he used them for the worship service as well. It is more difficult to determine which of these purposes he may have had in mind when he initially wrote the works. This conjectural matter will be pursued in the conclusion of the present study.

VII
Two Aspects of Performance Practice: Registration and Manual Change

Two elements of performance practice that are of special concern for the organ preludes are registration and manual change. Ever since the appearance of the editions of Karl Straube and Charles-Marie Widor and Albert Schweitzer in the early part of this century, these closely related topics have been the focus of much passionate and often controversial debate.[1] Unfortunately, the outcome of this debate has often been the continued advocacy of arbitrary procedures based more on late-nineteenth-century convention than on the sources, the style, and the historical context of the works themselves.[2] The purpose of the present discussion is to examine the historical and stylistic evidence pertaining to registration and manual change in the preludes in order to establish a more reliable guide for performance.

The Registration of the Preludes

The vast majority of Bach's organ works have been handed down without specific instructions for registration.[3] Two chorale-preludes, *Gottes Sohn ist kommen*, BWV 600, and *Ein feste Burg*, BWV 720, and the Concerto in d, BWV 596, call for specific stops, but these pieces must be considered exceptional cases.[4] A number of other compositions carry the general indication "in Organo pleno." Among the organ preludes this term appears in the sources with striking frequency, as one can observe from the following tabulation:

Work	Source	Location of Title[5]	Title[6]
Prelude & Fugue in g, BWV 535	Berlin, SPK: *P 320*	H	"Preludio con Fuga *pro Organo Pleno* in G moll"
	Berlin, SPK: *P 577*	H	"Preludio con Fuga *pro Organo Pleno* in G moll"
	Hamburg: Schubring Collection	H	"Preludio con Fuga *pro Organo pleno*"

Work	Source		Title
Toccata & Fugue in d, BWV 538	Berlin, SPK: *P 275*	H	"Preludia *in Organo Pleno* con Fuga"
	Berlin, SPK: *P 596*	TP	"Preludium con Fuga D♭ *in Organo Pleno* e Pedale Obligato"
	Yale: *LM 4839e*	H	"Preludio *in Organo Pleno* a 2. Clav: con Fuga"
Fantasia & Fugue in g, BWV 542	Berlin, SPK: *P 288*	TP	"Fantasia e Fuga in Gm: *Per l'Organo pieno* col Pedale Obligato"
Prelude & Fugue in a, BWV 543	Berlin, SPK: *P 505*	TP	"Preludio e Fuga *per l'Organo pieno* col Pedale obligato"
	Berlin, SPK: *AmB 60*	TP	"Preludio/Fuga *per l'Organo pieno*"
	MBLpz: *III.8.14*	TP	"Praeludium et Fuga, in A. moll. *für die volle Orgel*"
	-----	H	"Praeludium con Pedale. *pro Organo pleno*"
Prelude & Fugue in b, BWV 544	Berlin, SPK: *P 891*	H	"Praeludium *in Organo pleno*, pedal"
	BMLpz: *Poel. mus. Ms. 24*	TP	"Praeludium et Fuga in H moll *pro Organo pleno* cum Pedale oblig:"
	-----	H	"Praeludium *pro Organo pleno*"
	Oxford: Rosenthal Collection (Autograph)	H	"Praeludium *in Organo pleno* pedale"
	Yale: *LM 4839i*	TP	"Praeludium *für die volle Orgel* mit Obligatem Pedal"
	----	H	"Praeludium *pro Organo pleno* cum Pedale obligato"
Prelude & Fugue in C, BWV 545	Autograph (lost)	H	"Praeludium *in Organo pleno* pedaliter"[7]
	Berlin, SPK: *P 276*	TP	"Preludio e Fuga *per l'Organo pieno*"
	Berlin, SPK: *P 286*	H	"Praeludium *in Organo pleno* pedaliter"
	Berlin, SPK: *P 559*	TP	"Preludio e Fuga *per l'Organo pieno*"
	Berlin, SPK: *P 602*	TP	"Preludio e Fuga *per l'Organo pieno* con Pedal obligato"
	Berlin, SPK: *P 658*	H	"Praeludium *pro Organo pleno*, pedaliter, cum Pedale obligato"
	Berlin, SPK: *P 916*	H	"Preludio e Fuga *per l'Organo pleno*"
	Berlin, SPK: *AmB 60*	TP	"Preludio e Fuga *per l'Organo pieno*"
	MBLpz: *III.8.21*	H	"Praeludium et Fuga *in Organo pleno*, pedaliter"
	Stockholm: Stiftelsen Musikkulturens främjande	H	"Praeludium *in Organo pleno*, pedaliter"
	Yale: *LM 4839c*	H	"Praeludium et Fuga, *pro Organo pleno* cum Pedale"

Registration and Manual Change 157

Prelude & Fugue in c, BWV 546	Berlin, SPK: *P 596*	TP	"Praeludium et Fuga in C♭ *pro Organo pleno* pedaliter"
Prelude & Fugue in C, BWV 547	Berlin, SPK: *P 320*	H	"Praeludium cum Fuga. *pro Organo Pleno* in C dur"
	Berlin, SPK: *P 557*	H	"Praeludium cum Fuga; *pro Organo Pleno* in C dur"
	MBLpz: *Ms. 1*	TP	"Praeludium con Fuga ex C♯ *pro Organo pleno*"
Prelude & Fugue in e, BWV 548	MBLpz: *III.8.21*	H	"Praeludium pedaliter *pro Organo pleno*"
Prelude & Fugue in E♭, BWV 552	Original print of *Clavierübung III*	H	"Praeludium *pro Organo pleno*" "Fuga à 5. con pedale. *pro Organo pleno*"
Prelude in a, BWV 569	Berlin, SPK: *P 1105*	H	"Praeludium *pro Organo pleno*"
Passacaglia in c, BWV 582	Hauser copy (lost)	H(?)	"Passacalio (sic) con Pedale *pro Organo pleno*[8]

As the above list shows, twelve preludes, slightly more than one-third of Bach's total output in this genre, bear the phrase "pro Organo pleno," "in Organo pleno," "per l'Organo pleno," or "für die volle Orgel" in at least one source. No matter what language the scribe used—Latin, Italian, or German—the result is the same: a plenum registration is involved in each case. Since the instructions found in the manuscripts are so uniform, one must question whether the plenum registration might not apply to the entire prelude repertoire. As Hans Musch has convincingly shown,[9] the organ fugue was generally considered only in terms of *organum plenum* in Germany in the first half of the eighteenth century.[10] Is it possible the free prelude was treated likewise?

Several contemporary accounts indicate that *organum plenum* may indeed have been the standard registration for free preludes. Scheibe's description of prelude and fugue playing within the worship service, already mentioned in connection with the function of the free works,[11] seems to make this quite clear:

> I have yet to talk about the second manner of preluding—that is, when one improvises freely, without being bound to a chorale. *It must be remembered that this generally takes place with the full organ.* One should employ good and lively invention and should crown such a prelude or postlude with a fine and magnificent fugue.[12]

Scheibe's statement implies that the performance of a free organ prelude in conjunction with "the full organ" may have been an established tradition in Germany during Bach's lifetime. The report in Forkel's biography of Bach's preluding outside of the worship service substantiates this view:

> When Johann Sebastian Bach seated himself at the organ when there was no divine service . . . he used to choose some subject and to execute it in all the various forms or organ composition . . . *First, he used this theme for a prelude and fugue, with the full organ.* Then he showed his art of using the stops for a trio, a quartet, etc., always upon the same subject.[13]

To judge from Forkel's account, Bach generally opened his performances with a prelude and fugue "pro Organo pleno." He then turned to other genres, such as the "trio, quartet,[14] etc.," in order to illustrate his ability to register in a colorful manner. Forkel seems to say that where an organ prelude and fugue was concerned, registration did not come into question.[15] Bach would display his "art of registering" in the works which *followed* the opening prelude and fugue, i.e., the trio, the quartet, and chorale preludes.

In 1706 Friedrich Erhardt Niedt concluded his explanation of free preluding in *Handleitung zur Variation* with the remark: "This preluding takes place with the full organ or at least with a strong registration."[16] A half-century later Jacob Adlung treated the combination of free prelude and *organum plenum* as an accepted fact. In his discussion of prelude registration in the *Anleitung zu der musikalischen Gelährtheit* Adlung complained that many organists knew nothing of preluding before concerted music or a chorale except to "roar away on the full organ."[17] His remark suggests the custom of using a *plenum* registration for free preluding had infiltrated into the realm of preluding on a chorale or on concerted music, two occasions for which an imaginative organist might use other stop combinations (see above). In another section of the *Anleitung*, Adlung reminded his readers that it was still wise to employ a *plenum* registration for the postlude, the occasion he considered best for improvising or playing a full-length free prelude.[18]

In *Musica Mechanica Organoedi*, under the heading "Fantasirregister," Adlung again stressed the need for playing "in Organo pleno" at the beginning and end of the worship service.[19] In his opinion, a chorale-prelude which contained the complete chorale melody in one form or another demanded a certain variety of registration. By contrast, a chorale-prelude of the fantasia type, a genre close to the free prelude, required "das volle Werk."

In sum, both manuscript evidence and contemporary accounts suggest that during Bach's lifetime a registrational tradition existed which called for the use of *organum plenum* in conjunction with free preludes and fugues.

The *Plenum* Combination

Before examining how *organum plenum* practice applies specifically to Bach's organ preludes, it is necessary to discuss the exact connotation of the term "organum plenum" in the first half of the eighteenth century. Although the phrase "pro Organo pleno" appears frequently in the manuscripts of Bach and his contemporaries, the phrase "organum plenum" does not seem to be defined in any eighteenth-century lexicon. However, the German equivalent of "organum plenum," "die volle Orgel" or "das volle Werk," is discussed at great length in several eighteenth-century treatises on organ building and organ playing. These reports reveal that the term did not refer to the indiscriminate use of all or almost all the ranks of an instrument. It alluded rather to a specific group of stops whose ability to blend together as an ensemble was considered of utmost importance to organists and organ builders alike. An excellent *plenum* was considered a necessary attribute of every baroque organ.

Bach himself did not record his views on the *plenum* combination. Fortunately, Mattheson and Adlung described the registration in detail. Even though they do not assign precisely the same stops to the *plenum*, the amount of agreement between them is striking. In *Der vollkommene Capellmeister* Mattheson clearly considers *organum plenum* a particular registrational genre and places it in a special category by itself:

> Organ combinations are generally divided into two genres. To the first belongs the full organ, to the second belong all the remaining possibilities which can be realized especially through the use of different manuals and with weaker but nevertheless carefully selected stops.[20]

It is important to note here that Mattheson connects the use of several manuals with "the remaining possibilities" and not with "the full organ." In fact his suggestion for a four-manual graduated combination is listed under the "second species" even though it includes stops traditionally assigned to *organum plenum*.[21] For "das volle Werk" he specifically recommends the following:

> To the full organ belong the principals, the sorduns, the salicionals or salicets (Weiden-Pfeiffen), the Rausch-Pfeiffen, the octaves, the quints, the mixtures, the

scharfs (small mixtures with three ranks of pipes), the quintades, the zimbels, the nasats, the terzians, the sesquialteras, the superoctaves, and the posaunes in the pedal, not in the manual, for the posaunes are reed pipes which are excluded in the manual for the full organ. This is done because the posaune rattles too much on account of its pitch. On the other hand, when there is proper wind, it sounds splendid in the pedal because of the depth of its tone.[22]

In *Musica Mechanica Organoedi* Adlung recommends a *plenum* registration which parallels Mattheson's almost exactly. According to Adlung only stops which add either fullness or brightness to the ensemble should be employed.[23] For an even more brilliant sound he suggests drawing the *plenum* stops on another manual and coupling it into the main keyboard:

Anyone who would like to know what to draw in the manual for the plenum need only to remember this: One must have registers, which brighten. To this end the principal serves together with all the octaves and the quints and terzes and best of all the mixed voices such as the terzian, the sesquialtera, the mixtures, the scharfs, the cymbels and so forth. If one does not wish such a strong combination, then one should leave something out – whatever one wishes. But if one desires an even brighter plenum then one should pull the appropriate stops in another manual and couple it into the main keyboard. One must also have stops, however, which add gravity. For this purpose, the gedackts act as well as the quintaton 16', or even better the gedackt 16' or rohrflute 16' or a bourdon of similar size (according to what is available), the gedackt 8', quintaton 8', rohrflute 8', gemshorn 8', and so forth.[24]

What has been said about the manual plenum is also true for the pedal plenum for it must be very strong in order to be heard above the manual. One usually depends more on gravity in the pedal, although sometimes one brightens it as well. In order to obtain gravity one should use the contrabass 32', subbass 16', gedackt 8', principal 32' and 16', violon 16', and octave 8'. All these stops may be drawn together when the organ has enough wind (and especially when the pedal division has its own bellows). Sometimes one employs bright voices in the pedal, such as the octave 4' and 2' and perhaps mixtures too. If the organ does not have such stops, then one can bring manual registers into the pedal through the use of the coupler. If several bright ranks are already found in the pedal, then one does not need to use the coupler at all. The posaune 32' and 16' along with the trumpet and other reeds can be included in the plenum. Often the posaune 16' is sufficient, however, especially in rapid passages where 16' stops work better than 32' stops.[25]

To summarize these accounts, it can be said that the plenum combination as outlined by Bach's German contemporaries was built on the following principles:

In the manuals:
1. The principal chorus (all pitches) and mixtures are to be drawn plus any other stops (including 16′) which add either gravity or brightness to the total ensemble.
2. Reed stops are generally excluded from the manual plenum.
3. The *plenum* is concentrated in the sound produced on one manual (the Hauptwerk in most cases); the other manuals are used mainly to add strength or brightness to this one manual through coupling.

In the pedal:
1. The same general rule "1" above applies to the pedal as well. 32′ stops may be drawn if the music does not move too quickly.
2. Reed stops may be employed.
3. The manual divisions should not be coupled to the pedal division unless the latter is deficient in some respect.

On these general points Adlung and Mattheson agree. Soon after Bach's death the concept of *organum plenum* began to change: more and more stops were added in an effort to increase the volume of sound. This development foreshadows the nineteenth-century proclivity for an extremely loud *plenum*, an ideal which contrasts greatly with the carefully balanced ensemble of the baroque. Already in 1757, for instance, Friedrich Wilhelm Marpurg adds trumpets 16′, 8′, and 4′ to the manual *plenum*.[26] But during Bach's lifetime, the registration outlined by Mattheson and Adlung seems to have been the standard for free organ preludes.

The Use of Manual Change Within the Preludes

Contemporary accounts are much less clear about the practice of manual change within the context of *organum plenum*. As a consequence, one must turn again to the manuscript sources of the repertory. Of Bach's preludes, only two are handed down with indications for manual change: the Toccata in d ("Dorian"), BWV 538/1, and the Prelude in E♭, BWV 552/1. In both works manual change is notated in a very meticulous fashion.

In the Toccata, Bach used the words "Positiv" and "Oberwerk" to show where one should transfer from one keyboard to another.[27] Measures 30-32 illustrate this notation well:

In passages where the transition might be ambiguous, Bach further clarified the exact point of manual change through the beaming of individual notes. In m. 13, for example, a shift is made from the Oberwerk to the Positiv. The passage is not written thus:

but rather:

From the beaming of the notes it is clear that the manual change is to take place between the first and second sixteenth notes of the third

Registration and Manual Change 163

beat. In a similar fashion, the chords in m. 32 (illustrated above) are notated as eight separate eighth notes (♪♪♪♪♪♪♪♪) rather than four groups of two eighth notes (♫ ♫ ♫ ♫). Four groups of two eighth notes, the standard beaming for such a passage, would have obscured the manual change. One finds many instances of similarly irregular note beamings in Bach's concerto transcriptions for organ, BWV 592-596, where the precise grouping of notes is used to supplement "Ruckpositiv"-"Oberwerk" manual-change indications. Such unusual beamings, employed for the purpose of notating manual change, are strikingly absent in the manuscripts of all Bach organ preludes except the Toccata in d.

Aside from the specific manual-change instructions found in its text, the titles of the Toccata in many sources also indicate the piece was conceived for two keyboards. The remark "à due Clavier è Pedale" (or "à due Manuale è Pedale") which appears in five sources was one of the most common ways Bach labeled a two-manual piece. Analogous phrases appear in the titles of other works intended for two-manual performance: the six Trio Sonatas, BWV 525-530 ("Sonata 1 à 2 Clav. è Pedal," etc.), the five concerto transcriptions for organ ("Concerto à 2 Manuale è Pedale," etc.), chorale preludes such as *Herr Jesu Christ, dich zu uns wend*, BWV 655 ("Trio super *Herr Jesu Christ, dich zu uns wend*. à 2 Clav. è Pedale"), etc. They can also be found in certain harpsichord compositions such as the "Goldberg" Variations, BWV 988 ("Clavier Übung bestehend in einer Aria mit verschiedenen Veränderungen vors Clavicimbal mit 2 Manualen").

Even if the sources of the Toccata contained neither manual change indications nor the phrase "à due Clavier," one could still deduce from stylistic considerations that the work was intended for two keyboards. Aside from the unique formal structure of the piece, which is based on the interplay of two equal but contrasting manual ensembles, technical demands necessitate the use of two keyboards. For example, the following passage cannot be performed as written on one manual:

The runs in this passage involve rapid and extensive voice crossing and can be executed properly only through the use of two keyboards. Such passages commonly occur in Bach's works labeled "à due Manuale." In Trio Sonata No. 6 in G, BWV 530, for instance, similar voice crossings appear at m. 153 ff.:

This type of writing reveals that when Bach was composing a work for two manuals, he frequently exploited the possibility of extensive voice crossing. One need only examine the "Goldberg" Variations to see the extent to which he could apply this technique to best advantage. It is noteworthy that similar voice-crossing passages cannot be found in any of the organ preludes other than the Toccata in d. If two or more manuals were generally employed in the performance of organ preludes in the baroque, then it is somewhat puzzling why Bach, in a few instances at least, did not take full advantage of the opportunity to cross parts as he does in works marked "à 2 Clavier."

The use of two manuals in the Toccata in d does not preclude a *plenum* registration. The title on Michael Gotthard Fischer's manuscript

(Yale: *LM 4839e*), "Preludio in Organo Pleno à 2 Clav: con Fuga," supports this view. A *plenum* registration involving two equal but contrasting manuals must be regarded as an anomaly, however, and might have had something to do with the particular organ for which the Toccata was originally composed. Unfortunately, precise information is lacking about the two instruments most probably involved, the "Himmelsburg" Kapelle organ in Weimar and the Martinskirche organ in Kassel.

The Prelude in E♭, the second free organ prelude containing indications for manual change, was printed in 1739 as part of *Clavierübung* III. Since Bach was closely involved with the publication of the work[28] there is no reason to question the authenticity of the manual change instructions. In the Prelude in E♭ Bach utilized manual change for an entirely different reason than he did in the Toccata in d. Whereas the Toccata is built entirely upon the exchange of material between two manuals, the Prelude in E♭ requires two manuals only for the echo passage found in mm. 32-40 and in the analogous spot in mm. 111-119:

Bach notated the change of manuals in the Prelude by the words "piano" and "forte," a method he employed in other two-keyboard works such as the Italian Concerto, BWV 971, and the French Overture, BWV 831, which were published together as *Clavierübung* II in 1735. Within the context of these pieces, the terms "piano" and forte" do not necessarily imply a strong contrast of dynamics, but rather signify a change from a main manual (on an organ usually the Hauptwerk; on a harpsichord usually the lower keyboard[29]) to a secondary one.

The Prelude in E♭ raises a very important question about manual change. Did Bach really intend the entire work to be performed on one manual except for the two brief echo passages, mm. 32-40 and mm. 111-119 ? To judge from the text of the piece as it appears in *Clavierübung* III, he did. A comparison of the original prints of *Clavierübung* III and *Clavierübung* II supports this conclusion. In *Clavierübung* II the numerous and in many cases intricate manual changes are very carefully notated. In the first edition (1735) manual change is indicated through the use of: 1) the words "piano" and "forte," 2) braces showing the exact point at which the transfer of manuals is to take place, and 3) precise note beamings. In many passages several of these notational methods are employed simultaneously. At m. 53 in the first movement of the Italian Concerto, for instance, the change from the "piano" keyboard to the "forte" keyboard is indicated through the use of all three of the above:

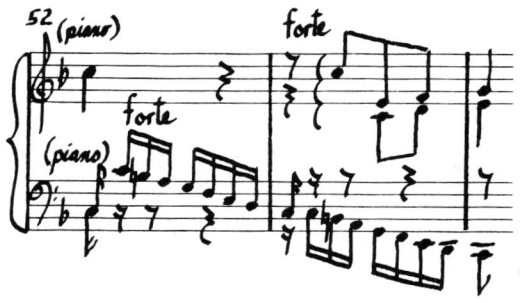

As a result, nothing is left to chance as far as manual changes are concerned. In fact, four of the corrections Bach made in the second edition of *Clavierübung* II helped to clarify further the exact point at which manual changes were to occur.[30] Considering the care with which Bach notated such changes in *Clavierübung* II, it is difficult to imagine he would have left most of the manual transfers to the discretion of the performer in *Clavierubüng* III. Both collections were printed by

Nuremberg publishers (Christoph Weigel, Jr. and Balthasar Schmid, respectively) whose publications display a high standard of neatness and accuracy.[31] Although a second edition of *Clavierübung* III never appeared, three different sets of handwritten corrections were incorporated into the original print.[32] There is no reason to doubt the authenticity of these corrections, and it is significant that none of them alter the original state of manual change in the Prelude in E♭. If Bach wanted passages other than mm. 32-40 and mm. 111-119 of the Prelude to be performed on a secondary manual, then it is curious he did not mark these spots "piano." To assume he left manual change to the liberty of the performer in *Clavierübung* III is to disregard the existence of a very meticulously printed first edition.

Turning to the remaining organ preludes, it is noteworthy that not one is handed down with any indication of manual change in its text or the remark "à due Clavier" in its title. Does this mean Bach intended all his organ preludes except the Toccata in d and the Prelude in E♭ to be performed on one manual, *organum plenum*? There is no manuscript or stylistic evidence that indicates the contrary.

The Prelude & Fugue in b, BWV 544, is a case in point. Bach's autograph (Oxford: Rosenthal Collection) calls for *plenum* registration ("Praeludium in Organo pleno pedale") and gives no indications for manual change. The Prelude contains three episodes, mm. 17-27, mm. 43-50, and mm. 74-70, which are traditionally performed on a secondary manual.[33] Bach notated the beginning of what is frequently termed the first "manual episode" in the following manner:

Excerpts from the Prelude & Fugue in b, courtesy of Universal

If he had actually intended this section, m. 17ff. to be performed on a secondary manual, would he not have indicated the change through the word "piano," through braces, or, at the very least, through beaming? It has been demonstrated that Bach consistently employed one or more of these three methods when notating a two-manual work. A different beaming, for example, would have indicated a manual change at m. 17:

A closer look at the autograph of the piece shows Bach deliberately avoided this reading. Initially, he broke the beams of the first two notes of the alto voice; he then changed his mind and extended the flags of the first sixteenth note downwards and to the right in order to join them with those of the next note:

When he arrived at the parallel passage in m. 63, his mind was made up, and he connected the two critical notes without hesitation:

Had Bach separated the flags in m. 17, the passage would have resembled m. 13 of the Toccata in d, where both the beaming of the notes and the word "Positiv" delineate a manual transfer.[34] Since no such indications are found in the autograph of the Prelude in b, one must assume Bach deemed manual change unnecessary.

The Fugue which follows the Prelude contains a long manual episode, mm. 28-61, which is also frequently performed on a secondary keyboard. In the autograph, m. 28 is notated in the following fashion:

If a change of manual was called for in this passage Bach surely would have stemmed the notes in m. 28 differently, perhaps:

Had Bach written m. 28 in this way, a manual change would have been required. Notationally the passage would have resembled m. 16 of the first movement of the Concerto in a, BWV 593, where a manual transfer is clearly indicated:

Since m. 28 of the Fugue is not notated in this manner, one must presume a different performance procedure is involved. Manuscript evidence suggests that a manual change is unnecessary.

One searches the sources of the other free works for signs which suggest manual change, but none can be found in any pieces other than the Toccata in d and the Prelude in E♭. It is quite possible, of course, that Bach intended certain sectional preludes such as the Fantasia in G, BWV 572, or the Passacaglia in c, BWV 582, or certain concerto-derived preludes such as the Prelude in c, BWV 546/1, or the Prelude in e, BWV 548/1, to be performed on more than one keyboard, and he may have informed his students of the practice orally. His meticulous notation of manual change in other works weighs against this procedure, however. The prevailing evidence suggests he wrote all but two of his preludes for one-manual performance.

The Use of a *Plenum* Registration Without Manual Change

An examination of other Bach organ, harpsichord, and orchestral works discloses that the uninterrupted use of *plenum* sound for five to ten minutes was not unusual in the baroque. Among the chorale preludes the well-known piece Fantasia super *"Komm heiliger Geist, Herre Gott,"* BWV 651, calls for 106 measures (in 4/4 time) of sustained *organum plenum*. The duration of this work, approximately six minutes, equals that of many preludes and fugues. The Prelude & Fugue in C, BWV 545, for instance, requires about the same amount of time to perform.

Of Bach's preludes, toccatas, and fantasias for harpsichord the vast majority were written for one manual and require no registrational change. All of the preludes and fugues in the two volumes of the Well-Tempered Clavier fall into this category. Many large toccatas, including the Toccata in f♯, BWV 910, the Toccata in d, BWV 913, the Toccata in e, BWV 914, and the Toccata in G, BWV 916, were also written for performance on one keyboard.

The manual change instructions found in the BG text of the Toccata in c, BWV 919, and the Toccata in D, BWV 912, are so erratic and musically out of context that one must consider them highly suspect. Do they stem from Bach or whimsical scribes? The copy of the Toccata in D found in the *Möller Handschrift*, for example, contains absolutely no "piano" or "forte" markings. The well-known Chromatic Fantasia & Fugue in d, BWV 903, may also contain manual change accretions. The numerous "piano" and "forte" markings which appear in the BG text do not stem from the famous contemporary manuscript, Berlin, SPK: *P 421* (dated "Dec. 6, 1730"), but rather from a posthumous source, Berlin, SPK: *P 577*, which seems to reflect an attempt to update the work to the more coloristic stop- and manual-changing style of late eighteenth-century keyboard fantasias.[35]

On a two-manual baroque harpsichord a full registration on the lower keyboard, with or without the upper manual coupled in, served as the equivalent of a plenum combination. This setting appears to have been standard for harpsichord toccatas, fantasias, and preludes such as those found in *Clavierübung* I and the Well-Tempered Clavier I and II. Works requiring two manuals, the Italian Concerto, the French Overture, or the "Goldberg" Variations, were exceptional and were clearly marked as such.

Among Bach's orchestral works the Brandenburg Concerto No. 3 in G, BWV 1048, utilizes a *plenum* sound throughout. In this concerto the instrumentarium (three violins, three violas, three cellos, and continuo) functions continuously as a tutti ensemble. Although Bach modifies the tutti sound at various points by reducing the texture of the music, concertino interludes per se are not a part of the work's formal structure. As a result, an orchestral *plenum* is maintained in the Concerto for over twelve minutes, the approximate duration of Bach's longest prelude and fugue, the Prelude & Fugue in e, BWV 548.

Five to ten minutes of uninterrupted *plenum* sound thus appears to have been a common characteristic of harpsichord, orchestral, and organ works in the first half of the eighteenth century. Justification for this registrational (or orchestral) practice can be found in the baroque doctrine of the affections. One of the basic tenets of this doctrine is that every composition or movement within a composition should embody only one affect. The performance of the organ preludes on one manual, *organum plenum*, both reflects and fulfills this aesthetic convention.

Conclusion

The present study must conclude with the humbling admission that our picture of Bach's prelude writing can be only fragmentary at best. This is not caused by a deficient source situation, for there is no reason to suppose — as there is in the case of the cantatas — that numerous works have been lost. It is attributable, rather, to the very nature of the genre itself. In the baroque the prelude was primarily an improvisational medium, a vehicle used by performers for extemporization. Only thirty-three Bach free organ preludes have been handed down, a figure that represents an average of less than one work for each year of the composer's career. As an organist famous throughout Germany for his fruitful invention, Bach must have improvised countless other pieces.

Committing his ideas to paper undoubtedly afforded him the opportunity to work out and refine his ideas to a greater extent than he was able to do when he played "aus dem Stegreif." Hence the works that have been preserved probably reflect the acme of his preluding skills at various points in his life. Still, there must have been many important transitional and experimental pieces which he did not set down on paper. These "missing links" prevent us from following the evolution of his prelude style in greater detail.

To judge from the material available, the Weimar years represent the decisive period for Bach's writing. In Arnstadt Bach mastered the fundamental skills of organ composition. The pieces that appear to date from that time — the "first fruits of his application of the art of organ playing," as the *Nekrolog* expressed it — already display a calculated design that sets them apart from the works of contemporary composers. In addition, they show even at this early date a distinct trend towards the prelude-fugue pair.

It was in Weimar, however, that the two most crucial changes in Bach's writing seem to have occurred: the adoption of the Italian concerto principle and the formal separation of prelude and fugue. From the concerto principle Bach derived a prelude style based on new melodic, harmonic, and structural precepts. This in turn enabled him to construct a large independent piece, a composition as carefully deliberated as the more traditional studied form, the fugue. The subsequent codification of the prelude-fugue pair was possible only after he considered the prelude and the fugue equally important compositional types. In Cöthen and Leipzig he apparently continued to modify and refine the prelude, but the general course of his writing has already been determined in Weimar. Thus for the preludes, Weimar was indeed "die goldene Zeit," to use Spitta's apt phrase. It was not only the period of great production, but also the time of unparalleled stylistic change.

This remarkable development may have been spurred by Bach's official duties at the Weimar court. In the discussion of function it was pointed out that the preludes could have served as liturgical works, as concert pieces, and as teaching material. In Arnstadt Bach's primary role was church organist. The preludes that seem to stem from those years do not exceed in size and scope what might be expected of a liturgical work.

In Weimar, however, Bach had new opportunities for performance. True, he was responsible for the religious services held in the "Himmelsburg" Kapelle, but he was also encouraged, or perhaps even commissioned,[1] to present special concerts on the organ for his employers, Duke Ernst August and Prince Johann Ernst. Furthermore, as his reputation grew, he was increasingly in demand as an organ examiner and recitalist outside Weimar. One can assume that for these events Bach wished to transcend the more straightforward church-oriented work and present, as Kräuter said, "incomparable things." Looking at the preludes that date from Weimar, one is impressed by their "incomparable" features. In terms of size they exceed by far anything Bach had written earlier. In terms of technique they show an unprecedented number of virtuoso elements. In terms of style they incorporate features of the most up-to-date music, the Italian instrumental concerto. In addition, their melodic material has an unusually direct, immediate appeal.

In light of this, it is possible Bach developed a larger, more ambitious prelude for special concerts in the Weimar chapel and elsewhere. The dimensions and virtuosic nature of pieces such as the Toccata in F, BWV 540/1, or the Toccata in d ("Dorian"), BWV 538/1, appear to preclude performance in a worship service, where time and taste would have been dictated by liturgical considerations. In a recital, however, Bach would have been able to expand his ideas without such constraints.

At the concert in the Katharinenkirche in Hamburg in 1720 Bach preluded on the chorale *An Wasserflüssen Babylon* for almost half an hour. Such a lengthy improvisation surely would not have been possible within the context of a worship service. In the Katharinenkirche recital

Bach undoubtedly wished to expand on a practice already familiar to his audience, preluding on a chorale. In a similar fashion, he may also have intended his free preludes for concerts, where they would have served as idealized examples of the type of work one might improvise, on a more modest scale, in a church service. That the "Dorian" Toccata & Fugue was written in Weimar and performed later at an inauguration in Kassel suggests that Bach liked to plan out these "idealized examples" ahead of time.

Although the hypothesis that Bach conceived his mature free preludes for recitals and dedications is attractive, one cannot rule out the possibility that the works originated for the worship service or teaching. Despite the constant protests of clergy and council members, virtuosic and fashionable elements found their way into German church music in the seventeenth and eighteenth centuries. The widespread practice of parodying demonstrates that the line between secular and sacred styles was far from distinct. For example, the pedal solos of the Toccata in F, BWV 540/1, or the Prelude & Fugue in a, BWV 543, are certainly no more virtuosic or "worldly" than the obbligato organ parts of the sinfonias to Cantata 29, *Wir danken dir, Gott, wir danken dir*, or Cantata 146, *Wir müssen durch viel Trübsal in das Reich Gottes eingehen*.[2] Moreover, contemporary theorists, when discussing the production of a prelude or a postlude in the worship service, constantly urged organists to play "something ambitious," to show the "extent of their inventiveness," to display "complete dexterity," and, in some instances, to "weave in a pedal solo." Taking this into account, there is no reason Bach could not have planned even his more expansive bravura preludes for the Lutheran service.

One also cannot eliminate teaching as a stimulus for the composition of some pieces. The preludes show a wide range of styles, and they cover the entire spectrum of technical difficulties. Bach may have devised them this way, intending them to serve as encompassing exercises for his better students.

Thus Bach may have written his preludes for the worship service, for organ examinations and recitals, or for teaching, and he probably used them for all three of these purposes. Such a conclusion reaffirms what we already know about Bach's pragmatic view of composition: the more versatile a work, the more it fulfilled the ideal role of music — to inspire and to educate. What Bach appears to have passed down to posterity, then, is a group of works emulated in the Lutheran service, performed in tests and concerts, and studied as masterful examples of the highest art of free preluding.

Notes

Introduction

1. Johann Nikolaus Forkel, *Über Johann Sebastian Bachs Leben, Kunst, und Kunstwerke* (Leipzig: Hoffmeister und Kühnel) 1802; C.L. Hilgenfeldt, *Johann Sebastian Bach's Leben, Wirken, und Werke* (Leipzig: Hoffmeister) 1850; Carl Heinrich Bitter, *Johann Sebastian Bach* (Berlin: F. Schneider) 1865; Philipp Spitta, *Johann Sebastian Bach* (Leipzig: Breitkopf und Härtel), Vol. I, 1873; Vol. II, 1879.

2. The most important of these are: N. Dufourcq, *J.S. Bach, le maître de l'orgue* (Paris: Editions du Cerf) 1948; Gotthold Frotscher, *Geschichte des Orgelspiels und der Orgelkomposition* (Berlin: Merseburger) 2nd Edition, 1959; Harvey Grace, *The Organ Works of Bach* (London: Novello) 1922; Hermann Keller, *The Organ Works of Bach*, Helen Hewitt, tr. (New York: C.F. Peters) 1967; and André Pirro, *Johann Sebastian Bach: The Organist and His Works for the Organ*, Wallace Goodrich, tr. (New York: G. Schirmer) 1902.

3. *Musikalisches Lexicon* (Leipzig: Wolffgang Deer) 1732, p. 584.

4. *Primae linae musicae vocalis, das ist: Kurze, leichte, gründliche und richtige Anweisung* (Freiburg: Elias Nicolaus Kuhsus), 1703, Appendix: "Ein Praeambulum ist eine kurze Harmonie, der entweder ein Organist auf der Orgel oder Musici Instrom. auf ihren Instrumenten nach ihrer Fantasia den ordentlichen Tonum vorspielen, in welchen sich der kommenden anfänget."

5. Buxtehude's multisectional works, for instance, are invariably labeled "Praeludium" rather than "Praeludium und Fuge" in the early sources. See the Critical Commentary in *Dietrich Buxtehude: Sämtliche Orgelwerke*, Klaus Beckmann, ed. (Wiesbaden: Breitkopf und Härtel), Vol. I (*Freie Orgelwerke*), 1972.

6. This matter is discussed in Chapters I and III.

7. The traditional title of this work, "Prelude & Fugue in a," cannot be traced directly to Bach and seems inappropriate, for it wrongly implies that BWV 551 is a prelude-fugue pair. The more neutral term "Prelude" reflects more accurately the multisectional design of the piece and therefore will be used in this study.

Chapter I

1. Viewed as prelude sources are manuscripts and prints which contain either an independent prelude or a prelude-fugue pair.

2. Recent handwriting studies undertaken in conjunction with the editing of the NBA have shown that four prelude sources long thought are to be autographs are, in fact, copies:

> Prelude & Fugue in C, BWV 531: Berlin, SPK: *P 274*, pp. 23-25, written by W.N. Mey (cf. Dietrich Kilian, NBA IV/5-6, KB)
>
> Prelude & Fugue in e, BWV 533: copy of Fugue only, Leipzig, Bach-Archiv: *Mus. ms. 2*, written by Johann Caspar Vogler (cf. Hans-Joachim Schulze, "'Das Stück im Goldpapier' – Ermittlungen zu einigen Bach-Abschriften des frühen 18. Jahrhunderts" in BJ 1978, pp. 19-42)
>
> Prelude & Fugue in C, BWV 545: Stockholm, Stiftelson Musikkulturens främjande, the so-called "Moscheles Autograph," actually written by Johann Caspar Vogler (cf. Schulze, "'Das Stück im Goldpapier'")
>
> Prelude & Fugue in C, BWV 547: Berlin, SPK: *P 274*, pp. 2-7, written by an anonymous scribe (cf. Kilian, NBA IV/5-6, KB)

3. Facsimilies: *Praeludium pro organo cum pedale obligato, di Joh. Seb. Bach* (Vienna: Universal) n.d., and *Praeludium pro organo cum pedale obligato di Joh. Seb. Bach* (London: Chiswick Press) 1942.

4. Facsimile: NBA IV/6, p. VII.

5. Facsimile (pp. 10 & 14 only): NBA IV/5, pp. VII & IX.

6. Facsimile: NBA IV/6, pp. VIII, IX, & X.

7. Facsimile (pp. 1, 3, & 4 only): NBA IV/5, pp. IX & X.

8. Friedrich Conrad Griepenkerl, Peters Edition II, p. i.

9. Wilhelm Rust, BG XV, p. xxx.

10. BDok III, #792.

11. Griepenkerl, Peters Edition I, p. iv.

12. See Manfred Tessmer, NBA IV/4, KB, pp. 14-16.

13. Ibid., p. 16.

14. A complete list of the prelude copies and copyists appears in Appendix I.

15. Since music students in the eighteenth century usually mimicked the calligraphy of their teachers, it is often difficult to distinguish the handwriting of different

individuals working within the same tradition. Until recently Kittel's handwriting was confused with that of his student Johann Nicolaus Gebhardi. See Yoshitake Kobayashi, *Franz Hauser und seine Bach-Handschriftensammlung* (Göttingen: Dissertation) 1973, p. 163ff.

16. This summary is based primarily on information appearing in Kilian, NBA IV/5-6.

17. Werner Wolffheim, "Die Möllersche Handschrift – ein unbekanntes Gegenstück zum Andreas Bach-Buch" in BJ 1912, pp. 42-60.

18. Alfred Dürr, "Neues über die Möllersche Handschrift" in BJ 1954, pp. 66-74.

19. Kilian, NBA IV/5-6, KB.

20. Hans-Joachim Schulze, *Studien zur Bach-Überlieferung im 18. Jahrhundert* (Rostock: Dissertation), 1978.

21. BDok II, #263. For a speculative but highly interesting discussion of Walther's collection see Ernest May, "J.G. Walther and the Lost Weimar Autographs of Bach Organ Works" in *Studies in Renaissance and Baroque Music in Honor of Arthur Mendel*, Robert Marshall, ed. (Kassel: Bärenreiter; Hackensack, N.J.: Joseph Boonin) 1974, pp. 264-282.

22. See Hermann Zietz, *Quellenkritische Untersuchungen an den Bach-Handschriften P 801, P 802, and P 803* (Hamburg: Karl Dieter Wagner) 1969.

23. For information on Krebs and his family see Karl Titel, "Krebs" in MGG, Vol. 7, Columns 1726-1736, and "Vom 'einzigen Krebs in meinem Bach' – Johann Ludwig Krebs als Bachschüler und Orgelkomponist" in *Musik und Kirche*, Vol. 46 (1976), pp. 172-181.

24. Printed in Marpurg's *Historische-Kritische Beyträge zur Aufnahme der Musik* (Berlin: Joh. Jacob Schutzens sel. Wittwe) 1754, pp. 439-445. See BDok III, #662.

25. This is the Prelude & Fugue in e, BWV 548, in Berlin, SPK: *P 274*. See above under "Autographs."

26. See Hans-Joachim Schulze, "Wie entstand die Bach-Sammlung Mempell-Preller?" in BJ 1974, pp. 104-122.

27. Kilian, NBA IV/5-6, KB.

28. Kobayashi, *Franz Hauser und seine Bach-Handschriftensammlung*, p. 92.

29. For a detailed description of Kittel's handwriting and that of his students see Kobayashi, *op. cit.*, pp. 92ff. and 156ff.

30. See Eva Renate Blechschmidt, *Die Amalien-Bibliothek* (Berlin: Merseburger) 1965. The collection is presently distributed between the Deutsche Staatsbibliothek in East Berlin and the Staatsbibliothek Preussischer Kulturbesitz in West Berlin.

31. See Hans-Joachim Schulze, "Die Bach-Überlieferung – Plädoyer für ein notwendiges Buch" in *Beiträge zur Musikwissenschaft*, Vol. 1 (1975) p. 53.

32. BDok III, #666.

33. See Max Schneider, "Das sogenannte 'Orgelkonzert d-moll von Friedemann Bach,'" in BJ 1911, pp. 23-36.

34. See Alfred Dürr, *Zur Chronologie der Leipziger Vokalwerke J.S. Bachs* (Kassel: Bärenreiter) Second Edition, 1976, p. 10ff.

35. BDok II, #957. Also mentioned in the inventory are "5 Präludien und 5 Fugen." These pieces may have been for organ, but it is more likely, judging from context, that they were intended for harpsichord.

36. Letters show that he sold some of his father's keyboard manuscripts to Forkel (BDok II, #792). The extent of these transactions is unknown.

37. Johann Nikolaus Forkel, *Musicalischer Almanach für Deutschland auf das Jahr 1782* (Leipzig: Schwickert), p. 120.

38. NBA IV/5-6, KB. See also Dietrich Kilian, "Dreisätzige Fassungen Bachscher Orgelwerke" in *Bach-Interpretationen*, Martin Geck, ed (Göttingen: Vandenhoeck & Ruprecht) 1969, p. 17.

39. See the Chiswick Press facsimile.

40. See Dürr, *Zur Chronologie*, p. 11ff.

41. The same holds true for another extremely popular piece, the Chromatic Fantasia & Fugue in d, BWV 903. See BG XXXVI, pp. xi-xlvii.

42. Nothing suggests that Bach himself ever assembled the preludes into a bound collection.

43. One can observe this phenomenon in the clavier repertoire as well. The autographs of many collections – the Well-Tempered Clavier, the Two- and Three-Part Inventions, etc. – survive while those of most single works – the toccatas, fantasias, etc. – do not.

44. Although Bach was acquainted with north-German organ tablature, he apparently used it only for notating corrections and completing pieces where lack of space prohibited the continuation of staff notation. Only one Bach organ work, the chorale-prelude *Gott, durch deine Güte*, BWV 724, is transmitted in tablature (in MBLpz: *III.8.4*, the *Andreas Bach Buch*).

The use of two-stave notation for free organ works with obbligato pedal also had its shortcomings, however, for in several prelude sources manual and pedal parts were wrongly interchanged. The Kittel-derived copy of the Prelude & Fugue in C, BWV 547, in Berlin, SPK: *P 320*, for instance, shows the pedal taking the fourth voice of the Fugue (m. 13ff. and m. 30ff.) rather than the fifth (m. 49ff.) as it should. It is easy to understand how the industrious copyist of *P 320* (or the industrious copyist of *P 320*'s *Vorlage*), encountering a fourth voice entering in the bass register, mistakenly assigned it to the pedal rather than the manual.

Eighteenth-century musicians must have been aware of such pitfalls, for in certain instances they sought ways to improve upon the conventional two-stave notation. At the Amalien-Bibliothek the Bach preludes were notated in the traditional fashion, but the pedal parts were written in red ink. This procedure, undoubtedly initiated by Kirnberger, successfully eliminated any ambiguity that might arise between the manual and pedal voices. Curiously, this technique, used extensively at the Amalien-Bibliothek, was not adopted elsewhere.

The modern method of notating the preludes on three staves did not become common practice until the nineteenth century. It first appears in handwritten copies of the preludes dating from around 1820 (Berlin, SPK: *P 922*, written in 1819 by Grasnick, for instance). Shortly thereafter it gained wide acceptance.

45. See Georg von Dadelsen, *Beiträge zur Chronologie der Werke Johann Sebastian Bachs* (Trossingen: Hohner Verlag) 1958, pp. 49-68.

46. The latter is only partially autograph. See Walter Emery, "The London Autograph of the 'Forty-Eight'" in *Music and Letters*, Vol. 34 (1953), pp. 106-123.

47. This includes a Leipzig autograph, Berlin, DStB: *P 271*, and numerous copies stemming from Weimar. For details see Hans Klotz, NBA IV/2, KB and NBA IV/3, KB.

48. See, however, Robert Marshall's comments on the two autographs of the Fantasia in c, BWV 906, in *Johann Sebastian Bach: Fantasia per il Cembalo*, Facsimile edition published for the members of the Neue Bachgesellschaft (Kassel: Bärenreiter) 1976.

49. There are no extant copies of the other prelude autographs.

50. This fact is often overlooked by those who cite the arrangement of the Prelude & Fugue in E$^\flat$ in *Clavierübung* III and contend that Bach intended the larger preludes and fugues as music for framing the Lutheran worship service, the prelude serving as prelude and the fugue serving as postlude. For additional comments on this matter see Chapter VI.

51. The sources of the Amalien-Bibliothek, written by professional copyists, are an exception.

52. Examples: Berlin, SPK: *P 923*, *P 1102*, and *P 1103*.

53. In the case of Buxtehude's free organ compositions the term "Praeludium Pedaliter" is used consistently in the early sources. In later materials it is supplanted by the phrase "Praeludium et Fuga." See the discussion in Chapter V and the Critical Commentary in *Dietrich Buxtehude: Sämtliche Orgelwerke*, Klaus Beckmann, ed., Vol. 1 (*Freie Orgelwerke*).

54. The Two- and Three-Part Inventions represent another example of title changes initiated by Bach. The pieces were originally called "Praeambula" and "Fantasie" rather than "Inventiones" and "Sinfonie."

55. For further discussion see Chapter III.

56. The texts of both pieces are printed in the NBA.

57. The texts of both pieces are printed in the NBA.

58. Although the variant BWV 545b presents intriguing questions (see *Johann Sebastian Bach: Prelude, Fugue & Trio in B♭*, Walter Emery, ed., London: Novello, 1965), it is obviously a corrupt form of BWV 545 and will not be considered in the present study.

59. See Robert Marshall, *The Compositional Process of J.S. Bach* (Princeton: Princeton University Press) 1972, Vol. I, pp. 157-233.

60. See Klotz, NBA IV/2, KB.

61. See Christoph Wolff, "Bach's 'Handexemplar' of the Goldberg Variations: A New Source" in *Journal of the American Musicological Society*, Vol. 39 (1976), pp. 224-241.

62. See Anne Bagnall et al., "Bach's 'Art of Fugue': An Examination of the Sources" in *Current Musicology*, Issue 19/1975, pp. 47-77.

63. See BG XIV, p. 205 (Prelude in C, BWV 846/1) or p. 213 (Prelude in d, BWV 850/1).

64. This is discussed in Frederick Neumann, "The Question of Rhythm in the Two Versions of Bach's French Ouverture, BWV 831," in *Studies in Renaissance and Baroque Music in Honor of Arthur Mendel*, pp. 183-194.

65. The only exception to this seems to have been the Nuremberg scribes, who changed Bach's works in order to make them less difficult to perform.

66. See the discussion of the Walther-Krebs circle, above.

67. Walther's copy of the Fantasia in G does differ from the standard text of the work (see BG XXXVIII, pp. xxiv-xxviii). These differences most probably reflect a now-lost Weimar version of the Fantasia rather than Walther revisions.

68. See Dietrich Kilian, "Studie über Bachs Fantasie und Fuge c-moll (BWV 562)" in *Hans Albrecht in Memoriam*, Wilfried Brennecke and Hans Hasse, eds. (Kassel: Bärenreiter), 1969, pp. 127-135.

69. The single exception to this is the Kittel-derived copy in Berlin, SPK: *P 320*, in which the final measures of the Fantasia are abridged.

70. See Chapter VI.

71. In the anonymous copy of the Prelude & Fugue in G, BWV 550, in Berlin, SPK: *P 1210*, Bach himself made the emendation, expanding one measure into two new ones.

72. See Chapters III, IV, and V.

Chapter II

1. Dürr, *Zur Chronologie* and *Studien über die frühen Kantaten J.S. Bachs* (Wiesbaden: Breitkopf und Härtel) Second Edition, 1977; and Dadelsen, *Beiträge*.

2. The most important of these chronologies are summarized in the table at the end of Chapter IV.

3. Schmieder, of course, did not have a satisfactory alternative. For matters of chronology he relied on the existing literature, and of this material Spitta's biography clearly represented the most scholarly attempt to date the free organ works.

4. Zietz, *Quellenkritische Untersuchungen*; Kilian, "Studie über Bachs Fantasie und Fuge c-moll (BWV 562)"; and Stephen Daw, "Copies of J.S. Bach by Walther and Krebs: A Study of the Mss. *P 801, P 802,* and *P 803*" in *Organ Yearbook*, Vol. 7 (1976), pp. 31-58.

5. See Schulze's comments on the matter in "Die Bach-Überlieferung."

6. Hans Klotz, "Bachs Orgeln und seine Orgelmusik" in *Musikforschung*, Vol. 3 (1950), pp. 189-203.

7. See Chapter VI. The isolated appearance of notes quite outside the normal pedal compass (f' in the Toccata in F, BWV 540/1; BB in the Fantasia in G, BWV 572) also implies Bach composed some pieces for organs which he did not have regularly at his disposal.

8. See Walter Emery, "Cadence and Chronology," in *Studies in Renaissance and Baroque Music in Honor of Arthur Mendel*, pp. 156-164.

9. Walter Emery, "Some Speculations on the Development of Bach's Organ Style" in *The Musical Times*, Vol. 107 (1966), pp. 596-603.

10. This point cannot be overemphasized. The Prelude & Fugue in b, BWV 544, for instance, is currently assigned to the years 1727-1731. This date is derived from the watermark of the surviving autograph (Oxford: Rosenthal Collection). Since this autograph is a *Reinschrift*, clearly copied from another, earlier source, it is quite possible – and indeed likely – that the Prelude & Fugue was composed sometime before 1727-1731. See the commentary on the work in Chapter IV.

11. Another characteristic of Bach's early notational style, the cancellation of flats with sharps rather than naturals, cannot be used as a chronological criterion because the surviving sources do not present a clear picture of the practice.

12. See Chapter I, where it is argued that most copyists writing in the eighteenth century preserved Bach's original text and notation.

13. A case in point: Spitta (and consequently Schmieder) assigned the Prelude & Fugue in d ("Dorian"), BWV 538, to Leipzig, 1727-1736. The work, however, is consistently handed down in the soprano clef and dorian notation, a fact that points to a pre-Cöthen origin. Stylistic evidence strongly supports this conclusion (see the commentary on the work in Chapter IV).

14. A detailed explanation of these forms is presented in Chapter III.

15. For example, Spitta's assignment of the Fantasia in G, BWV 572, to "Arnstadt, 1705/06" and the Toccata in d, BWV 565, to "Weimar, ca. 1709," contradicts contrapuntal evidence. In the Toccata four real parts are maintained with difficulty (cf. m. 52, m. 120, *inter alia*), whereas in the Fantasia perfect five-part writing is maintained throughout the lengthy Gravement section. If one accepts Spitta's dating of the Fantasia and the Toccata, then one must assume Bach's ability to write independent voices declined between 1706 and 1709!

16. This process can be observed in the Prelude & Fugue in A, BWV 536. An early variant of the work, BWV 536a, displays awkward part-writing. BWV 536, a later revision, shows substantial improvements.

17. The instances in which a prelude and a fugue were written independently and paired at a later date are discussed in Chapter V.

Chapter III

1. A large number of pieces were undoubtedly improvised but never written down. See the comments on this practice in Chapter V.

2. See, for example, Keller's treatment of the free works in *The Organ Works of Bach*.

3. Johann Mattheson, *Der vollkommene Capellmeister* (Hamburg: Christian Herold) 1739, p. 122.

4. Ibid, p. 235:

   ... die nette Anordnung aller Theilen und Umstände in der Melodie, oder in einer ganzen melodischen Werke, fast auf die Art, wie man ein Gebäude einrichtet und abzeichnet, einen Entwurff oder Riss machet, um anzuzeigen, wo ein Saal, eine Stube, eine Kammer, u.s.w. angeleget sollen.

5. No pedal indications appear in the sources of either work.

6. C.P.E. Bach's letter to Forkel of 1775 (BDok III, #803).

7. Cf. Pachelbel's Fantasia in C (DTB IV^1, #11) or Fischer's Preludes in E$^\flat$ and B from *Ariadne Musica*.

8. The *Livre d'Orgue* was issued in 1699 (Paris: Le Mercier) and 1711 (Paris: C. Ballard). Bach's autograph copy of the publication (Frankfurt, Stadt- und Universitätsbibliothek: *Mus. Hs. 1538*) appears to stem from the earlier edition.

9. See the discussion of the Fantasia in Chapter IV and the text of the unpublished early version in Appendix II.

10. In several manuscripts this coda is labeled "allegro."

11. Bach's writing breaks off at the bottom of a verso page in the extant autograph (Berlin, SPK: *P 490*).

12. It is noteworthy that the Canzona in d, BWV 588, and the Allabreve in D, BWV 589, both even more fugue-like than the Fantasias in b, C, and c, are transmitted as independent pieces in the sources.

13. This type of procedure can be seen in the 3-part Ricercare of the Musical Offering. The Ricercare resulted from an improvisation and consequently contains more digressions and passagework than most Bach fugues.

14. The trio is from the *Messe du Deuzième ton* in the *Livre d'Orgue* of 1688.

15. See Hermann Roth, "Bachs c-Moll-Passacaglia und die verwandten Werke Dietrich Buxtehudes" in *Monatsschrift für Gottesdienst und kirchliche Kunst*, Vol. 10, p. 18ff.; Werner Tell, "Das Formproblem der Passacaglia Bachs" in *Musik und Kirche*, Vol. 8 (1937), p. 102ff.; and the articles by Vogelsänger and Wolff cited below.

16. "Passacaglia und Chaconne in der Orgelmusik" in *Musik und Kirche*, Vol. 37 (1967), pp. 14-27, and "Zur Architektonik der Passacaglia J. S. Bachs" in *Musikforschung*, Vol. 25 (1972), pp. 40-50.

17. See "Die Architectur von Bachs Passacaglia" in *Acta organologica*, Vol. 3 (1969), pp. 183-194.

18. The "Thema Fugatum" is, in fact, the portion of the Passacaglia bass borrowed directly from Raison.

19. The double bar found in modern editions does not appear in any extant source.

20. Mattheson, in *Der vollkommene Capellmeister*, p. 478, describes *passaggio* as follows:

    Durch die Passaggi verstehen wir hie(r) geschwinde in dreigeschwänzten Noten bestehende Läuffe, wobei die Abwechselung der Hände zu thun findet. Man kan dieselbe aus vielen gedrückten oder in Kupffer gestochenen Sachen ersehen, wo gemeiniglich besagte Abwechselung mit R. und L., d. i., rechte und lincke Hand angedeutet zu werden pfleget. Die Passaggi müssen aber in diesem Stücke von dem diminutionibus und melismis unterschieden werden: indem diese einem gewissen melodischen Gang zum Grunde haben, den sie nur variiren, jene aber nichts singendes in sich fassen, sondern bloss der Fertigkeit halber, und solche zu zeigen, eingeführet werden.

21. In the process of revising the Prelude in a (see the early variant, BWV 543a, in NBA IV/6) Bach clarified these rhythmic relationships.

22. Only six are known today.

23. See the discussion of this point in Chapter IV.

24. The modern term "Prelude & Fugue" does not really apply to Buxtehude's works since many of them contain several fugues. In the early sources these pieces usually carry the more general title, "Praeludium." See the Critical Commentary in *Dietrich Buxtehude: Sämtliche Orgelwerke*, Klaus Beckmann, ed., Vol. 1 (*Freie Orgelwerke*).

25. See Chapter V.

26. This is demonstrated in Chapter IV.

27. See Chapter V.

28. This included compositions by Vivaldi, Torelli, Marcello, and others.

29. The influence of Italian instrumental style on Bach's cantata writing in Weimar is discussed at length in Dürr, *Studien*. Unfortunately, the related topic, the influence of Italian instrumental style on Bach's keyboard writing in Weimar, has not been subjected to an equally thorough study. Some useful information appears in Spitta I, pp. 392-460, and Hans Gunter Klein, *Der Einfluss der Vivaldischen Konzertform im Instrumental-Werk Johann Sebastian Bachs* (Strasbourg: Heitz) 1970.

30. The chronological implications of this relationship are discussed in Chapter IV.

31. Cf. the opening pedal solo of the Prelude in c, for example.

32. For an interesting discussion of the exchanges between keyboard, instrumental, and vocal idioms in the baroque see Manfred Bukofzer, *Music in the Baroque Era* (New York: W.W. Norton) 1947, pp. 9-19.

33. Cf. the opening theme of the Vivaldi-Bach Concerto in d, BWV 596, which is also unambiguously triadic.

34. From *L'Estro armonico* Bach transcribed Concertos #3 (=BWV 578), #8 (=BWV 593), #9 (=BWV 972), #10 (=BWV 1065), #11 (=BWV 596), and #12 (=BWV 976). From *La Stavaganza* he transcribed Concertos #1 (=BWV 980) and #6 (=BWV 975). From *Concerti a cinque stromenti* he transcribed Concertos #8 (=BWV 973) and #11 (=BWV 594). For a most interesting discussion of the possible circumstances behind these transcriptions see Hans Joachim Schulze, "J.S. Bach's Concerto-Arrangements for Organ — Studies or Commissioned Works?" in *Organ Yearbook*, Vol. 3 (1972), pp. 4-13.

35. Bach knew the Vivaldi concerto because he transcribed it for organ. It is logical to assume that he was also acquainted with the Buxtehude *Praeludium* since it appeared in the *Andreas Bach Buch*. I am indebted to Professor Christoph Wolff for pointing out to me the similarity between the opening of the Vivaldi concerto and the opening of the Toccata in F.

36. Dadelsen has presented convincing evidence that many *Orgelbüchlein* chorales, including "In dulci jubilo," were written in Weimar rather than in Cöthen as was previously assumed. Dadelsen specifically assigns "In dulci jubilo" to the period "ca. 1714." See *Beiträge*, p. 71ff.

37. See, for example, Keller, *The Organ Works of Bach*, pp. 118-119, or Klein, *Der Einfluss*, p. 76.

38. See Dürr, *Studien*, p. 69ff.

39. Contained in Berlin, DStB: *P 802*.

40. Walther's manuscript copy (Yale: *LM 4718*) presents an early version of BWV 529/2 which Bach apparently intended as a middle movement for the Prelude & Fugue in C, BWV 545. For further discussion of this point see Chapter V.

41. The "Vivace" indication appears only in the final version of the Prelude, which is represented solely by Bach's late autograph (New York: Hinrichsen Collection).

42. The chronological implications of this relationship are discussed in Chapter IV.

43. See Chapter I.

44. This is especially evident in the two versions of the Fugue (BWV 574 and BWV 574b) which contain a long, elaborate free ending.

45. DTB IV^1, #12.

46. The Toccata appears in the *Andreas Bach Buch*.

47. The thematic similarity between the Prelude in C and the opening of Cantata 65, *Sie werden aus Saba alle kommen*, has been noted often. In this case, the thematic likeness does not assure a close chronological relationship, for the treatment of the melody is quite different in each work.

48. See, for example, the middle movement of Vivaldi's Concerto in C (Ryom 208), which Bach transcribed for organ (=BWV 594). An interesting though by no means conclusive study of the instrumental recitative is Paul Mies's *Das instrumentale Rezitativ* (Bonn: Bouvier) 1968.

49. See Joshua Rifkin, "The Chronology of Bach's Saint Matthew Passion" in *Musical Quarterly*, Vol. 61 (1975), pp. 360-387.

50. See the discussion of the Fantasia elsewhere in this chapter.

51. It is also noteworthy that in both pieces the tonal areas touched upon by the ritornello are the same, that is: i, v, III & iv, and i.

52. Klein, in *Der Einfluss*, pp. 16-17, suggests a different division of the ritornello. The present analysis, however, seems to reflect to a greater degree Vivaldi's own manipulation of the ritornello in the movement.

53. See Dürr, *Zur Chronologie*, and Dadelsen, *Beiträge*.

54. To date the most extensive studies dealing with the opening choruses of Bach's cantatas are: Werner Neumann, *J.S. Bachs Chorfuge* (Leipzig: Breitkopf und Härtel), 2nd Edition, 1950; and Emil Platen, *Untersuchungen zur Struktur der Chorischen Choralbearbeitung Johann Sebastian Bachs* (Bonn: Friedrich Wilhelms-Universität) 1959.

55. This appellation is applied to cantatas whose text and music reflect the text and melody of a specific chorale. See Spitta II, p. 550, and Dürr, *Zur Chronologie*, pp. 43-47.

56. The anglicization "ritornel" is often used in reference to instrumental ritornelli in vocal works. This semantic distinction does not seem to have any historical basis and therefore is not employed here.

57. Although composed in 1731, Cantata #140 was undoubtedly intended as part of *Jahrgang* II. See Dürr, *Zur Chronologie*, p. 104; and *Bach: Cantata No. 140, Wachet auf ruft uns die Stimme*, A Norton Critical Score, Gerhard Herz, ed. (New York: W.W. Norton) 1972, p. 114.

Notes for Pages 68 to 83

58. See Herz's diagram of the movement in *Bach: Cantata No. 140*, p. 122.

59. The function and dating of these compositions is discussed in depth by Konrad Ameln in NBA III/1, KB. Although the sources do not permit an exact dating of *Komm, Jesu, komm*, both the style of the piece and the performance possibilities in Leipzig suggest it belongs to the period 1723-1729.

60. *Das neu-eröffnete Orchester* (Hamburg: auf Unkosten des Autoris) 1713, p. 413.

61. Several scholars, including Christoph Wolff and Luigi Tagliavini, have suggested that the pairs of eighth notes in the ritornello should be played inégal, ♩³♪ , rather than ♫ . If this hypothesis is correct, the overall number of rhythmic units would be reduced to four. Nevertheless, the ritornello would still exhibit a remarkable degree of rhythmic flexibility.

62. Compare, however, the opening measures of *Dies sind die heil'gen zehn Gebot'*, BWV 678, in which the rhythmic motion changes from ♩ → ♫ → ♬ .

63. See the Echo movement of Bach's French Ouverture, BWV 831, for example.

64. Bach's choice of keys a tritone apart was unquestionably intentional since he transposed the ouverture, which appears in an early form in Berlin, DStB: *P 226*, from c to b when he revised it for *Clavierübung* II.

65. See Robert L. Marshall, "Bach the Progressive: Observations on his Later Works" in *Musical Quarterly*, Vol. 62 (1976), pp. 313-357.

66. This matter is discussed in depth in Chapter V.

67. See Griepenkerl's comments on the matter in the Preface to the Peter's Edition, Vol. III, as well as the extended discussion in Chapter V of the present study.

68. Bach expanded other keyboard works in a similar manner, by "tacking on" additional measures at the beginning or end of them. During the engraving process of the Art of Fugue, for example, he added new endings to three of the simple fugues (BWV 1080/1, 2 & 3) and a new beginning to one of the double fugues (BWV 1080/10). See Anne Bagnall et al., "Bach's Art of Fugue: An Examination of the Sources," pp. 47-77.

69. DBT IV^1, #12 and #20.

70. M. Jacob Adlung was quick to point out the dual nature of the fantasia: "Man merke heirbey, dass man eine doppelte Art zu Fantasiren habe, (1) nach einem Tacte, es sei der gerade, oder ungerade, (2) ohne Tact, wie bey Recitativen gewöhnlich. Zu beiden muss man die Scholaren gewöhnen" (*Anleitung zu der musikalischen Gelährtheit* (Erfurt: J.D. Jungnicol) 1758, p. 750).

71. *Musikalisches Lexicon* (Leipzig: W. Deer) 1732, p. 233.

72. See Chapter V.

73. Cf. Buxtehude's *Praeludium* in e, BuxWV 143, Bruhn's *Praeludium* in G, or Reinken's *Praeludium* in G.

74. In the sources the Fantasia is transmitted both with and without the Fugue in g, BWV 542/2. The pairing of the two is discussed in Chapter V.

75. A very interesting discussion of the recitative in the Chromatic Fantasia appears in Rolf Dammann, *Der Musikbegriff im deutschen Barock* (Köln: Arno Volk Verlag) 1967, p. 368ff.

76. *Musikalisches Lexicon*, p. 239: "Fantasia ist der Effect guten Naturells so auch theils ex tempore sich äussert, da einer nach seinem Sinn etwas spielet, oder setzet, wie es ihm einfällt, ohne sich an gewisse Schrancken und Beschaffenheit des Tacts zu binden."

77. *Versuch über die wahre Art das Clavier zu spielen* (Berlin: George Ludewig Winter), Part I, 1753, p. 86:

Das Fantasiren ohne Tact scheint überhaupt zu Ausdrückung der Affecten besonders geschickt zu seyn, weil jede Tact-Art von Zwang mit sich führet. Man siehet wenigstens aus den Recitativen mit einer Begleitung, dass das Tempo und die Tact-Arten oft verändert werden mussen, um viele Affecten kurz hinter einander zu erregen und zu stillen. Der Tact ist alsdenn oft bloss der Schreib-Art wegen vorgezeichnet, ohne dass man hieran gebunden ist. Da wir nun ohne diese Umstände mit aller Freyheit, ohne Tact, durch Fantasien dieses auf unserm Instrumente bewerckstelligen können, so hat es dieserwegen einen besondern Vorzug.

78. C.P.E. Bach's own fantasias are a case in point.

79. See Wolfgang Plath's comments on this matter in NBA V/5, KB, pp. 67-68.

80. BR, p. 290; BDok II, #499:

Sie wissen, der berühmte Mann, welcher in unserer Stadt das grösste Lob der Musik, und die Bewunderung der Kenner hat, kömmt, wie man saget, nicht eher in den Stand, durch die Vermischung seiner Töne andere in Entzückung zu setzen, als bis er etwas vom Blatte gespielt, und seine Einbildungskraft in Bewegung gesetzt hat.

81. See the Source List in Appendix I.

82. This matter is discussed in Chapters IV and V. See also Dietrich Kilian, "J.S. Bachs Praeludium und Fuge d-moll, BWV 539 – Ein Arrangement aus dem 19. Jahrhundert?" in *Musikforschung*, Vol. 14 (1961), pp. 323-328.

83. See Chapter IV.

Chapter IV

1. See Chapter II.

2. The curriculum of the Michaelsschule is discussed in Gustav Fock, *Der junge Bach in Lüneburg* (Hamburg: Merseburger) 1950.

3. BDok II, #224.

4. The letter (BDok III, #803) contains a reference to Böhm as Bach's "Lehrmeister." The word "Lehrmeister" was subsequently crossed out, perhaps to preserve the impression, presented elsewhere, that Bach was a self-made musician.

5. BR, pp. 217-218; BDok III, #666:

   Hier zeigte er eigentlich die ersten Früchte seines Fleisses in der Kunst des Orgelspielens, und in der Composition, welche er grösstentheils nur durch das Betrachten der Wercke der damaligen berühmten und gründlichen Componisten und angewandtes eigenes Nachsinnen erlernet hatte. In der Orgelkunst nahm er sich Bruhnsens, Reinkens, Buxtehudens und einiger guter französischer Organisten ihre Werke zu Mustern. Hier in Arnstadt bewog ihn einsmals ein besonderer starker Trieb, den er hatte, so viel von guten Organisten, als ihm möglich war, zu hören, dass er, und zwar zu Fusse, eine Reise nach Lübek antrat, um den dasigen berühmten Organisten an der Marienkirche Diedrich Buxtehuden zu behorchen. Er hielt sich daselbst nicht ohne Nutzen, fast ein vierteljahr auf, und kehrete alsdenn wieder nach Arnstadt zurück.

6. The *raison d'être* of the work was the departure of Bach's brother Johann Jacob to join the Swedish Army. According to Bach's own genealogy, this event took place in 1704 (cf. BDok I, #184). Albert Protz, in "Zu Johann Sebastian Bachs 'Cappriccio sopra la lontananza del suo fratello delettissimo'" in *Musikforschung*, Vol. 10 (1957), pp. 405-408, argues that Johann Jacob did not leave for the Swedish Army until 1706. Protz's conclusions are based on hypothetical evidence and seem less trustworthy than Bach's account. The Capriccio is analysed in depth in Elke Krüger, *Stilistische Untersuchungen zu ausgewählten Klavierfugen Johann Sebastian Bachs* (Hamburg: Karl Dieter Wagner Musikalienhandlung) 1970.

7. See the discussion of these collections in Chapter I.

8. The commentary on each work summarizes to a great extent material presented in Chapters I and III. A detailed discussion of individual points can be found there.

9. *Beiträge*, pp. 73-76.

10. *Stilistische Untersuchungen*, p. 12ff.

11. In Bach's autograph the Fugue is a *Reinschrift*. The Prelude is also written neatly, though several emendations can be observed.

12. Spitta I, p. 580.

13. The Cantata was written for Dec. 30, 1714. Spitta believed it to have been composed in 1715.

14. BWV 533a, the variant published in NBA IV/6, appears to be a corrupt *manualiter* arrangement rather than an *Urfassung*. It was probably fashioned by J.G. Preller, who also may have been responsible for the *manualiter* version of the Canzona in d, BWV 588. Both arrangements are handed down solely in Preller manuscripts (in MBLpz: *Ms. 7*).

15. It is noteworthy that Böhm's fugues show a similarly relaxed approach to part-writing.

16. These recommendations are reprinted in BDok I, #83.

17. BDok III, #666.

18. These "incomparable things" could have been Bach's preludes, or, as Hans-Joachim Schulze has suggested, his organ transcriptions of Italian concertos. See Schulze, "J.S. Bach's Concerto-Arrangements for Organ – Studies or Commissioned Works?"

19. The court library is discussed in Schulze, "J.S. Bach's Concerto-Arrangements." Walther's collection is discussed in May, "J.G. Walther and the Lost Weimar Autographs of Bach's Organ Works."

20. The term "Bologna School" is commonly used to denote the seventeenth-century instrumental composers, active in Bologna, who developed the trio sonata, concerto grosso, and other important instrumental forms. The most famous representatives of the school are G.B. Vitali, Torelli, and Corelli.

21. The text of this unpublished variant is presented in Appendix II.

22. See Kilian, "Studie über Bachs Fantasia und Fuge c-moll (BWV 562)."

23. See Wolff, "Die Architektur von Bachs Passacaglia," pp. 190-192.

24. See Chapter V.

25. See Dürr, *Studien über die frühen Kantaten J.S. Bachs*, p. 102.

26. See Chapter V.

27. It also links the Fantasia in g with the Chromatic Fantasia in d for clavier, BWV 903, as noted in the previous chapter. Unfortunately, the similar treatment of recitative in the two works sheds no light on chronology, for the Chromatic Fantasia cannot be dated with certainty.

28. See Chapter V.

29. *L'Estro armonico* first appeared in 1711 and was generally available on the continent from 1712 on. The collection was issued by Roger in Amsterdam, Walsh in London, and Le Clerc in Paris. Schulze, in "J.S. Bach's Concerto-Arrangements for Organ – Studies or Commissioned Works?" suggests on the basis of circumstantial evidence that Bach first saw *L'Estro armonico* in the summer of 1713. Nothing weighs against the possibility that he had access to the collection at an even earlier date, however.

30. The most complete account of Bach's activities in Cöthen is found in Friedrich Smend, *Bach in Köthen* (Berlin: Christlicher Zeitschriftverlag) 1951.

31. Two such instances can be documented: the examination of the Paulinerkirche in Leipzig in 1717 and the recital in the Katharinenkirche in Hamburg in 1720.

32. See Chapter V.

33. Kilian, NBA V/5-6, KB.

34. Kilian, in NBA IV/5-6, KB, assigns this copy to an anonymous scribe. The handwriting appears to be that of Kellner, however.

35. The presentation copy of the Brandenburg Concertos (Berlin, DStB: *P 234*), is dated March 24, 1721. Several scholars have suggested that Concerto No. 2 was written somewhat earlier, around 1719. See Heinrich Besseler, NBA VII/2, KB, pp. 23-38, and Martin Geck, "Gattungstraditionen und Altersschichten in den Brandenburgischen Konzerten" in *Musikforschung,* Vol. 23 (1970), pp. 139-152.

36. In "Some Speculation on the Development of Bach's Organ Style" in *Musical Times,* Vol. 107 (1966), pp. 596-603, Walter Emery goes so far as to suggest that Bach may not have composed any preludes and fugues in Leipzig.

37. See the *stemma* on p. 107.

38. See the table at the end of Chapter IV.

39. Johann Tobias copied the Fantasia and mm. 1-89 of the Fugue; Johann Ludwig copied the remainder of the work.

40. See Hans-Joachim Schulze, "Wer intavolierte Johann Sebastian Bachs Lautenkompositionen?" in *Musikforschung,* Vol. 19 (1966), pp. 32-39.

41. Only those works which vary enough from their originals to merit a special BWV number are considered here.

42. See Kilian, "Studie über Bachs Fantasia und Fuge c-moll (BWV 562)."

43. It appears to be a composition by Johann David Heinichen. See Spitta II, p. 43, and Günter Hausswald, *Johann David Heinichens Instrumental-Werke* (Wolfenbüttel: Kallmeyer) 1937, p. 93.

44. "J.S. Bachs Praeludium und Fuge d-moll, BWV 539 – Ein Arrangement aus dem 19. Jahrhundert?"

45. Forkel, p. 82.

46. Spitta I and II.

47. *Bach-Werke-Verzeichnis.*

48. *The Organ Works of Bach.*

Chapter V

1. It is interesting to note that in North Germany this technique was used in other genres as well. See Buxtehude's cantatas or sonatas for violin, gamba, and continuo, for example. The most important discussions of the development of the north-German *Praeludium Pedaliter* are found in: Hans Klotz, *Über die Orgelkunst der Gotik, der Renaissance und des Barok* (Kassel: Bärenreiter) First Edition, 1934, p. 149ff.; Josef Hedar, *Dietrich Buxtehudes Orgelwerke* (Frankfurt: Wilhelmiana Musikverlag) 1951, pp. 123-198; Hans Jakob Pauly, *Die Fuge in den Orgelwerken Dietrich Buxtehudes* (Regensburg: G. Bosse) 1964, pp. 89-109; and *Dietrich Buxtehude: Sämtliche Orgelwerke*, Klaus Beckmann, ed., Volume 1 (*Freie Orgelwerke*), Critical Commentary.

2. *Blumen-Strauss* was issued without a publication date. *Ariadne Musica* has been preserved in editions from 1713 and 1715. Walther and Gerber cite earlier editions, of 1702 and 1710, respectively.

3. See Keller, *The Organ Works of Bach*, p. 28, or Gotthold Frotscher, *Geschichte des Orgelspiels* (Berlin: Merseburger) 2nd Edition, 1959, pp. 854-859.

4. See Chapter IV.

5. BDok III, #803.

6. This is especially evident in the Fugue in c on a theme by Legrenzi and the Fugue in c. Both end with a free coda that must have been balanced by a free introduction, undoubtedly improvised.

7. A case in point is Fischer's *Blumen-Strauss*, which provides only one prelude for every six fugues.

8. See the discussion of the composition in Chapter IV.

9. The post-compositional pairing of the Prelude in D with the Fugue in D is discussed below.

10. Of the fourteen extant sources of the Prelude & Fugue in D nine contain the Fugue alone, two contain the Prelude alone, and only three contain the entire work. Since a manuscript dating from before 1750, Stuttgart, Württembergische Landesbibliothek: *Cod. Mus. II, 288*, contains the complete composition along with the unambiguous remark "Volti Sequitur Fuga," it is reasonable to assume that the Prelude and Fugue were paired together during Bach's lifetime.

11. Discrepancies in pedal compass (Toccata: C-f″ ; Fugue: C-c′) suggest that the Toccata and the Fugue were written for different occasions and subsequently joined together. The sources support this conjecture, for of the sixteen extant copies of the work five contain the Toccata alone, seven contain the Fugue alone, and only four contain the entire work. Since three copies of the complete composition (in Berlin, DStB: *P 803* and Berlin, SPK: *P 277* and *P 290*) stem directly from the Bach circle, it is likely that the practice of pairing the Toccata and the Fugue originated with Bach himself.

12. Of the twenty-two sources for the Fantasia & Fugue, seventeen contain the Fugue alone, one contains the Fantasia alone, and five contain the entire work. Several factors indicate that the Fantasia and the Fugue had separate origins and may not have been paired together until a rather late date. First, only the Fugue is handed down in two different keys, F minor (five times) and G minor (twelve times). Since no F minor copies of the Fantasia exist, it seems probable that the Fugue was transposed before the Fantasia was paired with it. Second, the three oldest sources for the work (Berlin, DStB: *P 803* and Berlin, SPK: *P 288* and *P 598*) – the only ones that appear to date from before 1750 – contain the Fugue alone. Third, Mattheson's famous citation of the Fugue in the *Grosse General-Bass-Schule* (1731) includes no mention whatsoever of the Fantasia. Finally, in all eighteenth-century manuscripts the Fugue is consistently notated with a "dorian" key signature, i.e., G minor = one flat, f minor = three flats. The Fantasia, on the other hand, is always notated in modern key signature, i.e., g minor = two flats. The sources which contain the complete work preserve this notational discrepancy. This suggests that Bach himself may never have copied out the Fantasia and the Fugue as a pair, for if he had done so he surely would have equalized the accidentals.

Griepenkerl, who published the Fantasia with the Fugue for the first time in Volume II of the Peters Edition, gave as precedent "eine alte Abschrift der Fantasie aus meiner Sammlung . . . nach deren Schluss sich das Thema der Fuge, als zu ihr gehörig, angedeutet findet" (Peters Edition II, Foreword). This "alte Abschrift," which may have been an attempt to capture on paper an oral tradition of pairing the Fantasia with the Fugue, has disappeared.

The five extant copies of the complete Fantasia & Fugue – all unknown to Griepenkerl – are post-1750 sources. Since three of these manuscripts (Berlin, SPK: *P 288* and *P 595* and Berlin, DStB: *AmB 531*) can be associated with the Bach circle, it is most probable that the practice of pairing the Fantasia with the Fugue stems from Bach himself.

13. See Kilian, "Dreisätzige Fassungen Bachscher Orgelwerke."

14. See Walter Gerstenberg, "Zur Verbindung von Praeludium und Fuge bei J.S. Bach" in *Bericht des Internationalen Musikwissenschaftlichen Kongresses*, Lüneburg, 1950, pp. 126-129.

15. Griepenkerl, who paired the Prelude and the Fugue in the Peters Edition, thereby establishing the modern tradition of performing the two together, stated that his action was "nicht willkürlich, sondern einer alten Überlieferung folgend, die mir Forkel schon vor vierzig Jahren mitteilte" (Peters Edition, Vol. III, Foreword).

16. This can be verified by comparing the Amalien-Bibliothek copies of Buxtehude's works with earlier sources. See the Critical Commentary in *Dietrich Buxtehude: Sämtliche Orgelwerke*, Klaus Beckmann, ed., Volume I (*Freie Orgelwerke*).

17. Cf. Berlin, SPK: *P 320* and *P 557*.

18. See Chapters III and IV.

Chapter VI

1. Forkel, pp. 32 and 40.

2. Peters Edition, Vol. IV, pp. i and ii.

3. Spitta, Vol. 2, pp. 122-123.

4. Ibid., Vol. 1, p. 404 and pp. 634-635.

5. The tradition of performing cantatas during communion is discussed by William Scheide in "Zum Verhältnis von Textdrucken und musikalischen Quellen der Kirchenkantaten Johann Sebastian Bachs" in BJ 1976, pp. 79-94.

6. BR, p. 70; BDok I, #178:

    1) Praeludieret. 2) *Motetta.* 3) Praeludieret auf das Kyrie, so gantz musiciret wird. 4) Intoniret vor dem Altar. 5) Epistola verlesen. 6) Wird die Litaney gesungen. 7) Praelud: auf den Choral. 8) Evangelium verlesen. 9) Praelud. auf die Haupt Music. 10) Der Glaube gesungen. 11) Die Predigt. 12) Nach der Predigt, wie gewöhnlich einige Verse aus einem Liede gesungen. 13) Verba Institutionis. 14) Praelud. auf die Music. Und nach selbiger wechselsweise praelud. v Choräle gesungen, biss die Communion zu Ende & *sic porrò*.

7. Bach's order of service was intended for a substitute, who may not have needed any instructions for the short section of *Hauptgottesdienst* following the Eucharist: the Dismissal, the Blessing, and the Postlude. Bach's concluding phrase, "and so forth," may refer to this post-Eucharist material. The most important sources for our knowledge of the Leipzig liturgy between 1700 and 1750 are the *Leipziger*

Kirchen-Andachten (Leipzig, 1694), the *Leipziger Kirchen-Staat* (Leipzig, 1710), Christian Gerber's *Historie der Kirchen Ceremonien in Sachsen* (Leipzig: Saueressig, 1732), and Johann Christoph Rost's *Nachricht* (Leipzig, manuscript, 1716 *et sequitur*). These sources agree with Bach's order in all essentials, and similarly omit any reference to an organ postlude. As Spitta observed (Vol. 2, p. 123), Johann Adolph Scheibe, a Bach student and Leipziger, treated postluding as a *fait acquis* in *Der Critische Musicus* (see quotations, below). This might imply that postludes were a tradition in Leipzig even though they were not mentioned in contemporary orders of service.

8. The order for *Vespergottesdienst* is presented in *Leipziger Kirchen-Staat* and other eighteenth-century documents. *Vespergottesdienst* did not include Communion, and it generally contained concerted music only on feast days. Johann Samuel Petri, in *Anleitung zur praktischen Musik* (Leipzig: Breitkopf, 1782, p. 297), specifically mentions the use of free preludes before weddings, which included concerted music when commissioned. Several sources cite the use of an organ prelude before the commemoration service for Queen Eberhardine held in the Paulinerkirche in Leipzig on October 17, 1727 (see BDok II, #230-232).

9. *Der Vollkommene Capellmeister*, p. 477:

Unter der Anleitung zum fantasiren verstehen wir auch zwar das Vorspiel, aber hauptsächlich das Nachspiel, und weil man darin (zumahl auf der Orgel) mehr Freiheit und Zeit hat, als bey dem Vorspiel, so wollen wir desto weitläuffiger davon handeln, indem es an beiden Orten ein gutes Hülffs-Mittel abgeben kan.

10. Ibid., p. 473:

Uiberhaupt leidet die Kirche im Vorspiel bey weitem nicht so viel Umschweifes und Ausdehnung, als im Nachspiel. Wie den auch von her die künstlichsten Organisten ihre besten Einfälle zum sogenannten Ausgange aufzuheben pflegen. Es ist aber solches Nachspiel sonst nirgends gebräuchlich, als in der Kirche.

11. Ibid., p. 474:

Was das Fugenspiel betrifft, ist solches zweierley. Eine Art der Fugen gehört zur wircklichen Ausführung der Choräle, und da werden die Fugensätze aus der Melodie der Gesänge selbst genommen. Die andre beziehet sich auf das Vor- und Nachspiel, als ein Theil oder eine Folge desselben: und da nimmt oder macht man sich die Themata nach Gefallen.

12. *Der Critische Musicus* (Hamburg: Thomas von Wierings Erben), July 14, 1739, p. 159:

Ich muss noch von der zwoten Art zu präludiren, wenn man nemlich nach freyer Willkühr und ohne Absicht auf einen Choral, präludiret, erinnern dass solches insgemein mit dem vollen Werke geschiehet, dass man dabey auf gute und lebhafte Erfindung zu sehen hat, und dass man endlich ein solches Vorspiel oder Nachspiel mit einer guten und prächtigen Fuge auszieren soll, Weil ich hierzu vornemlich rechne, wenn man zum Anfange das Gottesdienstes, oder auch zum Ausgange spielet, und man dazu folglich oft sehr viel Zeit hat, etwas rechtes auszuführen, so kann auch ein Organist ganz leicht zeigen, wie weit sich seine Erfindung erstreckt, und wie geschickt er ist.

13. *Anleitung zur praktischen Musik*, pp. 297-298:

> Die Ermunterung und Ergänzung der Zuhörer anbelangend, so ist dem Organisten bey einem Präludio vor einer Trauung, beim Ausgange der Gemeinde aus der Kirche (wie in einigen Städten gebräuchlich ist), vor dem Te Deum, und in mehreren der gleichen Fällen wohl erlaubt, alle seine Kunst auszukramen, und sich mit dem vollen Werke in feurigen thematischen oder fugirenden Präludiis, Pedalsolos und dergleichen Sachen hören zu lassen.

14. *Von den wichtigsten Pflichten eines Organisten* (Halle: auf Kosten des Verfassers, 1787), p. 139:

> Unter dem Nachspiele . . . versteh ich diejenigen freyen Fantasien, welche an vielen Orten beym Ende des Gottesdienstes gewöhnlich sind. In der Hauptsache kommen sie mit dem gemeinen Vorspielen überein; wiewohl hier die Fuge auch einen schicklichen Platz fände. Vielleicht wäre dies der bequemste Zeitpunkt, in welchem der Organist seine ganze Fertigkeit zeigen, ein Pedalsolo einweben, und alles, was ihn die Kunst darbietet, anwenden konnte. Schweift er dabey aus, so ist der Unfug, welchen er dadurch anrichtet, hierbey nicht so beträchtlich; den der grösste Theil der Gemeinde – hört nicht mehr davon.

15. They certainly would not have been performed *sub communione*, as it is occasionally suggested.

16. In collections stemming from South Germany or Austria, where short free organ works were used within the Catholic service, one often finds preludes and fugues arranged in some type of tonal order. See, for example, F.X.A. Murschhauser's *Octi-Tonium Novem Organicum* (1696), J.K.F. Fischer's *Ariadne Musica* (1702) or *Blumen-Strauss* (ca. 1730), or Gottlieb Muffat's *72 Versell Sammt 12 Toccaten* (1726).

17. *Handleitung zur Variation* (Hamburg: B. Schiller) 1706, Chapter XII:

> Musicalisch zu verstehen ist es (das Praeludium) ein Anfang ehe ein recht gesetztes Musicalisches Stücke angefangen wird, dass auff der Orgel in wehrenten (anderer Instrumenten) Stimmen der Organiste was spielet damit die Instrumentisten reine Stimmen und die Sänger den Thon fassen können, dass denen Zuhörern kein Verdruss durchs Stimmen verursachet wird. Solch Praeludium oder Praeludiren kan ein jeder so lange spielen als er will, oder biss die Instrumentisten reine gestimmet haben und ihme ein Zeichen gegeben wird, auffzuhalten.

18. *Von den wichtigsten Pflichten*, pp. 136-137:

> In diesen Tonarten muss sich der Organist eine Zeitlang aufhalten, damit die Musicirenden ihre Saiteninstrumente richtig stimmen können. Alsdenn erst geht er, durch eine gutgewählte Modulation, in den Hauptton des Stücks über; allein

der Hörner, Trompeten, Pauken, u. wegen, muss er noch eine Weite in dem Tone, worin diese Instrumente stehen, moduliren; das darf aber nicht allein der Ton seyn, aus welchem der erste Satz des Kirchenstückes geht; denn theils können diese Instrumente erste in einem der folgenden Sätze eintreten; theils sind sie auch wohl aus einem andern Tone gesetz; folglich muss der Organist hierauf aufmerksam seyn, und die Partitur vorher durchsehen.

19. *Anleitung zur praktischen Musik*, pp. 298-299:

Ein Präludium vor einer Musik muss schon nach der Musik eingerichtet seyn, und ein geübter Organist lässt es nicht genung seyn, seine Generalbassstimme wegen des Anfangstons anzuseyn; sondern er sieht sich seinem Bass in Vergleichung mit der ersten Violine, oder (welches noch besser ist) die Partitur einmal an, um zu wissen, welches Tempo and der Affekt der Musik eigentlich seyn solle, und mit was für Noten die erste Violine anfange.

20. See, for example, the diminutive *intonationi* of Andrea and Giovanni Gabrieli.

21. For details of the *Chor-* and *Kammerton* practices in Weimar and Leipzig see Dürr, *Studien über die frühen Kantaten Johann Sebastian Bachs*, pp. 74-79.

22. See Hans Löffler, "*J.S. Bachs Orgelprüfungen*" in BJ 1925, pp. 91-100. Löffler's article represents the first attempt to gather together all the data on Bach's organ examinations. It is now outdated, however, and some of the information it presents is incorrect.

23. BDok II, #7.

24. BDok II, #18.

25. BDok I, #84; BDok II, #50, #50a.

26. BDok II, #76-78, #85, #594.

27. BDok I, #86.

28. BDok I, #87; BDok II, #85-89.

29. BDok II, #163, #164, #181.

30. BDok II, #183, #183a.

31. Ibid.

32. BDok II, #298.

33. BDok II, #316-318, #321, #522.

34. BDok II, #365, #372.

35. BDok II, #453, #460.

36. BDok II, #486.

37. BDok II, #519, #740.

38. BDok I, #89; BDok II, #545.

39. BDok I, #90; BDok II, #546-551.

40. BDok II, #561. Spitta believed Bach also played a dedicatory recital in the Blasiuskirche in Mühlhausen on Reformation Sunday in 1709 (See Spitta I, pp. 394-395). Spitta presents a convincing case: Bach drew up the plans for rebuilding the Blasiuskirche instrument while he was organist there, and it is not improbable that the church council might have bid him back from Weimar to test the organ when it was completed in 1709. In addition, the registration indications given in Johann Tobias Krebs's copy of Bach's early chorale-prelude *Ein feste Burg ist unser Gott*, BWV 720, call for stops found specifically in the rebuilt Mühlhausen instrument. Nevertheless, there is no documentary evidence of a Bach examination or inauguration in Mühlhausen in 1709. Thus Spitta's proposal must remain a hypothesis.

41. BDok III, #740.

42. BR, p. 276; BDok III, #801:

Das erste, was er bey einer Orgelprobe that, war dieses: Er sagte zum Spass, vor allen Dingen muss ich wissen, ob die Orgel eine gute Lunge hat, um dieses zu erforschen, zog er alles Klingende an, u. spielte so vollstimmig, als möglich. Hier wurden die Orgelbauer oft für Schrecken ganz blass.

43. See Chapter VII.

44. See Chapter VII.

45. BR, pp. 127-128; BDok II, #316:

Es ist die im hiesigen Stifft St. Martini, oder der so genannten grossen Kirche grosse und Kostbahre Orgel, woran bey nahe 3. Jahr gearbeitet, endlich durch den Orgel bauer Herr Nicolaus Becker von Mühlhausen nach heutiger Art eingerichtet, und zu seiner perfection gebracht worden. Nachdem dann nun dieses Werck auff Hohen Obrigkeitlichen Befehl durch den Berühmten Organisten und Music Directorem Herr Bach von Leipzig mit zuziehung des hiesigen Hoff und Stadt Organisten Herrn Carl Möller examiniret werden wird, in ohngezweiffelter Hoffnung, dass solche die erwünschte probe erhält, so soll diesem selbige künfftigen Sontag geliebts Gott in öffentlicher versamlunge vollkommen gespielet und mit einer Musicalischen harmonie inauguriret werden. Man wünschet, dass so thanes, zur Ehre Gottes Hauptsächlich gereichendes Werck der gantzen Gemeinde und einem jeden und ins besondere zur auffmunterung gereichen möge.

46. Michael Gotthard Fischer's handwritten copy of the Toccata & Fugue (Yale: *LM 4839e*) contains the remark "bey der Probe der grossen Orgel in Cassel von S. Bach gespielt." Fischer was a student of Johann Christian Kittel, who in turn had studied with Bach. I am indebted to Dietrich Kilian for drawing my attention to Fischer's comment.

47. BR, p. 236; BDok II, #522:

Princeps sane hereditarius Hassiae Fridericvs Bachio tunc temporis, Organum, vt resitutum ad limam vocaret Cassellas Lipsia accersito eademue facilitate pedibus veluti alatis transtra haec, vocum grauitate reboantia, fulgurisque in morem aures praesentium terebrantia, percurrente, adeo Virum cum stupore est admiratus, ut annulum gemma distinctum, digitoque suo detractum, finito hoc musico fragore, ei dono daret. Quod munus, si pedum agilitas meruit, quid quaeso daturus fuisset Princeps, (cui soli tunc hanc gratiam faciebat,) si & manus in subsidium vocasset.

48. See Chapter IV.

49. Connecting at least some of the preludes with Bach's out-of-town duties helps to explain one facet of the repertoire: the great variety of ranges found in the pieces. Most of the works adhere to a relatively restricted manual and pedal compass, one encountered frequently on the organs of the time: CD - c''' in the manuals, CD - c' in the pedal. Certain compositions require notes outside this range: C♯ and d''' in the manuals, BB, C♯, d', e', and f' in the pedal. These notes appeared less regularly on baroque instruments. If Bach was writing for twenty or thirty different organs and wished to take full advantage of the manual and pedal compass of each, then the dissimilar ranges of the free works become quite understandable.

Hans Klotz, in "Bachs Orgeln und Seine Orgelmusik," attempted to establish a chronology of the organ works by matching the ranges of the pieces with the ranges of Bach's instruments. There are two problems with this approach. First, as Walter Emery pointed out in "The Compass of Bach's Organs as Evidence of the Date of his Works" in *The Organ*, Vol. 32 (1952), pp. 92-100, the manual and pedal compasses of many of the organs at Bach's disposal are not known. Second, in light of the present discussion of function, Klotz's study seems to be too restricted. He considered only the instruments in Arnstadt, Mühlhausen, Weimar, Weissenfels, Cöthen, and Leipzig, and did not take into account the organs Bach played for examinations and inaugurations.

50. The early history of the north-German organ concert is traced in Johann Hennings and Wilhelm Stahl, *Musikgeschichte Lübecks* (Kassel: Bärenreiter) 1952, Vol. 2.; Oskar Söhngen, "Die Lübecker Abendmusiken als Kirchengeschichtliches und Theologisches Problem" in *Musik und Kirche*, Vol. 27 (1957), pp. 181-191; Georg Karstadt, *Die "extraordinairen Abendmusiken" Dietrich Buxtehudes* (Lübeck: Verlag Max Schmidt) 1962; and Walter Blankenburg, "Zur Geschichte des Kirchen-

konzerts" in *Musik und Kirche*, Vol. 44 (1974), pp. 165-175.

51. BDok II, #102, #253; BDok III, #666, #681, #739.

52. BDok II, #193.

53. BDok II, #294, #323.

54. BDok II, #389, #390.

55. BDok II, #554. According to Forkel (p. 9f.), Bach played all the organs in Potsdam. One can also assume Bach was required to give a recital of some sort when he applied for organist positions in Mühlhausen (1707), Weimar (1708), and Halle (1713). A Mühlhausen "Probe" is mentioned in the church records (see BDok II, #19), but no details are given.

56. BR, pp. 315-316; Forkel, p. 40:

Wenn Joh. Seb. Bach ausser den gottesdienstlichen Versammlungen sich an die Orgel setzte, wozu er sehr oft durch Fremde aufgefordert wurde, so wählte er sich irgend ein Thema, und führte es in allen Formen von Orgelstücken so aus, dass es stets sein Stoff blieb, wenn er auch zwey oder mehrere Stunden ununterbrochen gespielt hätte. Zuerst gebrauchte er dieses Thema zu einem Vorspiel und einer Fuge mit vollem Werk. Sodann erschien seine Kunst des Registrirens für ein Trio, ein Quatuor etc. immer über dasselbe Thema. Ferner folgte ein Choral, um dessen Melodie wiederum das erste Thema in 3 oder 4 verschiedenen Stimmen auf die mannigfaltigste Art herum spielte. Endlich wurde der Beschluss mit dem vollen Werke durch eine Fuge gemacht, worin entweder nur eine andere Bearbeitung des erstern Thema herrschte, oder noch eines oder auch nach Beschaffenheit desselben zwey andere beygemischt wurden.

57. Spitta I, pp. 634-635.

58. These arguments are summarized in Keller, *The Organ Works of Bach*, pp. 112-113.

59. BDok III, #58a: "Nun weiss ich auch, dass Hr. Bach nach Verfertigung dieser neuen Orgel in Weimar absonderlich anfänglich gewiss unvergleichliche Sachen darauf spilen wird, konnte also auch hierinnen noch vil sehen, hören und decopirt bekommen."

60. BR, p. 442; BDok II, #239:

Ich möchte wünschen dass er Herrn Bachen auff der Orgel mahl hörete, er wahrhafftig sich vor ihm, wie auch Keiner in Braunschweig, nicht auffdecken darff, ich habe so was noch niemahls gehöret, und ich mus meine Spielart gantz anders ändern, denn es nichts zu rechnen ist, wie auch im General Bass, ich werde so Gott wil und mir gesund lässt, ungemein fleissig, denn ich bin recht begierig Herrn Bachen seine art zu lernen.

61. BR, p. 441; BDok II, #268:

> Als ich neulich zu Leipzig in der Oster-Messe war . . . hatte ich das Glück, den weltberühmten Herrn Bachen zu hören. Ich meinte, der Italiänische Frescobaldi hatte alle Clavir-Kunst allein gefressen, und Carissimi wäre ein allertheuerster und allerliebster Organist; Allein wenn man die 2. Italiäner in eine Wagschale zusammen mit ihrer Kunst, und den Teutschen Bachen in die andere setzen solte, so würde dieser sehr praeponderiren, und die andere 2. in die Lufft marchiren. Ich habe hernach auch zu Halle den wohl renommirten Herrn Kirchhof auf der Orgel gehöret, dessen Finger die Gratien also regierten, dass ich ausrief: Schade, dass dieser 2. Clavier-Spieler zu Leipzig und zu Halle, ihre Hände dermahleinst verfaulen sollen!

62. BDok III, #803.

63. According to Ernst Ludwig Gerber, Bach started his students on the Two- and Three-Part Inventions, then proceeded to suites, and then to the Well-Tempered Clavier. See BDok III, #948, and Alfred Dürr, "Heinrich Nicolaus Gerber als Schüler Bachs" in BJ 1978, pp. 7-18.

Chapter VII

1. Straube, in his *Praktische-Ausgabe* of Volume II of the Peters Edition (Leipzig: C.F. Peters, 1913), and Widor and Schweitzer, in *Johann Sebastian Bach: Complete Organ Works*, Vols. 1-5 (New York: G. Schirmer, 1912) made suggestions for manual change and registration that differed sharply from the more eighteenth-century-oriented views of Griepenkerl and Roitzsch, editors of the original Peters Edition (1844-1852).

2. See Hans Klotz, *Über die Orgelkunst der Gotik, der Renaissance und des Barock*, 1st Edition, pp. 251-277, or 2nd Edition, pp. 386-393; Klotz, "Originale Spielanweisungen in Bachs Orgelwerken und ihre Konsequenzen für die Interpretation" in *Bach-Interpretationen*, pp. 112-118; or Hermann Keller, *The Organ Works of Bach*, pp. 38-58.

3. See, for example, the *Orgelbüchlein* or *Clavierübung* III.

4. In his *Handexemplar* of the "Schübler" Chorales (Princeton: Scheide Collection) Bach designated the pitches but not the types of stops to be used. See Christoph Wolff, "Bachs Handexemplar der Schübler-Choräle" in BJ 1977, pp. 120-129.

5. H = Heading (*Überschrift*); TP = Title page.

6. The portion of the title that pertains to registration has been italicized.

7. BG XV, p. xxi.

8. Kobayashi, *Franz Hauser und seine Bach-Handschriften-Sammlung*, p. 72. Hauser's copy of the Passacaglia is of great importance because it is one of two sources which apparently reflect the text of Bach's revised autograph. Unfortunately all three sources, the autograph and the two copies of it, have disappeared.

9. Hans Musch, "Von der Einheit der grossen Orgelfuge Johann Sebastian Bachs" in *Musik und Kirche*, Vol. 44 (1974), pp. 267-279.

10. Striking evidence of this tradition, as Musch points out, is found in Bach's organ transcription (BWV 596) of Vivaldi's Concerto in d, Op. III, No. 11. While Vivaldi's original calls for "piano" and "forte" in the Fugue (labeled "Allegro" by Vivaldi), Bach's transcription of the movement uses *plenum* throughout, with no manual changes.

11. See Chapter VI.

12. *Der Critische Musicus*, Tuesday, July 14, 1739, p. 159. The original text is presented in Chapter VI. The italics have been added for emphasis.

13. BR, p. 315. Forkel, p. 40. The original German text is given in Chapter VI. The italics have been added for emphasis.

14. Quartets for organ were quite common in the French repertoire, where they were considered a virtuoso vehicle for displaying an organist's registrational and digital mastery. These pieces were commonly written for three manuals and pedal, with one hand (usually the right) playing on two keyboards at the same time. One well-known example was published by Louis Marchand (whom Bach supposedly vanquished in 1717) in his *Première suite de pièces d'orgue du premier ton* (1732). This collection has been reprinted in *Archives des Maîtres de l'orgue*.

15. See Musch's comments on the same quote in "Von der Einheit," p. 268.

16. *Handleitung zur Variation*, Chapter XII: "Welches Praeludiren mit dem vollen Wercke oder doch sonst starck angezogen geschiehet."

17. *Anleitung zu der musikalischen Gelährtheit*, Ch. I, Sec. 206, No. 5: "Manche wissen vor der Musik oder einem Chorale nichts, als das Toben des vollen Werks."

18. Ibid., Ch. 8, Sec. 206, No. 6: "Zum Ausgange aus der Kirche wird mehrentheils zusammen gezogen; doch leidet auch diese Zeit ihre Ausnahme." See the discussion of this quote in Chapter VI.

19. *Musica Mechanica Organoedi* (Berlin: Friedrich Wilhelm Birnstiel) 1768, Sec. 236: "Beym Anfange und Beschluss des Gottesdienstes lässt es besser mit dem vollen Werke zu spielen."

20. *Der vollkommene Capellmeister*, Ch. 24, Sec. 74: "Uiberhaupt theilen sich die Orgel-Züge in zwo Gattungen. Zur ersten gehört das volle Werk; zur andern

zehlet man alle übrige vielfältige Veränderungen, die sich mit verschiedenen Clavieren besonders, und mit schwächern, ausgesuchten Stimmen machen lassen."

21. Ibid., Ch. 24, Sec. 83. Mattheson's suggestion:

Im Werke: Principal 16, Octave 8, Octave 4, Octave 2, Rauschpfeiffe 2 fach, Mixtur.

Im Ruckpositive: Principal 8, Quintadeen 8, Octave 4, Sesquialtern 2 und etwa ein Quintflötgen von 1 1/2 f.

In der Brust: Principal 8, Octave 4, Scharff, welches nicht so vielfach als die Mixtur.

Im Oberwerke: Principal 8 und Scharff: das ist genug zur vierten Stuffe. Bey allen diessen aber müste man nehmen:

Im Pedal: Principal 32, Gross-Posaun 32, Principal 16, Posaun 16, Octave 8, Trommet 8, Octave 4, Schallmey 4, Mixtur, und Rauschpfeiffe.

22. Ibid., Ch. 24, Sec. 76:

Es gehören zum vollen Werk die Principale, die Sordunen, die Salicionale oder Salicete (Weiden-Pfeiffen), die Rausch-Pfeiffen, die Octaven, die Quinten, Mixturen, Scharffen (kleine Mixturen von drey Pfeiffen), Quintadeen, Zimbeln, Nasat, die Terzien, Sesquialtern, Super-Octaven, Posaunen im Pedal, nicht im Manual: denn die Posaunen sind ein Rohr-Werk, welches aus dem Manual, bey volle Orgel zugeschlossen bleibet; indem es dasselbst, wegen der Höhe, zu sehr schnarren würde; da es hergegen wegen der Tiefe des Klanges, im Pedal prächtig lautet, wenn die Mundstücke, wie billig, gefüttert sind.

23. *Musica Mechanica Organoedi*, p. 168. While *Musica* was published in 1768, Adlung states that he assembled most of the material during the period 1723-1727.

24. Ibid., p. 169:

Wollte jemand wissen, was im Manuale zum vollen Werke zu ziehen, der merke nur so viel: Man muss Register haben, die schärfen. Dazu dient das Principal, sammt allen Oktaven; item die Quinten, Terzen; und am meisten schärfen die gemischten Stimmen, als das Terzian, Sesquialter, Mixturen, Scharf, Cimbelregister, etc. Will Man es nicht allzustark haben; so lass man etwas weg, was man will. Soll es aber noch schärfer werden; so ziehe man die Register des andern Clavieres eben so, und koppele sie zusammen. Man muss aber auch Register haben, die die Gravität geben. Dazu dienen die Gedackte, als die Quintatön 16', oder besser das Gedackt 16', oder Rohrflöte 16', oder der gleich grosse Bordun; (wie man sie hat) Gedackt 8', Quintatön 8', Rohrflöte 8', Gemshorn 8', & c.

25. Ibid, p. 171:

> Was von den Manualstimmen gesagt ist, das gilt auch im Pedale. Denn das muss im vollen Werke auch stark seyn, dass man es gegen das Manual höre. Doch sieht man da mehr auf die Gravität; zuweilen schärft man es auch. Die Gravität befördern der Contrabass 32', Subbass 16', Gedackt 8', Principal 32' und 16', Violon 16', Oktave 8'. Diese können alle zugleich gezogen werden, wenn eine Orgel satt Wind hat, und sonderlich etliche Bälge besonders zum Pedale gehören. Zuweilen macht man schärfende Stimmen ins Pedal, z. Ex. Oktave 4' und 2', auch wol Mixturen. Die können auch gebraucht werden. Hat man aber solche schärfende Stimmen nicht, so kann man die Manualstimmen durch das Koppel ins Pedal bringen: sind aber ohne Koppel die Manualstimmen dem Pedale gemein, so braucht man es nicht. Die Posaune 32' und 16' sammt der Trompete können, wie auch die anderen Schnarrwerke, auch dabey seyn. Sonst aber kann die Posaune 16' genug seyn. Zumal man im geschwinden Spielen die 16-füssigen Register bequemer gebraucht, als die 32-füssigen.

26. *Historische-kritische Beiträge zur Aufnahne der Musik* (Berlin: Gottlieb August Lange), Part III (1957), p. 502.

27. Although the autograph of the "Dorian" Toccata has disappeared, it is safe to assume that the indications for manual change stem from Bach. The consistent appearance of these indications in the surviving sources and the unusual structure of the work support this supposition.

28. See Manfred Tessmer, NBA IV/4, KB, pp. 14-16.

29. The 8' strings on the lower keyboard of an eighteenth-century harpsichord were usually plucked further away from the nut than the 8' strings of the upper manual. Hence the lower 8' had a somewhat richer, fuller sound than the upper 8', which had a more nasal tone. The contrast between the two was chiefly one of timbre, however, and not dynamics.

30. J.A. Fuller-Maitland, "A Set of Bach's Proof-Sheets" in *Sammelbände der Internationalen Musikgesellschaft*, Vol. 2 (1900-1901), pp. 643-650.

31. See *Die Nürnberger Musikverleger und die Familie Bach*, Willi Wörthmüller, ed. (Zirndorf: Druckerei Bollman) 1973.

32. Tessmer, NBA IV/4, KB, p. 14ff.

33. See Widor and Schweitzer's recommendations in *Johann Sebastian Bach: Complete Organ Works*, Vol. 4, pp. xix-xxii; Straube, Peters Edition, Vol. II, *Praktische Ausgabe*, pp. 113-126; Klotz, *Über die Orgelkunst der Gotik, der Renaissance und des Barock*, 1st Edition, p. 275, 2nd Edition, p. 391; or Keller, *The Organ Works of Bach*, p. 158.

34. See p. 162.

35. It is interesting to note that knee levers, pedals, and similar devices enabling rapid stop changes on the harpsichord did not begin to emerge until after the initial impact of the piano-forte spread through Europe, i.e., not until after ca. 1740-1750.

Conclusion

1. See Schulze, "J.S. Bach's Concerto-Arrangements for Organ – Studies or Commissioned Works?"

2. Both cantata movements stem from secular works. The Sinfonia to Cantata 29 was arranged from the Preludio of the E-Major Partita for Solo Violin, BWV 1006; the Sinfonia to Cantata 146 was arranged from the first movement of the Concerto in d for Harpsichord, BWV 1052.

Appendix I

1. TP = Title page; H = Heading (*Überschrift*)

2. Blechschmidt = Blechschmidt, *Die Amalien-Bibliothek;* Dadelsen = Dadelsen, *Beiträge zur Chronologie;* Dürr = Dürr, "Neues über die Möllersche Handschrift"; Griepenkerl = Griepenkerl, Peters Edition, Vol. II, Foreword, Kast = Kast, *Die Bach-Handschriften der Berliner Staatsbibliothek;* Kilian = Kilian, NBA IV/5-6 KB (Manuscript); Krause = Krause, *Handschriften der Werke J.S. Bachs in der Musikbibliothek der Stadt Leipzig;* Rust = Rust, BG, Vol. XV, Foreword; Schulze = Schulze, "'Das Stück im Goldpapier'"; Wolffheim = Wolffheim, "Die Möllersche Handschrift – ein unbekanntes Gegenstück zum Andreas Bach-Buch;" Zietz = Zietz, *Quellenkritische Untersuchungen.*

3. According to Manfred Tessmer, NBA, IV/4, KB, all extant manuscript copies of the *Prelude & Fugue in E♭* reflect the text of the printed edition.

Appendix I
Source List

Prelude & Fugue in C, BWV 531

Source	Title[1]	Scribe[2]
Berlin, SPK: *P 274*	"Praeludium Pedaliter" (H)	Kast: J.P. Kellner Kilian: W.N. Mey?
Berlin, SPK: *P 286*	"C dur Praeludium Pedaliter" (TP) "Praeludium Pedaliter" (H)	Kast: anon. scribe, 18th cen. Kilian: anon. scribe, 2nd half of 18th cen.
Berlin, SPK: *P 308*	"Praeludio e Fuga. C dur per Org: pedaliter" (TP) "Praeludium con Fuga pedaliter" (H)	Kast: anon. scribe, 19th cen. Kilian: anon. scribe, 1st half of 19th cen.
Berlin, SPK: *P 913*	"Praeludium con Fuga pedaliter" (TP) "Praeludium" (H)	Kast: F.A. Grasnick (ca. 1820) Kilian: F.A. Grasnick
Berlin, SPK: *Mus. ms. 40644 (Möller Handschrift)*	"Praeludium Pedaliter" (H)	Wolffheim: J.G. Walther Dürr: J. Bernhard Bach, the younger Kilian: J. Bernhard Bach, the elder
Göttingen, Bach-Institut	"Praeludium et Fuga" (H)	Kilian: anon. scribe, 18th cen. (Nürnberg circle?)
Göttingen, Bach-Institut	"Praeludium con Fuga" (H)	Kilian: L. Scholz
Hamburg: Schubring Collection	"Preludio" (H)	Kilian: J. Schubring
Stuttgart, Württembergische Landesbibliothek: *Cod. mus. II, 288*	"Praeludium et Fuga C#" (H)	Kilian: L. Sichart? ("1740")
Washington, Library of Congress: *ML 96/ B186*	"Praeludium pedaliter" (H)	Kilian: anon. scribe, 18th cen. Schulze: Gerlach, between 1720 and 1723

Prelude & Fugue in D, BWV 532

Source	Title	Scribe
Berlin, SPK: *P 204*	"Piece d'Orgue" (H)	Kast: C.F.G. Schwencke, 1781 Kilian: C.F.G. Schwencke, 1781

Source	Title	Scribe
Berlin, SPK: *P 287* (Prelude only)	"Preludio. ex Clavicembalo" (TP) "Preludio" (H)	Kast: anon. scribe, 2nd half of 18th cen. Kilian: anon. scribe, 2nd half of 18th cen.
Berlin, SPK: *P 291*	"Piece d'Orgue" (H)	Kast: anon. scribe, 2nd half of 18th cen. Kilian: anon. scribe, 2nd half of 18th cen.
Berlin, SPK: *P 567* (Fugue, in C, only)	"Thema pedaliter" (H)	Kast: J.F. Doles? Kilian: J.F. Doles?
Berlin, SPK: *P 595* (Fugue only)	"Fuga. Ex D♮. Pedaliter" (TP) "Fuga" (H)	Kast: J. Ringk Kilian: J. Ringk
Berlin, SPK: *P 834* (Fugue, in F, only)	"Fuga" (H)	Kast: anon. scribe, ca. 1800 Kilian: anon. scribe, 1st half of 19th cen.
Berlin, SPK: *P 924* (Fugue only)	"Fuga. pedaliter" (H)	Kast: F.A. Grasnick Kilian: F.A. Grasnick
Berlin, SPK: *P 1095* (Fugue only)	"Fuga. in D♮ " (TP) "Fuga" (H)	Kast: J.N. Mempell Kilian: J.N. Mempell
Brussels, Bib. Royale: *MS 4093* (Fugue only)	"Fuga" (H)	Kilian: anon. scribe, 2nd half of 18th cen.
Göttingen, Bach-Insitut (Fugue only)	"Fuga" (H)	Kilian: anon. scribe, 18th cen. (Nürnberg circle?)
Hamburg: Schubring Collection (Fugue only)	"Fuga" (H)	Kilian: J. Schubring
Leipzig, MBLpz: *Ms. 7* (Prelude only)	"Praeludium in D. dur." (H)	Krause: J.N. Mempell?
Leipzig, MBLpz: *III.8.20* (Fugue only)	"Fuga" (H)	Krause: J.F. Doles
Stuttgart: Württembergische Landesbibliothek: *Cod. mus. II, 288*	"Praeludium Concertato ex D♯. con Pedale" (H)	Kilian: L. Sichart?

Prelude & Fugue in e, BWV 533

Source	Title	Scribe
Berlin, SPK: *P 282*	"Praeludium e Fuga ped. ex. E moll" (H)	Kast: anon. scribe, 19th cen. Kilian: anon. scribe, beginning of 19th cen.
Berlin, SPK: *P 287*	"Praeludium et Fuga ped. ex E. moll" (TP) "Praeludium" (H)	Kast: Michel Kilian: Michel
Berlin, SPK: *P 289*	"Praeludium et Fuga ped. ex E mol" (TP)	Kast: anon. scribe, 2nd half of 18th cen. Kilian: anon. scribe, 2nd half of 18th cen.

Source	Title	Scribe
Berlin, SPK: *P 301* (Prelude only)	"Praeludium" (H)	Kast: anon. scribe, ca. 1800 in Vienna Kilian: anon. scribe, 1st half of 19th cen.
Berlin, SPK: *P 319*	"Praeludium et Fuga ped: ex E. moll" (H)	Kast: J.C. Westphal, Jr. Kilian: J.C. Westphal, Jr.
Berlin, SPK: *P 320*	"Praeludium" (H)	Kast: J.C. Kittel Kilian: L.E. Gebhardi?
Berlin, SPK: *P 425*	"Praeludium con Fuga. ex E Moll. pedaliter" (TP) "Praeludium" (H)	Kast: J. Ringk Kilian: J. Ringk
Berlin, SPK: *P 557* (Prelude only)	"Praeludium" (H)	Kast: F.A. Grasnick Kilian: F.A. Grasnick
Berlin, SPK: *P 671*	"Praeludium und Fuge" (H)	Kast: F.A. Grasnick Kilian: F.A. Grasnick
Berlin, SPK: *P 804* (Fugue only)	"Fuga ex ac.: E♭" (TB) "Fuga" (H)	Kast: "A.C."? Kilian: "C.A."?, "A.C."? "E.A."?, "E.C.A."?
Berlin, SPK: *P 923*	"Praeludium und Fuga" (H)	Kast: anon. scribe, ca. 1800 Kilian: J.F.W. Kühnau
Berlin, DStB: *Mus. ms. 30289*	"Praeludium et Fuga" (H)	Kast: anon. scribe, 18th cen. Kilian: copyist for J.F.W. Kühnau?, ca. 1830
Göttingen: Bach-Institut (Fugue only)	"Fuga" (H)	Kilian: anon. scribe, 18th cen. (Nürnberg Circle?)
Hamburg: Schubring Collection	"Praeludium und Fuge für die Orgel" (H)	Kilian: J. Schubring
Leipzig, Bach-Archiv: *Mus.ms. 2* (Fugue only)	"Fuga. pedaliter" (H)	Kilian: Anonymous 18 Schulze: Johann Caspar Vogler
New Haven, Yale: *LM 4838*	"Praeludium" (H)	Kilian: J.C.H. Rinck

Prelude & Fugue in e, BWV 533a

Source	Title	Scribe
Leipzig, MBLpz: *Ms. 7*	"Praeludium et Fuga in E moll" (H)	Krause: J.G. Preller

Prelude & Fugue in f, BWV 534

Source	Title	Scribe
Leipzig, MBLpz: *III.8.21*	"Praeludium et Fuga ex F moll pedaliter" (H)	Krause: J.A. Dröbs

Prelude & Fugue in g, BWV 535

Source	Title	Scribe
Berlin, SPK: *P 288*	"G. moll. Praeludium con Fuga Pedaliter" (TP) "Praeludium" (H)	Kast: anon. scribe, 2nd half of 18th cen. Kilian: anon. scribe, 2nd half of 18th cen.
Berlin, SPK: *P 320*	"Preludio con Fuga pro Organo Pleno in G moll" (H)	Kast: Kittel Kilian: L.E. Gebhardi?
Berlin, SPK: *P 557*	"Preludio con Fuga pro Organo Pleno in G moll" (H)	Kast: F.A. Grasnick Kilian: F.A. Grasnick
Berlin, SPK: *P 804* (Prelude only)	"Praeludium in G♭" (H)	Kast: J.P. Kellner Kilian: J.P. Kellner or W.N. Mey
Berlin, SPK: *P 1097*	"Praeludium et Fuga ex G moll con Pedale pro Organo Pleno" (TP) "Pralud. con Ped: (pro Organo pleno) (H)	Kast: J.C. Oley? Kilian: J.C. Oley?
Berlin, SPK: *P 1098*	"Preludio con Pedale ex G mol." (TP) "Prel: con Ped." (H)	Kast: J.G. Preller Kilian: J.G. Preller
Göttingen: Bach-Institut	"Praeludio et Fuga. G♭. con Pedal." (TP) "Praeludium con Pedal" (H)	Kilian: anon. scribe, 1st half (?) of 18th cen.
Hamburg: Schubring Collection	"Preludio con Fuga pro Organo pleno" (H)	Kilian: J. Schubring
Leipzig, MBLpz: *Poel. mus. Ms. 19*	"Praeludium und Fuga in G moll" (TP)	Krause: J.G. Weigand
Leipzig; MBLpz: *III.8.7*	"Preludio con Fuga per il Organo" (TP) "Preludio" (H)	Krause: scribe from Bach's circle; autograph corrections, 1740-1750

Prelude & Fugue in g, BWV 535a

Source	Title	Scribe
Berlin, SPK: *Mus. ms. 40644 (Möller Handschrift)*	"Praeludium cum Fuga ex G♭. Pedaliter" (H)	J.S. Bach Dadelsen: before 1707 Kilian: before 1708

Prelude & Fugue in A, BWV 536

Source	Title	Scribe
Berlin, SPK: *P 804*	"Praeludium in A♯ cum Pedale" (H)	Kast: J.P. Kellner & an anon. scribe Kilian: J.P. Kellner & an anon. scribe, 1st half of 18th cen.

Appendix I

| Berlin, SPK: *P 837* | "Preludio con Pedalo" (H) | Kast: anon. scribe
Kilian: anon. scribe, 1st half of 19th cen. |

Prelude & Fugue in A, BWV 536a

Source	Title	Scribe
Frankfurt: Guhr Collection (Lost)	?	Griepenkerl: J.S. Bach
Göttingen: Bach-Institut	"Preludio con Fuga. con Pedale" (H)	Kilian: L. Scholz
Göttingen: Bach-Institut (Fugue only)	"Fuga a Tempo" (H)	Kilian: L. Scholz

Fantasia and Fugue in c, BWV 537

Source	Title	Scribe
Berlin, DStB: *P 803*	"Fantasia con Fuga pro Organo" (TP) "Fantasia pro Organo" (H)	Kast: J.T. Krebs & J.L. Krebs, 1751 Kilian: J.T. Krebs & J.L. Krebs, 1751 Zietz: J.T. Krebs & J.L. Krebs, 1751

Toccata & Fugue in d ("Dorian"), BWV 538

Source	Title	Scribe
Berlin, SPK: *P 275*	"Praeludia in Organo Pleno con Fuga" (H)	Kast: J.G. Palschau Kilian: J.G. Palschau
Berlin, SPK: *P 277*	"Preludio" (H)	Kast: Anonymous 401 Kilian: Anon. 1 of the Amalien-Bibliothek, 2nd half of 18th cen.
Berlin, SPK: *P 282*	"Toccata p. l'Organo à due manuale e Pedale colla Fuga" (H)	Kast: anon. scribe, 19th cen. Kilian: anon. scribe, beginning of 19th cen.
Berlin, SPK: *P 286*	"D moll Toccata per l'Organo à due Clav: è Pedale col la Fuga" (TP)	Kast: Anonymous 300 Kilian: anon. scribe
Berlin, SPK: *P 290*	"Preludio" (H)	Kast: Anonymous 303 Kilian: Anonymous 303, 2nd half of 18th cen.
Berlin, SPK: *P 319*	"Toccata. per l'Organo, D. moll. à due Clav: è Pedale col la Fuga" (H)	Kast: J.C. Westphal, Jr. Kilian: J.C. Westphal, Jr.
Berlin, SPK: *P 416*	"Toccata con Fuga ex D. ♮ (Pedal)" (H)	Kast: anon. scribe, 2nd half of 18th cen. Kilian: anon. scribe, 2nd half of 18th cen.

Source	Title	Scribe
Berlin, SPK: *P 596*	"Preludium con Fuga D♭ in Organo Pleno è Pedale Obligato" (TP) "Preludium" (H)	Kast: "Kauffmann", 18th cen. ? Kilian: "Kauffmann", 18th cen.
Berlin, DStB: *P 803*	"Toccata con Fuga D♭" (H)	Kast: J.G. Walther Kilian: J.G. Walther Zietz: J.G. Walther, ca. 1712
Berlin, SPK: *P 837*	"Praeludium" (H)	Kast: anon. scribe, 1st half of 19th cen. Kilian: anon. scribe, 1st half of 19th cen.
Berlin, SPK: *P 1099*	"Toccata ex D mol. per l'Organo. â due Clavier e Pedal. col la Fuga" (TP) "Toccata" (H)	Kast: J.G. Preller Kilian: J.G. Preller
Hamburg: Schubring Collection (Toccata only)	"Toccata" (H)	Kilian: J. Schubring
Leipzig, MBLpz: *III.8.16*	"Praeludium con Fuga (D moll)" (TP)	Krause: J.A. Dröbs, beginning of 19th cen.
New Haven, Yale: *LM 4839e*	"Preludio in Organo Pleno à 2. Clav: con Fuga" (H)	Kilian: M.G. Fischer
New Haven, Yale: *LM 4842h* (Fugue only)	"Fuga" (H)	Kilian: L. Scholz
Vienna; Gesellschaft der Musikfreunde: *VII 14399a/B* (Fugue only)	"Fuga ex D. moll. a voc: 4. con Pedale Obligato" (TP) "Fuga. à Voc. 4. con Pedale Obligato" (H)	Kilian: anon. scribe, 2nd half of 18th cen.(?)

Prelude & Fugue in d, BWV 539

Source	Title	Scribe
Berlin, SPK: *P 213* (Fugue only)	"Fuga" (H)	Kast: anon. scribe, 2nd half of 18th cen. Kilian: anon. copyist, Amalien-Bibliothek
Berlin, SPK: *P 282* (Fugue only)	"Fuga" (H)	Kast: anon. scribe, 19th cen. Kilian: anon. scribe, beginning of 19th cen.
Berlin, SPK: *P 304* (Fugue only)	"Fuga" (H)	Kast: anon. scribe, active in Vienna ca. 1800 Kilian: anon. scribe, 1st half of 19th cen.
Berlin, SPK: *P 517*	"Praeludium und Fuge für die Orgel mit obligatem Pedal" (TP) "Praeludium" (H)	Kast: W.F.E. Bach? Kilian: anon. scribe, before 1829.
Berlin, DStB: *AmB 606* (Fugue only)	"Fuga" (H)	Kilian: Anonymous 29 of the Amalien-Bibliothek

Appendix I

Toccata & Fugue in F, BWV 540

Source	Title	Scribe
Berlin, SPK: *P 277*	"Preludio" (H)	Kast: Anonymous 401
		Kilian: Anonymous 1 of the Amalien-Bibliothek, 2nd half of 18th cen.
Berlin, SPK: *P 282* (Fugue only)	"Fuga (a Organo pedaliter)" (H)	Kast: anon. scribe, 19th cen.
		Kilian: anon. scribe, beginning of 19th cen.
Berlin, SPK: *P 287* (Fugue only)	"F dur. Fuga pro Organo pedaliter" (TP) "Fuga" (H)	Kast: anon. scribe, 2nd half of 18th cen.
		Kilian: anon. scribe, 2nd half of 18th cen.
Berlin, SPK: *P 289* (Toccata only)	"Toccata col Pedali Obligato" (H)	Kast: anon. scribe, 2nd half of 18th cen.
		Kilian: anon. scribe, 2nd half of 18th cen.
Berlin, SPK: *P 290*	"Preludio" (H)	Kast: Anonymous 303
		Kilian: Anonymous 303, 2nd half of 18th cen.
Berlin, SPK: *P 409* (Fugue only)	"Fuga" (H)	Kast: anon. scribe, 2nd half of 18th cen.
		Kilian: anon. scribe, 1st half of 19th cen.
Berlin, SPK: *P 596*	"Toccata in F♮ pedaliter" (TP) "Preludium" (H)	Kast: "Kauffmann" (?) Kilian: "Kauffmann," 18th cen.
Berlin, DStB: *P 803*	"Toccata col pedale obligato" (TP)	Kast: Toccata: J.T. Krebs Fugue: J.L. Krebs
		Kilian: Toccata: J.T. Krebs Fugue: J.L. Krebs
		Zietz: Toccata: J.T. Krebs, ca. 1714 Fugue: J.L. Krebs, before 1731
Berlin, SPK: *P 1009* (Toccata only)	"Toccata" (H)	Kast: J.C. Kittel? Kilian: J.C. Kittel?
Berlin, DStB: *Mus. ms 30387* (Toccata only)	"Toccata in F dur" (H)	Kast: J.A. Dröbs? Kilian: J.A. Dröbs
Hamburg: Schubring Collection (Toccata only)	"Preludio" (H)	Kilian: J. Schubring
Leipzig, MBLpz: *Ms. 3* (Fugue only)	"Fuga ex. F. dur. Pedaliter" (TP) "Fuga" (H)	Krause: J.A.G. Wechmar?
Leipzig, MBLpz: *Poel. mus. Ms. 16* (Toccata only)	"Toccata in F. dur... con obligato Pedale" (TP) "Toccata" (H)	Krause: W. Saalborn?, beginning of 19th cen.

216 *The Organ Preludes of J. S. Bach*

Leipzig, MBLpz: *Poel. mus. Ms. 28* (Fugue only)	"Fuga in F♮ . pro Org: Pedaliter" (TP) "Fuga" (H)	Krause: anon. scribe, end of 18th cen.
Leipzig, MBLpz: *III.8.29* (Fugue only)	"Fuga" (H)	Krause: J.A. Dröbs, beginning of 19th cen.

Prelude & Fugue in G, BWV 541

Source	Title	Scribe
Berlin, SPK: *P 288*	"Praeludium con Fuga Pedalit: ex G♮" (TP) "Praeludium Pedaliter" (H)	Kast: J.P. Kellner Kilian: J.P. Kellner, with emendations of J.C. Westphal, Jr.
Berlin, SPK: *P 290*	"Preludio" (H)	Kast: Anonymous 303 Kilian: Anonymous 303, 2nd half of 18th cen.
Berlin, SPK: *P 319*	"Praeludium con fuga pro Organo cum Pedale obligato ex G♮ " (H)	Kast: J.C. Westphal, Jr. Kilian: J.C. Westphal, Jr.
Berlin, SPK: *P 320*	"Praeludium pro Organo" (H)	Kast: J.C. Kittel Kilian: L.E. Gebhardi?
Berlin, SPK: *P 557*	"Praeludium pro Organo" (H)	Kast: F.A. Grasnick Kilian: F.A. Grasnick
Berlin, SPK: *P 595*	"Praeludium pedaliter" (H)	Kast: J. Ringk Kilian: J. Ringk
Berlin, SPK: *P 597*	"Preludio e Fuga per l'Organo con Pedale obligato" (TP) "Preludio" (H)	Kast: anon. scribe, 2nd half of 18th cen. Kilian: anon. scribe, 2nd half of 18th cen.
Berlin, SPK: *P 837*	"Praeludium" (H)	Kast: anon. scribe, 1st half of 19th cen. Kilian: anon. scribe, 1st half of 19th cen.
Berlin, DStB: *AmB 543*	"Praeludium pro Organo cum pedale obligato" (TP) "Praeludium (H)	Kilian: Anonymous 2 of the Amalien-Bibliothek
Brussels, Bibliothèque Royale: *II.3914*	"Praeludium und Fuga aus G dur" (TP) "Praeludium pro Organo" (H)	Kilian: K.C. Kegel?
Hamburg: Schubring Collection	"Praeludium (und) Fuga" (H)	Kilian: J. Schubring
Leipzig: MBLpz: *Ms. 7*	"Praeludium et Fuga ex G dur" (TP) "Praeludium Pedaliter" (H)	Krause: J.N. Mempell?
New Haven, Yale: *LM 4839d*	"Praeludium pro Organo" (H)	Kilian: M.G. Fischer
New York: Hinrichsen Collection	"Praeludium pro Organo con Pedal: obligat:" (H)	J.S. Bach Kilian: between 1733 and 1742

Appendix I

Fantasia & Fugue in g, BWV 542

Source	Title	Scribe
Berlin, SPK: *P 203* (Fugue only)	"Fuga" (H)	Kast: J.S. Borsch Kilian: J.S. Borsch
Berlin, SPK: *P 204* (Fugue, in f, only)	"Fuga" (H)	Kast: C.F.G. Schwencke Kilian: C.F.G. Schwencke
Berlin, SPK: *P 282* (Fugue only)	"Fuga (ex G moll pro Organo cum Pedale obligato" (H)	Kast: anon. scribe, 19th cen.
Berlin, SPK: *P 287* (Fugue, in f, only)	"Orgel Fuga. Das allerbeste Pedal-Stück vom Herrn Johann Sebastian Bach" (TP) "Thema" (H)	Kast: J.S. Borsch Kilian: J.S. Borsch
Berlin, SPK: *P 288* (Fugue only)	"Fuga ex G mol pro Organo pleno cum Pedale obligato" (TP) "Fuga ex G mol." (H)	Kast: J.P. Kellner Kilian: J.P. Kellner
Berlin, SPK: *P 288*	"Fantasia e Fuga in Gm: Per l'Organo pieno col Pedale Obligato" (TP) "Fantasia" (H)	Kast: anon. scribe, 2nd half of 18th cen. Kilian: anon. scribe, ca. 1800
Berlin, SPK: *P 290* (Fugue only)	"Fuga" (H)	Kast: Anonymous 303 Kilian: Anonymous 303, 2nd half of 18th cen.
Berlin, SPK: *P 320* (Fugue only)	"Fuga"	Kast: J.C. Kittel Kilian: L.E. Gebhardi?
Berlin, SPK: *P 518* (Fugue, in f, only)	"Orgel-Fuga aus F moll" (TP) "Thema Fuga" (H)	Kast: anon. scribe, ca. 1800 Kilian: anon. scribe, ca. 1800
Berlin, SPK: *P 557* (Fugue, in f, only)	"Fuga"	Kast: F.A. Grasnick Kilian: F.A. Grasnick
Berlin, SPK: *P 595*	"Fantasia con Fuga. con pedale, G♭" (TP) "Fantasia" (H)	Kast: anon. scribe, 18th cen. Kilian: anon. scribe, 2nd half of 18th cen.
Berlin, SPK: *P 598* (Fugue only)	"Fuga con Pedale" (H)	Kast: J.F. Agricola Kilian: J.F. Agricola, ca. 1738-1740
Berlin, DStB: *P 803* (Fugue only)	"Fuga" (H)	Kast: J.T. Krebs Kilian: J.T. Krebs Zietz: J.T. Krebs, ca. 1714
Berlin, SPK: *P 837* (Fugue only)	"Fuga" (H)	Kast: anon. scribe, 1st half of 19th cen. Kilian: anon. scribe, 1st half of 19th cen.
Berlin, SPK: *P 924*	"Fantasia con Fuga con Pedale" (H)	Kast: F.A. Grasnick Kilian: F.A. Grasnick
Berlin, SPK: *P 1071*	"Fantasie pour l'Orgue" (H)	Kast: anon. scribe, ca. 1800 Kilian: A. Kühnau?
Berlin, SPK: *P 1100* (Fugue only)	"Fuga ex G moll. con Pedale, pro Organo pleno" (TP) "Fuga" (H)	Kast: J.C. Oley Kilian: J.C. Oley

218 The Organ Preludes of J. S. Bach

Source	Title	Scribe
Berlin, DStB: *AmB 531*	"Fantasia" (H)	Kilian: Anonymous 34 of the Amalien-Bibliothek
Hamburg: Schubring Collection (Fugue only)	"Fuga" (H)	Kilian: J. Schubring
Leipzig, MBLpz: *Ms. 4* (Fugue only)	------	Krause: anon. scribe
Leipzig, MBLpz: *Poel. mus. Ms. 21* (Fugue only)	"Fuga ... in G moll" (H)	Krause: J.G. Weigand
Leipzig, MBLpz: *III.8.20* (Fantasia only)	"Fantasia" (H)	Krause: J.A. Dröbs, beginning of 19th cen.
New Haven, Yale: *LM 4838* (Fugue, in f, only)	"Fuga ... beteitelt das allerbeste Pedal Stück" (H)	Kilian: J.C.H. Rinck

Prelude & Fugue in a, BWV 543

Source	Title	Scribe
Berlin, SPK: *P 276*	"Preludio e Fuga per L'Organo (TP) "Preludio" (H)	Kast: Anonymous 401 Kilian: Anonymous 1 of the Amalien-Bibliothek
Berlin, SPK: *P 290*	"Preludio" (H)	Kast: Anonymous 303 Kilian: Anonymous 303, 2nd half of 18th cen.
Berlin, SPK: *P 505*	"Preludio e Fuga per l'Organo pieno col Pedale obligato" (TP) "Preludio" (H)	Kast: F.A. Grasnick, 1817 Kilian: F.A. Grasnick, 1817
Berlin, SPK: *P 819*	"Praeludium" (H)	Kast: anon. scribe, ca. 1800 Kilian: F.A. Grasnick?
Berlin, SPK: *P 837*	"Preludio" (H)	Kast: anon. scribe, 1st half of 19th cen. Kilian: anon. scribe, 1st half of 19th cen.
Berlin, SPK: *AmB 54*	"Preludio" (H)	Kilian: Anonymous 1 of the Amalien-Bibliothek
Berlin, SPK: *AmB 60*	"Preludio (und) Fuga per l'Organo pieno" (TP) "Preludio" (H)	Kilian: anon. scribe, working in Berlin after 1754
Leipzig, MBLpz: *III.8.14*	"Praeludium et Fuga in A moll für die volle Orgel" (TP) "Praeludium con Pedale. pro Organo pleno" (H)	Krause: J.A. Dröbs

Prelude & Fugue in a, BWV 543a

Source	Title	Scribe
Berlin, SPK: *P 288*	"Praeludium cum Fuga ex A♭ pedaliter" (TP)	Kast: J.P. Kellner? Kilian; J.P. Kellner?

Appendix I

Source	Title	Scribe
Berlin, DstB: *P 803*	"Praeludium con Fuga" (TP) "Praeludium" (H)	Kast: anon. scribe, 2nd half of 18th cen. Kilian: anon. scribe, 2nd (?) half of 18th cen. Zietz: anon. scribe
New Haven, Yale: *LM 4839g*	"Praeludium et Fuga in A moll pedaliter pro Organo" (TP) "Praeludium" (H)	Kilian: M.G. Fischer

Prelude & Fugue in b, BWV 544

Source	Title	Scribe
Berlin, SPK: *P 276*	"Preludio e Fuga per L'Organo" (TP) "Preludio" (H)	Kast: Anonymous 401 Kilian: Anonymous 1 of the Amalien-Bibliothek
Berlin, SPK: *P 290*	"Preludio" (H)	Kast: Anonymous 303 Kilian: Anonymous 303, 2nd half of 18th cen.
Berlin, SPK: *P 560*	"Preludio e Fuga per L'Organo" (TP) "Preludio" (H)	Kast: anon. scribe, ca. 1800 Kilian: Anonymous 2 (?) of the Amalien-Bibliothek
Berlin, SPK: *P 837*	"Praeludium" (H)	Kast: anon. scribe, 1st half of 19th cen. Kilian: anon. scribe, 1st half of 19th cen.
Berlin, SPK: *P 891*	"Praeludium in H mol. pro Organo cum pedale obligato" (TP) "Praeludium in Organo pleno, pedal" (H)	Kast: J.P. Kellner Kilian: J.P. Kellner
Berlin, SPK: *P 922*	"Preludio" (H)	Kast: F.A. Grasnick Kilian: F.A. Grasnick
Berlin, SPK: *AmB 54*	"Preludio" (H)	Kilian: Anonymous 1 of the Amalien-Bibliothek
Berlin, SPK: *AmB 60*	"Preludio (e) Fuga per L'Organo" (TP) "Preludio" (H)	Kilian: anon. scribe, working in Berlin after 1754
Leipzig, MBLpz: *Ms. 1*	"Praeludium con Fuga in H mol. pro Organo cum pedale obligato" (TP) "Praeludium" (H)	Krause: J.A.G. Wechmar?
Leipzig, MBLpz: *Poel. mus. Ms. 24*	"Praeludium et Fuga in H moll pro Organo pleno cum Pedale oblig." (TP) "Praeludium pro Organo pleno" (H)	Krause: J.G. Weigand, ca. 1817
Leipzig, MBLpz: *III.8.21*	"Praeludium con Fuga obligato pedaliter" (H)	Krause: J.A. Dröbs, beginning of 19th cen.
New Haven, Yale: *LM 4839i*	"Praeludium für die volle Orgel mit Obligatem Pedal" (TP) "Praeludium pro Organo pleno cum Pedale obligato" (H)	Kilian: anon. scribe, ca. 1800
Oxford: Rosenthal Collection	"Präludium pro Organo cum pedale obligato" (TP) "Praeludium in Organo pleno pedale" (H)	J.S. Bach Kilian: between 1727 and 1731

Prelude & Fugue in C, BWV 545

Source	Title	Scribe
Berlin, SPK: *P 276*	"Preludio e Fuga per l'Organo pieno" (TP) "Preludio" (H)	Kast: Anonymous 401 Kilian: Anonymous 1 of the Amalien-Bibliothek, 2nd half of 18th cen.
Berlin, SPK: *P 282* (with BWV 529/2)	"Praeludium (in Organo pleno/Praeludium e Fuga p. Organo obligato)" (H)	Kast: anon. scribe, ca. 1800 Kilian: anon. scribe, beginning of 19th cen.
Berlin, SPK: *P 286* (with BWV 529/2)	"C dur Praeludium pro Organo. cum Pedale obligato" (TP) "Praeludium in Organo pleno pedaliter" (H)	Kast: J.P. Kellner Kilian: J.P. Kellner
Berlin, SPK: *P 290*	"Preludio" (H)	Kast: Anonymous 303 Kilian: Anonymous 303, 2nd half of 18th cen.
Berlin, SPK: *P 559*	"Preludio e Fuga per L'Organo pieno" (TP) "Preludio" (H)	Kast: anon. scribe, ca. 1800 Kilian: Anonymous 6 of the Amalien-Bibliothek?
Berlin, SPK: *P 602*	"Preludio e Fuga Per L'Organo pieno con Pedale obligato" (TP) "Preludio" (H)	Kast: anon. scribe, 2nd half of 18th cen. Kilian: anon. scribe, working in Berlin, 2nd half of 18th cen.
Berlin, SPK: *P 658*	"Praeludium pro Organo pleno. pedaliter. cum Pedale obligato" (H)	Kast: J.C. Kittel Kilian: M.G. Fischer, 1792
Berlin, SPK: *P 816* (Fugue only)	-------	Kast: anon. scribe, ca. 1800 Kilian: G.L. Walchius? 1817?
Berlin, SPK: *P 837*	"Preludio" (H)	Kast: anon. scribe, 1st half of 19th cen. Kilian: anon. scribe, 1st half of 19th cen.
Berlin, SPK: *P 916* (Prelude only)	-------	Kast: anon. scribe, ca. 1800 Kilian: G.L. Walchius? 1817?
Berlin, SPK: *AmB 54*	"Preludio" (H)	Kilian: Anonymous 1 of the Amalien-Bibliothek
Berlin, SPK: *AmB 60*	"Preludio e fuga per l'Organo pieno" (TP) "Preludio" (H)	Kilian: anon. scribe, working in Berlin after 1754
Leipzig: Clauss Collection (Lost)	"Praeludium pro Organo cum Pedale obligato... C major" (TP) "Praeludium in Organo pleno pedaliter" (H)	Rust: J.S. Bach
Leipzig, MBLpz: *III.8.21*	"Praeludium et Fuga in Organo pleno, pedaliter" (H)	Krause: J.A. Dröbs
New Haven, Yale: *LM 4718* (with BWV 529/2)	"Preludio con Fuga e Trio" (TP)	Kilian: J.G. Walther, before 1717

Appendix I

New Haven, Yale: *LM 4839c*
"Praeludium et Fuga. pro Organo pleno cum Pedale" (H)
Kilian: M.G. Fischer

Stockholm: Stiftelsen Musikkulturens främjande (with BWV 529/2)
"Praeludium in Organo pleno, pedaliter" (H)
Kilian: Anonymous 18
Schulze: Johann Caspar Vogler

Prelude & Fugue in C, BWV 545a

Source	Title	Scribe
Berlin, SPK: *P 290* (Prelude only)	"Praeludium Pedaliter" (H)	Kast: Anonymous 303 Kilian: Anonymous 303, 2nd half of 18th cen.
Berlin, SPK: *P 521* (Fugue only)	"Fuga" (H)	Kast: anon. scribe, 19th cen. Kilian: anon. scribe, 1st half of 19th cen.
Leipzig, MBLpz: *Poel. mus. Ms. 12*	"Praeludium et Fuga" (TP) "Praeludium" (H)	Krause: anon. scribe, ca. 1780-1790

Prelude & Fugue in c, BWV 546

Source	Title	Scribe
Berlin, SPK: *P 276*	"Preludio e Fuga per L'Organo" (TP) "Preludio" (H)	Kast: Anonymous 401 Kilian: Anonymous 1 of the Amalien-Bibliothek
Berlin, SPK: *P 286*	"Praeludium cum fuga ex C mol. pro Organo cum Pedale obligato" (TP) "Praeludium pro Organo cum Pedale obligato" (H)	Kast: J.P. Kellner Kilian: J.P. Kellner
Berlin, SPK: *P 290*	"Preludio" (H)	Kast: Anonymous 303 Kilian: Anonymous 303, 2nd half of 18th cen.
Berlin, SPK: *P 320*	"Praeludium con Fuga pro Organo cum Pedale Obligato" (H)	Kast: Kittel Kilian: L.E. Gebhardi?
Berlin, SPK: *P 557*	"Praeludium cum Fuga pro Organo cum Pedale Obligato" (H)	Kast: F.A. Grasnick Kilian: F.A. Grasnick
Berlin, SPK: *P 596*	"Praeludium et Fuga, in C♭ pro Organo pleno con Pedale obligato" (TP) "Praeludium" (H)	Kast: "Kauffmann"? Kilian: Kauffman, 18th cen.
Berlin, SPK: *P 837*	"Preludio" (H)	Kast: anon. scribe, 1st half of 19th cen.
Berlin, SPK: *AmB 54*	"Preludio" (H)	Kilian: Anonymous 1 of the Amalien-Bibliothek
Berlin, SPK: *AmB 60*	"Preludio e Fuga per l'Organo con Pedale obligato" (TP) "Preludio" (H)	Kilian: anon. scribe, working in Berlin after 1754

Source	Title	Scribe
Brussels, Bibliothèque Royale: *II.3915*	"Praeludium con Fuga pro Organo con Pedale Obligato" (TP) "Praeludium" (H)	Kilian: anon. scribe, beginning of 19th cen.
Leipzig, MBLpz: *III.8.22*	"Praeludium con Fuga pour Organo con Pedale obligato" (H)	Krause: anon. scribe, beginning of 19th cen.
New Haven, Yale: *LM 4839f*	"Preludio" (H)	Kilian: anon. scribe, ca. 1800

Prelude & Fugue in C, BWV 547

Source	Title	Scribe
Berlin, SPK: *P 274*	"Praeludium pro Organo pedal" (TP) "Praeludium" (H)	Kast: J.P. Kellner Kilian: anon. scribe, 1st half of 18th cen.
Berlin, SPK: *P 276*	"Preludio e Fuga per L'Organo" (TP) "Preludio" (H)	Kast: Anonymous 401 Kilian: Anonymous 1 of the Amalien-Bibliothek
Berlin, SPK: *P 286*	"Praeludium ex C dur et Fuga ex C dur" (TP) "Praeludium" (H)	Kast: Forkel? Kilian: anon. scribe, 2nd half of 18th cen.
Berlin, SPK: *P 290*	"Preludio" (H)	Kast: Anonymous 303 Kilian: Anonymous 303, 2nd half of 18th cen.
Berlin, SPK: *P 320*	"Praeludium cum Fuga pro Organo Pleno in C dur" (H)	Kast: J.C. Kittel Killian: L.E. Gebhardi?
Berlin, SPK: *P 557*	"Praeludium cum Fuga; pro Organo Pleno in C Dur" (H)	Kast: F.A. Grasnick Kilian: F.A. Grasnick
Berlin, SPK: *P 837*	"Preludio" (H)	Kast: anon. scribe, 1st half of 19th cen. Kilian: anon. scribe, 1st half of 19th cen.
Berlin, SPK: *AmB 54*	"Preludio" (H)	Kilian: Anonymous 1 of the Amalien-Bibliothek
Berlin, SPK: *AmB 60*	"Preludio e Fuga per L'Organo" (TP) "Preludio" (H)	Kilian: anon. scribe, working in Berlin after 1754
Brussels: Bibliothèque Royale: *II.3914*	"Praeludium und Fuga aus C dur für die Orgel" (TP) "Praeludium con Fuga" (H)	Kilian: K.C. Kegel
Leipzig, MBLpz: *Ms. 1*	"Praeludium con Fuga ex C# pro organo pleno" (TP) "Praeludium" (H)	Krause: J.A.G. Wechmar
Leipzig, MBLpz: *Poel. mus. Ms. 32*	"Preludio con Fuga per il Organo" (H)	Krause: C.F. Penzel?
New Haven, Yale: *LM 5056*	"Praeludium et Fuga a C dur" (H)	Kilian: J. Becker, after 1779

Appendix I

Prelude & Fugue in e, BWV 548

Source	Title	Scribe
Berlin, SPK: *P 228* (Fugue only)	"Fuga pro Organo pedaliter" (TP) "Fuga" (H)	Kast: anon. scribe, working for Breitkopf in 1st half of 19th cen. Kilian: anon. scribe, working for Breitkopf in 1st half of 19th cen.
Berlin, SPK: *P 274*	"Praeludium et Fuga in E mol. pro Organo pedaliter" (TP) "Praeludium pedaliter pro Organo" (H)	Prelude, Fugue mm. 1-20: J.S. Bach Kilian: between 1727-1731 Fugue, m. 21ff.: Kast: J.P. Kellner Kilian: J.P. Kellner?
Berlin, SPK: *P 276*	"Preludio e Fuga per L'Organo" (TP) "Preludio" (H)	Kast: Anonymous 401 Kilian: Anonymous 1 of the Amalien-Bibliothek
Berlin, SPK: *P 287*	"Praeludium ex E mol. Fuga ex E moll" (TP) "Praeludium pedaliter pro Organo" (H)	Kast: J.N. Forkel? Kilian: anon. scribe, 2nd half of 18th cen.
Berlin, SPK: *P 290*	"Preludio" (H)	Kast: Anonymous 303 Kilian: Anonymous 303, 2nd half of 18th cen.
Berlin, SPK: *P 553*	"Praeludium et Fuga ex E moll" (TP) "Praeludium pedaliter pro Organo" (H)	Kast: anon. scribe, ca. 1800 Kilian: anon. scribe, ca. 1800
Berlin, SPK: *P 837*	"Preludio" (H)	Kast: anon. scribe, 1st half of 19th cen. Kilian: anon. scribe, 1st half of 19th cen.
Berlin, SPK: *AmB 54*	"Preludio" (H)	Kilian: Anonymous 1 of the Amalien-Bibliothek
Berlin, SPK: *AmB 60*	"Preludio e Fuga per l'Organo" (H)	Kilian: anon. scribe, working in Berlin after 1754
Leipzig, MBLpz: *Ms. 1*	"Praeludium et Fuga in E mol pro Organo pedaliter" (TP) "Praeludium pro Organo pedaliter" (H)	Krause: J.A.G. Wechmar
Leipzig, MBLpz: *Ms. 7*	"Praeludium et Fuga pro Organo Pedaliter" (TP) "Praeludium" (H)	Krause: anon. scribe, working with J.N. Mempell
Leipzig, MBLpz: *Poel. mus. Ms. 14* (Fugue only, incomplete)	"Fuga in E moll" (TP) "Fuga in E moll" (H)	Krause: J.G. Weigand, ca. 1815-1820
Leipzig, MBLpz: *Poel. mus. Ms. 15*	"E minor Praeludium pro Organo pedaliter con Fuga in E moll" (TP) "Präludium pedal: pro Organo" (H)	Krause: J.G. Weigand
Leipzig, MBLpz: *III.8.21*	"Praeludium pedaliter pro Organo pleno" (H)	Krause: J.A. Dröbs
New Haven, Yale: *LM 4839h*	"Praeludium et Fuga ex E Mol. Pedaliter" (TP) "Praeludium" (TP)	Kilian: anon. scribe, ca. 1800

The Organ Preludes of J. S. Bach

New Haven, Yale: *LM 5056*	"Praeludium pedaliter pro Organo" (H)	Kilian: J. Becker, after 1779
Vienna: Laichmann Collection	"Praeludium ped. pro Organo" (H)	Kilian: Anonymous 5a, after 1730

Prelude & Fugue in c, BWV 549

Source	Title	Scribe
Berlin, SPK: *P 282*	"Praeludium (pedaliter)" (H)	Kast: anon. scribe, 19th cen. Kilian: anon. scribe, beginning of 19th cen.
Berlin, SPK: *P 287*	"Praeludium et Fuga ped: ex C. moll" (TP) "Preludium pedaliter" (H)	Kast: Michel Kilian: Michel
Berlin, SPK: *P 289*	"Praeludium et Fuga ped. ex C mol." (TP)	Kast: anon. scribe, 2nd half of 18th cen. Kilian: anon. scribe, 2nd half of 18th cen.
Berlin, SPK: *P 301*	"Preludium" (H)	Kast: anon. scribe, active in Vienna ca. 1800 Kilian: anon. scribe, 1st half of 19th cen.
Berlin, SPK: *P 319*	"Praeludium et Fuga ped. ex C. moll" (TP) "Praeludium pedaliter" (H)	Kast: J.C. Westphal, Jr. Kilian: J.C. Westphal, Jr.
Berlin, SPK: *P 320*	"Praeludium" (H)	Kast: J.C. Kittel Kilian: L.E. Gebhardi?
Leipzig, MBLpz: *III.8.22*	"Praeludium et Fuga" (H)	Krause: anon. scribe, beginning of 19th cen.
New Haven, Yale: *LM 4838*	"Praeludium Pedaliter" (H)	Kilian: J.C.H. Rinck
Stift Göttweig: *J.S. Bachs Nr. 35*	"Praeludium pedaliter" (H)	Kilian: A. Fuchs

Prelude & Fugue in d, BWV 549a

Source	Title	Scribe
Berlin, SPK: *P 218*	"Preludium Pedaliter" (H)	Kast: anon. scribe, 18th cen. Kilian: anon. scribe, 2nd half of 18th cen. (=Anonymous 2 of the Amalien-Bibliothek?)
Berlin, SPK: *P 308*	"Preludio e Fuga in C mol (Dm)...per Organo" (TP) "Praeludium ô Fantasia...cum fuga" (H)	Kast: anon. scribe, 19th cen. Kilian: anon. scribe, 1st half of 19th cen.
Berlin, SPK: *Mus. ms. 40644 (Möller Handschrift)*	"Praeludium ô Fantasia. Pedaliter. ex D♭" (H)	Wolffheim: J.G. Walther Dürr: J. Bernhard Bach, the younger Kilian: J. Bernhard Bach, the elder
Hamburg: Schubring Collection	"Preludio" (H)	Kilian: J. Schubring

Appendix I

Prelude & Fugue in G, BWV 550

Source	Title	Scribe
Berlin, SPK: *P 287*	"Preludio con Fuga in G. dur" (TP)	Kast: Michel Kilian: Michel
Berlin, SPK: *P 512*	"Preludio e Fuga G♮ per l'Organo con Pedale obligato" (H)	Kast: F.A. Grasnick Kilian: F.A. Grasnick
Berlin, SPK: *P 642*	"Praeludium" (H)	Kast: anon. scribe, 19th cen. Kilian: anon. scribe, 1st half of 19th cen.
Berlin, SPK: *P 924*	"Praeludium" (H)	Kast: F.A. Grasnick Kilian: F.A. Grasnick
Berlin, SPK: *P 1090*	"Praeludium" (H)	Kast: G.A. Homilius Kilian: G.A. Homilius
Berlin, SPK: *P 1210*	"Praeludium pedaliter" (TP) "Praeludium" (H)	Kast: J.C.G. Bach Kilian: anon. scribe, 1st half of 18th cen., with autograph corrections
Brussels, Bibliothèque Royale: *II.4093*	"Preludio con Fuga" (H)	Kilian: anon. scribe, 2nd half of 18th cen.
Göttingen: Bach-Institut (Prelude only)	"Preludio" (H)	Kilian: L. Scholz
Leipzig, MBLpz: *Ms. 7*	"Praeludio (und Fuge) in G dur con Pedale" (TP)	Krause: J.N. Mempell?
New Haven, Yale: *LM 4839a*	"G. Major. Praeludium et Fuga per il Organo" (H)	Kilian: anon. scribe, ca. 1800

Prelude in a, BWV 551

Source	Title	Scribe
Berlin, SPK: *P 595*	"Praeludium con Fuga ex A Moll pedaliter" (H)	Kast: J. Ringk Kilian: J. Ringk
Berlin, SPK: *P 642*	"Praeludium con Fuga" (H)	Kast: anon. scribe, 19th cen. Kilian: anon. scribe, 1st half of 19th cen.
Berlin, SPK: *P 924*	"Praeludium con Fuga pedaliter" (H)	Kast: F.A. Grasnick Kilian: F.A. Grasnick
Leipzig, MBLpz: *Ms. 7* (mm. 1-11 missing)	"Fuga. in A mol." (H)	Krause: J.N. Mempell?
Leipzig, MBLpz: *III.8.20*	"Preludium con Fuga" (H)	Krause: J.A. Dröbs, beginning of 19th cen.

Prelude & Fugue in E♭, BWV 552

Source	Title	Scribe
Clavierübung III (1739)[3]	Prelude: "Praeludium pro Organo pleno" (H) Fugue: "Fuga à 5. con pedale. pro Organo pleno" (H)	Printed by Balthasar Schmid, Nürnberg

Fantasia & Fugue (incomplete) in c, BWV 562

Source	Title	Scribe
Berlin, SPK: *P 277* (Fantasia only)	"Fantasia. a 5. Voc" (H)	Kast: Anonymous 401 Kilian: Anonymous 1 of the Amalien-Bibliothek
Berlin, SPK: *P 288* (Fantasia only)	"Fantasia in C♮ pro Organo â 5. Voc. cum Pedali obligato" (TP) "Fantasia pro Organo a 5 Voc: cum pedale obligato" (H)	Kast: J.P. Kellner Kilian: J.P. Kellner
Berlin, SPK: *P 290* (Fantasia only)	"Fantasia a 5 Voc:" (H)	Kast: Anonymous 303 Kilian: Anonymous 303, 2nd half of 18th cen.
Berlin, SPK: *P 320* (Fantasia only)	"Fantasia pro Organo à 5 Voc. con Pedale Obligato" (H)	Kast: J.C. Kittel Kilian: L.E. Gebhardi?
Berlin, SPK: *P 490* (Fantasia; Fugue, mm. 1-27)	"Fantasia pro Organo a 5 Vocum cum Pedali obligato" (H)	J.S. Bach Dadelsen: Fugue: between 1735-1744/46 Kilian: Fantasia: 1720's or 1730's Fugue: ca. 1745
Berlin, SPK: *P 533* (Fantasia only)	"Fantasia à 5 Voc. l'Organo con ped: oblig." (H)	Kast: J.F. Agricola Kilian: J.F. Agricola, ca. 1738-1740
Berlin, SPK: *P 557* (Fantasia only)	"Fantasia pro Organo â 5 Voc con Pedale Obligato" (H)	Kast: F.A. Grasnick Kilian: F.A. Grasnick
Brussels: Bibliothèque Royale: *XY 15.137* (Fugue, mm. 1-27, only)	"Fuga. a 5" (H)	?
Brussels: Bibliothèque Royale: *XY 15.140* (Fugue, mm. 1-27, only)	"Fuga. a 5" (H)	?
Leipzig, MBLpz: *Ms. 1* (Fantasia only)	"Fantasia pro Organo ex C mol. à 5 Vox. Cum Pedal obligato" (TP)	Krause: J.A.G. Wechmar?

Fantasia & Fugue in c, BWV 562/1a & BWV 546/2a

Source	Title	Scribe
Berlin, SPK: *P 519*	"Praeludium (con fuga) pro Organo cum Pedali obligato" (TP) "Fantasia pro Organo cum Pedali obligato" (H)	Kast: anon. scribe, 19th cen. Kilian: anon. scribe, 1st half of 19th cen.

Appendix I

Berlin, SPK: *P 1104*	"PRAELUDIUM Pro Organo cum Pedal: Obligato" (TP) "Fantasia pro. Organo cum pedali obligato" (H)	Kast: anon. scribe, 18th cen. Kilian: J.C. Oley?

Fantasia con Imitazione in b, BWV 563

Source	Title	Scribe
Berlin, SPK: *P 279*	"Fantasia ex H moll con Imitatione" (TP) "Fantasia" (H)	Kast: anon. scribe, ca. 1800 Kilian: anon. scribe, beginning of 19th cen.
Berlin, SPK: *P 308*	"Fantasia" (H)	Kast: A. Werner?, 19th cen. Kilian: anon. scribe, 1st half of 19th cen.
Berlin, SPK: *P 804*, pp. 67-68 (Fantasia only)	-------	Kast: J.P. Kellner Kilian: J.P. Kellner?
Berlin, SPK: *P 804*, pp. 341-343 (Imitazione only)	"Fantasia in H-moll" (TP)	Kast: W.N. Mey Kilian: W.N. Mey
Berlin, SPK: *P 1091*	"Fantasia" (H)	Kast: anon. scribe, 2nd half of 18th cen. Kilian: anon. scribe, 2nd half of 18th cen.
Berlin, DStB: *Mus. ms. 30069*	"Fantasia" (H)	Kast: anon. scribe, 19th cen. Kilian: F.A. Grasnick
Leipzig, MBLpz: *III.8.4* (*Andreas Bach Buch*)	"Fantasia" (H)	Wolffheim: J.G. Walther Dürr: J. Bernhard Bach, the younger Kilian: J. Bernhard Bach, the elder

Toccata, Adagio, & Fugue in C, BWV 564

Source	Title	Scribe
Berlin, SPK: *P 286*	"Toccata ex C♮ pedaliter" (TP) "Praeludium" (H)	Kast: J.P. Kellner Kilian: J.P. Kellner
Berlin, SPK: *P 308*	"Toccata in C per Organo con pedale" (TP) "Toccata pedaliter" (H)	Kast: anon. scribe, 19th cen. Kilian: anon. scribe, beginning of 19th cen.
Berlin, DStB: *P 803*	"Toccata ped: ex C" (H)	Kast: anon. scribe, 2nd half of 18th cen. Kilian: anon. scribe, 1st half of 18th cen. Zietz: anon. scribe
Berlin, SPK: *P 1071* (Toccata only)	"C.♮ Pedaliter. Toccata" (H)	Kast: anon. scribe, ca. 1800 Kilian: A. Kühnel?

228 The Organ Preludes of J. S. Bach

Berlin, SPK: *P 1101*	"Toccata. pedaliter" (H)	Kast: anon. scribe, 18th cen. Kilian: anon. scribe, 2nd half of 18th cen.
Berlin, SPK: *P 1102* (Fugue only)	"Fuga" (H)	Kast: anon. scribe, 18th cen. Kilian: anon. scribe, 2nd (?) half of 18th cen.
Berlin, SPK: *P 1103* (Toccata and Fugue only)	"Toccata Pedaliter" (H)	Kast: anon. scribe, 18th cen. Kilian: anon. scribe, 2nd half of 18th cen.
Brussels, Bibliothèque Royale: *II.4093*	"TOCCATA" (H)	Kilian: anon. scribe, 2nd half of 18th cen.
Stift Göttweig: *J.S. Bach Nr. 34*	"Fuga" (H)	Kilian: anon. scribe, working with A. Fuchs

Toccata in d, BWV 565

Source	Title	Scribe
Berlin, SPK: *P 595*	"Toccata con Fuga pedaliter ex d♯" (TP)	Kast: J. Ringk Kilian: J. Ringk
Berlin, SPK: *P 642*	"Toccata" (H)	Kast: anon. scribe, 19th cen. Kilian: anon. scribe, 1st half of 19th cen.
Berlin, SPK: *P 924*	"Toccata con Fuga pedaliter" (H)	Kast: F.A. Grasnick Kilian: F.A. Grasnick
Hamburg: Schubring Collection	"Toccata" (H)	Kilian: J. Schubring
Leipzig, MBLpz: *III.8.20*	"Adagio" (H)	Krause: J.A. Dröbs, beginning of 19th cen.

Toccata in E, BWV 566

Source	Title	Scribe
Berlin, SPK: *P 203* (in C)	"Praeludium Concertato" (H)	Kast: C.F.G. Schwencke Kilian: C.F.G. Schwencke
Berlin, SPK: *P 277* (In C, mm. 1-122 only)	"Preludio" (H)	Kast: Anonymous 401 Kilian: Anonymous 1 of the Amalien-Bibliothek
Berlin, SPK: *P 286* (in C)	"Praeludium con Fuga. Pedal in C♮" (TP)	Kast: J.P. Kellner
Berlin, SPK: *P 320* (mm. 1-122 only)	"Praeludium Concertato con Fuga" (H) "Praeludium" (H)	Kilian: J.P. Kellner Kast: J.C. Kittel Kilian: L.E. Gebhardi?
Berlin, SPK: *P 416* (in C)	"Praeludium et Fuga pro Organo. Modi maioris C" (TP) "Praeludium" (H)	Kast: anon. scribe, 2nd half of 18th cen. Kilian: anon. scribe, 2nd half of 18th cen.
Berlin, SPK: *P 504* (mm. 123-229 only)	"Preludio e Fuga per l'Organo con Pedale obligato" (TP) "Preludio con Fuga" (H)	Kast: F.A. Grasnick, 1819 Kilian: F.A. Grasnick, 1819

Appendix I

Berlin, SPK: *P 557* (mm. 1-122 only)	"Praeludium" (H)	Kast: F.A. Grasnick Kilian: F.A. Grasnick
Berlin, SPK: *P 658* (in C)	"Praeludium" (H)	Kast: J.C. Kittel Kilian: M.G. Fischer, 1792
Berlin, DStB: *P 803* (in C)	"Praeludium con Fuga" (H)	Kast: J.T. Krebs Kilian: J.T. Krebs Zietz: J.T. Krebs, ca. 1714
Berlin, SPK: *P 837* (in C)	"Praeludium Concertato" (H)	Kast: anon. scribe, 1st half of 19th cen. Kilian: anon. scribe, 1st half of 19th cen.
Berlin, DStB: *AmB 544*	"Preludio ou Fantasia con Pedal" (TP) "Praeludium" (H)	Kilian: Anonymous 2 of the Amalien-Bibliothek

Prelude in G, BWV 568

Source	Title	Scribe
Berlin, SPK: *P 301*	"Praeludium con Pedale" (H)	Kast: anon. scribe, working in Vienna ca. 1800 Kilian: anon. scribe, 1st half of 19th cen.
Berlin, SPK: *P 303*	"Preludium con Pedale" (H)	Kast: anon. scribe, working in Vienna ca. 1800 Kilian: anon. scribe, 1st half of 19th cen.
Berlin, SPK: *P 515*	"Praeludium con Pedale" (H)	Kast: anon. scribe, 19th cen. Kilian: anon. scribe, 1st half of 19th cen.
Berlin, SPK: *P 1107*	"Praeludium con Pedale" (H)	Kast: anon. scribe, 18th cen. Kilian: anon. scribe, 2nd half of 18th cen.
Brussels, Bibliothèque Royale: *II.3917*	"Praeludium con Pedale" (H)	Kilian: anon. scribe, ca. 1830
Stift Göttweig: *J.S. Bach Nr. 34*	"Präludium (con Pedale)" (H)	Kilian: A. Fuchs

Prelude in a, BWV 569

Source	Title	Scribe
Berlin, SPK: *P 288*	"Praeludium ex A. moll. Pedaliter" (TP)	Kast: J.P. Kellner Kilian: J.P. Kellner

Berlin, DStB: *P 801*	"Praeludium pro Organo pleno con Pedale" (TP)
	"Praeludium" (H)
		Kast: J.G. Walther
		Kilian:
		  Title page: J.L. Krebs
		  Musical text: J.G. Walther
		Zietz:
		  Title page: J.L. Krebs
		  Musical text: J.G. Walther, ca. 1712

Berlin, SPK: *P 837*	-------	Kast: anon. scribe, 19th cen. Kilian: anon. scribe, 1st half of 19th cen.
Berlin, SPK: *P 1105*	"Praeludium pro Organo pleno con Pedale" (H)	Kast: Anonymous 703 (M.G. Fischer?) Kilian: anon. scribe, 2nd half of 18th cen.
Brussels, Bibliothèque Royale: *II.3913*	"Praeludium für die Orgel" (TP) "Praeludium" (H)	Kilian: K.C. Kegel
Leipzig, MBLpz: *Ms. 7*	"Praeludium" (H)	Krause: J.G. Preller
Leipzig, MBLpz: *III.8.16*	"Preludium" (H)	Krause: J.A. Dröbs
New Haven, Yale: *LM 4842e*	"Praeludium ex A♭"(H)	Kilian: anon. scribe, ca. 1800

Fantasia in C, BWV 570

Source	Title	Scribe
Berlin, SPK: *P 279*	"Fantasia ex C dur" (TP) "Fantasia" (H)	Kast: anon. scribe, ca. 1800 Kilian: anon. scribe, beginning of 19th cen.
Berlin, SPK: *P 308*	"Fantasia" (H)	Kast: anon. scribe, 19th cen. Kilian: anon. scribe, 1st half of 19th cen.
Berlin, SPK: *P 804*	"Fantasia" (H)	Kast: J.P. Kellner Kilian: J.P. Kellner?
Berlin, DStB: *Mus. ms. 30069*	"Fantasia" (H)	Kast: anon. scribe, 19th cen. Kilian: F.A. Grasnick
Leipzig, MBLpz: *III.8.4* (*Andreas Bach Buch*)	"Fantasia" (H)	Wolffheim: J.G. Walther Dürr: J. Bernhard Bach, the younger Kilian: J. Bernhard Bach, the elder

Fantasia in G, BWV 572

Source	Title	Scribe
Berlin, SPK: *P 288*, pp. 1-9	"Piece d'Orgue ex G♮ " (TP) "Piece d'Orgue" (H)	Kast: anon. scribe, 2nd half of 18th cen. Kilian: anon. scribe, 2nd half of 18th cen.
Berlin, SPK: *P 288*, pp. 11-19	"Piece d'Orgue in G♮ " (TP)	Kast: J.P. Kellner Kilian: J.P. Kellner
Berlin, SPK: *P 288*, pp. 22-31	"Piece d'Orgue a 5. avec le Pédale continue" (TP)	Kast: anon. scribe, 2nd half of 18th cen. Kilian: anon. scribe, ca. 1800
Berlin, SPK: *P 320*	"Piece d'Orgue à 5 Voc...con Pedale" (H)	Kast: J.C. Kittel Kilian: L.E. Gebhardi?
Berlin, SPK: *P 414* (12/8 section only)	"Praeludium" (H)	Kast: anon. scribe, ca. 1800

Appendix I

Berlin, SPK: *P 510*	"Piece d'Orgue à 5. Voc.. con Pedale" (H)	Kast: F.A. Grasnick, 1821
Berlin, DStB: *P 801*	"Piece d'Orgue" (TP)	Kast: J.G. Walther
	"Piece d'Orgue" (H)	Zietz: J.G. Walther, ca. 1712
Berlin, SPK: *P 837*	"Piece d'Orgue" (H)	Kast: anon. scribe, 1st half of 19th cen.
		Kilian: anon. scribe, 1st half of 19th cen.
Berlin, SPK: *P 1092*	"Piece d'Orgue a 5 avec La Pedalle continu" (TP)	Kast: Anonymous 5b
	"Piece d'Orgue" (H)	
Berlin, DStB: Mus. ms. 30386	"Preludio per l'Organo â 5. Voc. col Pedale obligato" (TP)	Kast: anon. scribe
Berlin, SPK: *AmB 54*	"Preludio per l'Organo col Pedale obligato" (TP)	Kilian: Anonymous 1 of the Amalien-Bibliothek
	"Preludio" (H)	
Berlin, DStB: *AmB 541*	"Preludio per l'Organo col Pedal obligato" (TP)	Bleckschmidt: Anonymous VI of the Amalien-Bibliothek
Göttingen: Bach-Institut (12/8 section only)	-------	?
New Haven, Yale: *LM 4838*	"Piece d'Orgue a 5. avec la Pedale" (H)	Kilian: J.C.H. Rinck
New Haven, Yale: *LM 4842h* (12/8 section only)	"Fantasia" (H)	Kilian: L. Scholz
Stift Göttweig: *J.S. Bach Nr. 34* (12/8 section only)	"Fantasie u. Fuge (sic) für Orgel und Pedal" (H)	Kilian: A. Fuchs
Stift Göttweig: *J.S. Bach Nr. 34* (12/8 section only)	"Fantasie für Orgel mit oblig. Pedal" (H)	Kilian: A. Fuchs

Fantasia in C (incomplete), BWV 573

Source	Title	Scribe
Berlin, SPK: *P 224* (*Klavierbüchlein für Anna Magdalena Bach*, 1722)	"Fantasia pro Organo"	J.S. Bach Dadelsen: 1722-1723 Kilian: ca. 1722

Passacaglia in c, BWV 582

Source	Title	Scribe
Berlin, SPK: *P 274*	"Passacalia en C♭ con Pedale" (H)	Kast: anon. scribe Kilian: anon. scribe, 1st half of 18th cen.
Berlin, SPK: *P 277*	"Passacalia" (H)	Kast: Anonymous 401 Kilian: Anonymous 1 of the Amalien-Bibliothek

Berlin, SPK: *P 279*	"Passacalia ex C moll con Pedale" (TP)	Kast: anon. scribe, ca. 1800
	"Passacaglia ex C moll con Pedale" (H)	Kilian: anon. scribe, beginning of 19th cen.
Berlin, SPK: *P 286*	"Passacalia ex C♭ Con Pedale" (TP)	Kast: anon. scribe, 18th cen.
		Kilian: anon. scribe, 2nd half of 18th cen.
Berlin, SPK: *P 290*	"Passacalia" (H)	Kast: Anonymous 303
		Kast: Anonymous 303, 2nd half of 18th cen.
Berlin, SPK: *P 320*	"Passatalia in C♭ per l'Organo" (H)	Kast: J.C. Kittel
		Kilian: L.E. Gebhardi?
Berlin, SPK: *P 557*	"Passacaglia in C♭ per l'Organo" (H)	Kast: F.A. Grasnick
		Kilian: F.A. Grasnick
Berlin, SPK: *P 601*	"Passacalia in C♭ Con Pedale" (TP)	Kast: "FrC"
	"Passacalia" (H)	
Berlin, DStB: *P 803*	"Passacaglia" (TP)	Kast: J.T. Krebs
		Zietz: J.T. Krebs, ca. 1714
Göttingen: Bach-Institut (Abridged version)	-------	Kilian: L. Scholz
Göttingen: Bach-Institut (Abridged version)	"Passaglia (sic)" (H)	Kilian: L. Scholz
Leipzig, MBLpz: *Ms. R. 16* (mm. 233-292 only)	-------	Wolffheim: J.G. Walther
		Dürr: J. Bernhard Bach, the younger
		Kilian: J. Bernhard Bach, the elder
Leipzig, MBLpz: *III.8.4* (*Andreas Bach Buch*)	"Passacalia. ex C♭ con Pedale" (H)	Wolffheim: J.G. Walther
		Dürr: J. Bernhard Bach, the younger
		Kilian: J. Bernhard Bach, the elder

Appendix II
The Fantasia & Fugue in C Minor, BWV 562/1a & BWV 546/2a

Edited from the Manuscript
Berlin, SPK: P 1104

Fantasia pro Organo cum pedal obligato

Vertendo Sequitur Fuga

Appendix II

Appendix II

Appendix II

Bibliography

Music Editions and Facsimiles

Collected Editions of Bach's Free Organ Works

Johann Sebastian Bach: Complete Organ Works, Albert Schweitzer and Charles-Marie Widor, eds. (New York: G. Schirmer) Vols. 1-5, 1912.

Johann Sebastian Bach. Neue Ausgabe sämtlicher Werke (Neue Bach-Ausgabe), issued under the auspices of the Johann-Sebastian-Bach-Institut, Göttingen, and the Bach-Archiv, Leipzig (Kassel: Bärenreiter; Leipzig: VEB Deutscher Verlag für Musik) Vol. IV/4 (Manfred Tessmer, ed.) 1969; Vol. IV/5 (Dietrich Kilian, ed.) 1972; Vol. IV/6 (Dietrich Kilian, ed.) 1964.

Johann Sebastian Bach's Kompositionen für die Orgel, Friedrich Conrad Griepenkerl and Ferdinand Roitzsch, eds. (Leipzig: C.F. Peters), Vols. 1-4, 1844-1846.

Johann Sebastian Bach's Werke (Bach-Gesamtausgabe), issued under the auspices of the Bach-Gesellschaft (Leipzig: Breitkopf und Härtel) Vol. III (C.F. Becker, ed.) 1853; Vol. XV (Wilhelm Rust, ed.) 1865; Vol. XXXVIII (Ernst Naumann, ed.) 1888.

Facsimiles

Bach, Johann Sebastian. *Fantasia per il Cembalo* (BWV 906), Facsimile edition of the autograph score with commentary by Robert Marshall (Kassel: Bärenreiter) 1976.

_____. *Praeludium pro organo cum pedale obligato* (BWV 544), Facsimile edition of the autograph score (London: Chiswick Press) 1942.

_____. *Praeludium pro organo cum pedale obligato* (BWV 544), Facsimile edition of the autograph score (Vienna: Universal) n.d.

Miscellaneous Editions

Bach, Johann Sebastian. *Kompositionen für die Orgel, Praktische-Ausgabe* of the Peters Edition. Vol. II, Karl Straube, ed. (Leipzig: C.F. Peters) 1913.

_____. *Wachet auf, ruft uns die Stimme* (BWV 140), a Norton Critical Score, Gerhard Herz, ed. (New York: W.W. Norton) 1972.

Buxtehude, Dietrich. *Sämtliche Orgel-Werke*, Klaus Beckmann, ed. (Wiesbaden: Breitkopf und Härtel) Volume I (Freie Orgelwerke), 1972.

Documents

Bach-Dokumente, issued under the auspices of the Bach-Archiv, Leipzig (Kassel: Bärenreiter; Leipzig: VEB Deutscher Verlag für Musik) Volume I, 1963; Volume II, 1969; Volume III, 1972.

Literature

Adlung, M. Jacob. *Anleitung zu der musikalischen Gelährtheit* (Erfurt: J.D. Jungnicol) 1758.

_____. *Musica Mechanica Organoedi* (Berlin: Friedrich Wilhelm Birnstiel) 1768.

Bach, Carl Philipp Emanuel. *Versuch über die wahre Art das Clavier zu Spielen* (Berlin: George Ludewig Winter), Part I, 1753.

Bagnall, Anne, et al. "Bach's 'Art of Fugue': An Examination of the Sources" in *Current Musicology*, Issue 19/1975, pp. 47-77.

Beyer, Johann Samuel. *Primae linae musicae vocalis, das ist: Kurze, leichte, gründliche, und richtige Anweisung* (Freiburg: Elias Nicolaus Kuhsus) 1703.

Blankenburg, Walter. "Zur Geschichte des Kirchenkonzerts" in *Musik und Kirche*, Vol. 44 (1974), pp. 165-175.

Blechschmidt, Eva Renate. *Die Amalien-Bibliothek* (Berlin: Verlag Merseburger) 1965.

Dadelsen, Georg von. *Beiträge zur Chronologie der Werke Johann Sebastian Bachs* (Trossingen: Hohner Verlag) 1958.

_____. *Bemerkungen zur Handschrift J.S. Bachs seiner Familie und seines Kreises* (Trossingen: Hohner Verlag) 1957.

_____. "Die 'Fassung letzter Hand' in der Musik" in *Acta Musicologica*, Vol. 33 (1961), pp. 1-14.

Dahlhaus, Carl. "Bachs Konzertante Fugen" in *Bach-Jahrbuch*, Vol. 42 (1955), pp. 45-72.

Dammann, Rolf. *Der Musikbegriff im deutschen Barock* (Cologne: Arno Volk Verlag) 1967.

David, Hans T. and Mendel. Arthur, *The Bach Reader* (New York: W.W. Norton) 1945; Revised Edition, 1966.

Bibliography

Daw, Stephen. "Copies of J.S. Bach by Walther and Krebs: a Study of the Mss. P 801, P 802, and P 803" in *Organ Yearbook*, Vol. 7 (1976), pp. 31-58.

Dietrich, Fritz. "Analogieformen in Bachs Tokkaten und Präludien für die Orgel" in *Bach-Jahrbuch*, Vol. 28 (1931), pp. 51-71.

Dürr, Alfred. "Neues über die Möllersche Handschrift" in *Bach-Jahrbuch*, Vol. 41 (1954), pp. 66-74.

_____. *Studien über die frühen Kantaten J.S. Bachs* (Leipzig: Breitkopf und Härtel) 1951; Second Edition, 1977.

_____. "Zur Chronologie der Handschrift Johann Christoph Altnickols und Johann Friedrich Agricolas" in *Bach-Jahrbuch*, Vol. 56 (1970), pp. 44-65.

_____. *Zur Chronologie der Leipziger Vokalwerke* (Kassel: Bärenreiter) 1957; Second Edition, 1976.

Emery, Walter. "Cadence and Chronology" in *Studies in Renaissance and Baroque Music in Honor of Arthur Mendel*, Robert Marshall, ed. (Kassel: Bärenreiter; Hackensack, N.J.: Joseph Boonin) 1974, pp. 156-164.

_____. "The Compass of Bach's Organs as Evidence of the Date of his Works" in *The Organ*, Vol. 32 (1952), pp. 92-100.

_____. "The London Autograph of 'The Forty-Eight'" in *Music and Letters*, Vol. 34 (1953), pp. 106-123.

_____. "Some Speculations on the Development of Bach's Organ Style" in *The Musical Times*, Vol. 107 (1966), pp. 596-603.

Fock, Gustav. *Der junge Bach in Lüneburg* (Hamburg: Merseburger) 1950.

Forkel, Johann Nikolaus. *Über Johann Sebastian Bachs Leben, Kunst, und Kunstwerke* (Leipzig: Hoffmeister und Kühnel) 1802; Modern edition by Joseph M. Müller-Blattau (Kassel: Bärenreiter) 1942.

Frotscher, Gotthold. *Geschichte des Orgelspiels und der Orgelkomposition* (Berlin: Merseburger) 1935; Second Edition, 2 vols., 1959.

_____. "Zur Problematik der Bach-Orgel" in *Bach-Jahrbuch*, Vol. 31 (1935), pp. 107-121.

Fuller-Maitland, J.A.. "A Set of Bach's Proof-Sheets" in *Sammelbände der Internationalen Musikgesellschaft*, Vol. 2 (1900-1901), pp. 643-650.

Geck, Martin. "Gattungstraditionen und Altersschichten in den Brandenburgischen Konzerten" in *Musikforschung*, Vol. 23 (1970), pp. 139-152.

Gerstenberg, Walter. *Die Zeitmasse und ihre Ordnungen in Bachs Musik* (Einbeck: Carl Schleicher & Schull) 1952.

_____."Zur Verbindung von Präludium und Fuge bei J.S. Bach" in *Bericht des Internationalen Musikwissenschaftlichen Kongresses*, Lüneburg, 1950, pp. 126-129.

Hedar, Josef. *Dietrich Buxtehudes Orgelwerke* (Frankfurt: Wilhelmiana Musikverlag) 1951.

Hering. "J.S. Bachs Klavier-Toccaten" in *Bach-Jahrbuch*, Vol. 40 (1953), pp. 72-86.

Kast, Paul. *Die Bach-Handschriften der Berliner Staatsbibliothek* (Trossingen: Hohner Verlag) 1957.

Keller, Hermann. *The Organ Works of Bach*, Helen Hewitt, tr. (New York: C.F. Peters) 1967.

Kilian, Dietrich. "Dreisätzige Fassungen Bachscher Orgelwerke" in *Bach-Interpretationen*, Martin Geck, ed. (Göttingen: Vandenhoeck & Ruprecht) 1969, pp. 12-21.

_____. "J.S. Bachs Praeludium und Fuge d-moll, BWV 539 – Ein Arrangement aus dem 19. Jahrhundert?" in *Musikforschung*, Vol. 14 (1961), pp. 323-328.

_____. "Studie über Bachs Fantasie und Fuge c-moll (BWV 562)" in *Hans Albrecht in Memoriam*, Wilfried Brennecke and Hans Hasse, eds. (Kassel: Bärenreiter) 1969, pp. 127-135.

Klein, Hans-Günter. *Der Einfluss der Vivaldischen Konzertform im Instrumental-Werk Johann Sebastian Bachs* (Baden-Baden: Heitz) 1970.

Kloppers, Jacobus. "A Criterion for Manual Changes in the Organ Works of Bach" in *Organ Yearbook*, Vol. 7 (1976), pp. 47-62.

_____. *Die Interpretation und Wiedergabe der Orgelwerke Bachs* (Frankfurt: Dissertation) 1965.

Klotz, Hans. "Bachs Orgeln und seine Orgelmusik" in *Musikforschung*, Vol. 3 (1950), pp. 189-203.

_____. "Johann Sebastian Bach und die Orgel" in *Musik und Kirche*, Vol. 32 (1962), pp. 49-55.

_____. "Originale Spielanweisungen in Bachs Orgelwerken und ihre Konsequenzen für die Interpretation" in *Bach-Interpretationen*, Martin Geck, ed. (Göttingen: Vandenhoeck & Ruprecht) 1969, pp. 112-118.

_____. *Über die Orgelkunst der Gotik, der Renaissance und des Barock* (Kassel: Bärenreiter) First Edition, 1934; Second Edition, 1975.

Kobayashi, Yoshitake. *Franz Hauser und Seine Bach-Handschriftensammlung* (Göttingen: Dissertation) 1973.

Krause, Peter. *Handschriften der Werke J.S. Bachs in der Musikbibliothek der Stadt Leipzig* (Leipzig: Musikbibliothek der Stadt Leipzig) 1964.

Krüger, Elke. *Stilistische Untersuchungen zu ausgewählten frühen Klavierfugen Johann Sebastian Bachs* (Hamburg: Karl Dieter Wagner Musikalienhandlung) 1970.

Lenz, Christfried. *Studien zur Satztechnik Bachs* (Heidelberg: Dissertation) 1970.

Löffler, Hans. "J.S. Bach's Orgelprüfungen" in *Bach-Jahrbuch*, Vol. 22 (1925), pp. 93-100.

_____. "Die Schüler Johann Sebastian Bachs" in *Bach-Jahrbuch*, Vol. 50 (1953), pp. 5-28.

Mahrenholz, Christhard. "Johann Sebastian Bach und der Gottesdienst seiner Zeit" in *Musik und Kirche*, Vol. 20 (1950), pp. 145-158.

Marpurg, Friedrich Wilhelm. *Historische-kritische Beiträge zur Aufnahme der Musik* (Berlin: Gottlieb August Lange), Part III, 1757.

Marshall, Robert L. "Bach the Progressive: Observations on his Later Works" in *Musical Quarterly*, Vol. 62 (1976), pp. 313-357.

_____. *The Compositional Process of J.S. Bach* (Princeton: Princeton University Press) 2 vols., 1972.

Mattheson, Johann. *Das neu-eröffnete Orchester* (Hamburg: auf Unkosten des Autoris) 1713.

_____. *Der vollkommene Capellmeister* (Hamburg: Christian Herold) 1739.

May, Ernest. "J.G. Walther and the Lost Weimar Autographs of Bach's Organ Works" in *Studies in Renaissance and Baroque Music in Honor of Arthur Mendel*, Robert Marshall, ed. (Kassel: Bärenreiter; Hackensack, N.J.: Joseph Boonin), 1974, pp. 264-282.

Mies, Paul. *Das instrumentale Rezitativ* (Bonn: Bouvier) 1968.

Musch, Hans. "Von der Einheit der grossen Orgelfuge Johann Sebastian Bachs" in *Musik und Kirche*, Vol. 44 (1974), pp. 267-279.

Neumann, Frederick. "The Question of Rhythm in the Two Versions of Bach's French Ouverture, BWV 831" in *Studies in Renaissance and Baroque Music in Honor of Arthur Mendel*, Robert Marshall, ed. (Kassel: Bärenreiter; Hackensack, N.J.: Joseph Boonin) 1974, pp. 183-194.

Neumann, Werner. *J.S. Bachs Chorfuge* (Leipzig: Breitkopf und Härtel) 2nd Edition, 1950.

Niedt, Friedrich Erhardt. *Handleitung zur Variation* (Hamburg: B. Schiller) 1706.

Oppel, Reinhard. "Bachs D-dur Praeludium und Fuge für Orgel" in *Zeitschrift für Musikwissenschaft*, Vol. 2 (1919-1920), pp. 149-156.

Pauly, Jakob. *Die fuge in den Orgelwerken Dietrich Buxtehudes* (Regensburg: G. Bosse) 1964.

Platen, Emil. *Untersuchungen zur Struktur der Chorischen Choralbearbeitung Johann Sebastian Bachs* (Bonn: Rheinische Friedrich Wilhelms-Universität) 1959.

Protz, Albert. "Zu Johann Sebastian Bachs 'Capriccio sopra la lontananza del suo fratello dilettissimo'" in *Musikforschung*, Vol. 10 (1957), pp. 405-408.

Riedel, Friedrich Wilhelm. "Strenger und Frier Stil in der nord- und süddeutschen Musik für Tasteninstrumente des 17. Jahrhunderts" in *Nord-deutsche und nordeuropäische Musik — Kieler Schriften zur Musikwissenschaft*, Vol. 16 (1965), pp. 63-70.

Rietschel, Georg. *Die Aufgabe der Orgel im Gottesdienste bis in das 18. Jahrhundert* (Hildesheim: Georg Olms Verlag) 1971.

Rifkin, Joshua. "The Chronology of Bach's Saint Matthew Passion" in *Musical Quarterly*, Vol. 61 (1975), pp. 360-387.

Scheibe, Johann Adolph. *Der Critische Musicus* (Hamburg: Thomas von Wierings Erben) 1739.

Scheide, William. "Zum Verhältnis von Textdrucken und musikalischen Quellen der Kirchenkantaten Johann Sebastian Bachs" in *Bach-Jahrbuch*, Vol. 62 (1976), pp. 70-94.

Schleuning, Peter. "'Diese Fantasie ist einzig . . .' Das Recitativ in Bachs Chromatischer Fantasia und seine Bedeutung für die Ausbildung der Freien Fantasie" in *Bach Interpretationen*, M. Geck, ed. (Göttingen: Vandenhoeck & Ruprecht) 1969, pp. 57-73.

Schmieder, Wolfgang. *Thematisch-Systematisches Verzeichnis der Musikalischen Werke von Johann Sebastian Bach (Bach-Werke-Verzeichnis)* (Wiesbaden: Breitkopf und Härtel; Leipzig: VEB Deutscher Verlag für Musik) 1950.

Schneider, Max. "Das sogennante 'Orgelkonzert d-moll von Friedemann Bach'" in *Bach-Jahrbuch*, Vol. 8 (1911), pp. 23-36.

Schrammek, W. "Über die 'Organisten-Probe' zur Zeit Johann Sebastian Bachs" in *Bach-Fest-Bücher der Neuen Bachgesellschaft*, 1957, pp. 65-70.

Bibliography

Schünemann, Georg. "J.G. Walther und H. Bokemeyer. Eine Musikerfreundschaft um Sebastian Bach" in *Bach-Jahrbuch*, Vol. 30 (1933), pp. 86-118.

Schulze, Hans-Joachim. "Die Bach-Überlieferung – Plädoyer für ein notwendiges Buch" in *Beiträge zur Musikwissenschaft*, Vol. 1 (1975), pp. 45-57.

_____. "J.S. Bach's Concerto-Arrangements for Organ – Studies or Commissioned Works?" in *Organ Yearbook*, Vol. 3 (1972), pp. 4-13.

_____. *Studien zur Bach-Überlieferung im 18. Jahrhundert* (Rostock: Dissertation), 1978.

_____. "'Das Stück im Goldpapier' – Ermittlungen zu einigen Bach-Abschriften des frühen 18. Jahrhunderts" in *Bach-Jahrbuch*, Volume 64 (1978), pp. 19-42.

_____. "Wer intavolierte Johann Sebastian Bachs Lautenkompositionen?" in *Musikforschung*, Vol. 19 (1966), pp. 32-39.

_____, "Wie entstand die Bach-Sammlung Mempell-Preller?" in *Bach-Jahrbuch*, Vol. 60 (1974), pp. 104-122.

Seitz, Reinhard. "Die Orgelcompositionen des Schülerkreises um Johann Sebastian Bach" in *Bach-Jahrbuch*, Vol. 32 (1935), pp. 33-96.

Siegele, Ulrich. "Zur Verbindung von Präludium und Fuge bei J.S. Bach" in *Bericht des Internationalen Musikwissenschaftlichen Kongresses*, Kassel, 1963, pp. 164-167.

Smend, Friedrich. *Bach in Köthen* (Berlin: Christlicher Zeitschriftverlag) 1951.

Spitta, Philipp. *Johann Sebastian Bach* (Leipzig: Breitkopf und Härtel) Volume I, 1873; Volume II, 1879.

Stiller, Günther. *Johann Sebastian Bach und das Leipziger gottesdienstliche Leben seiner Zeit* (Kassel: Bärenreiter) 1970.

Tittel, Karl. *Die musikalischen Vertreter der Familie Krebs mit besonderer Berücksichtigung der Bachschüler Johann Tobias und Johann Ludwig* (Marburg: Dissertation) 1963.

_____. "Vom 'einzigen Krebs in meinem Bach' – Johann Ludwig Krebs als Bachschüler und Orgelkomponist" in *Musik und Kirche*, Volume 46 (1976), pp. 172-181.

_____. "Welche unter J.S. Bachs Namen geführten Orgelwerke sind Johann Tobias bzw. Johann Ludwig Krebs zuzuschreiben?" in *Bach-Jahrbuch*, Volume 52 (1966), pp. 102-137.

Vogelsänger, Siegfried. "Zur Architektonik der Passacaglia J.S. Bachs" in *Musikforschung*, Volume 25 (1972), pp. 40-50.

Walther, Johann Gottfried. *Musikalisches Lexicon* (Leipzig: Wolffgang Deer) 1732.

Weiss, Wisso. *Die Wasserzeichen in den Bach-Dokumenten* (Manuscript) 1962.

Wolff, Christoph. "Die Architektur von Bachs Passacaglia" in *Acta Organologica*, Vol. 3 (1968), pp. 183-194.

_____. "Bach's 'Handexemplar' of the Goldberg Variations: A New Source" in *Journal of the American Musicological Society*, Vol. 39 (1976), pp. 224-241.

_____. "Bemerkungen zu Siegfried Vogelsängers Aufsatz 'Zur Architektonik der Passacaglia J.S. Bachs'" in *Musikforschung*, Vol. 25 (1972), pp. 488-489.

Wolffheim, Werner. "Die Möllersche Handschrift—ein unbekanntes Gegenstück zum Andreas Bach-Buch" in *Bach-Jahrbuch*, Vol. 9 (1912), pp. 42-60.

Zavarsky, Ernest. "Zum Pedalspiel des jungen Johann Sebastian Bachs" in *Musikforschung*, Vol. 18 (1965), pp. 370-378.

Zietz, Hermann. *Quellenkritische Untersuchungen an den Bach-Handschriften P 801, P 802, und P 803* (Hamburg: Karl Dieter Wagner) 1969.

Index

Adlung, Jacob, 158
  on fantasia, 189 n. 70
  on registration, 160
Agricola, Johann Friedrich, 9, 10
Albrecht, Johann, 145
Altenburg, 146
Amalien-Bibliothek, 9
Andreas Bach Buch. See Leipzig, Musikbibliothek der Stadt Leipzig, *III.8.4*
Anna Amalia, Princess, 9
Anonymous 303, 9
Ariadne Musica. See Fischer, J.K.F., works
Arnstadt, 103
  Bach's activities in, 94-95
  Bach's examination of the Neue Kirche organ, 145
ars inveniendi, 31
Art of Fugue, *See* Bach, J.S., works
Auflagebogen, 16
autographs, Bach, 5
  lost, 10-12

Bach, Carl Philipp Emanuel, 1, 6, 10-11
  as head of Hamburg circle, 9
  on his father's teaching, 152
Bach, Johann Bernard, the elder, 7
Bach, Johann Bernhard, the younger, 7
Bach, Johann Christian, 7, 11
Bach, Johann Christoph, 94
Bach, Johann Christoph Friedrich, 11
Bach, Johann Gottfried Bernhardt, 146
Bach, Johann Jacob, 191 n.6
Bach, Johann Sebastian
  as organ examiner, 145-48
  as recitalist, 148-52
  as teacher, 152-53
  works:
    Allebreve in D for Organ, BWV 589, 4, 185 n.12
    Art of Fugue, BWV 1080, 22
    Brandenburg Concerto No. 2 in F, BWV 1047, 60
    Brandenburg Concerto No. 3 in G, BWV 1048, 171
    Brandenburg Concerto No. 4 in G, BWV 1049, 53
    Canonic Variations on *Vom Himmel hoch*, BWV 769, 15
    Cantata 3, *Ach Gott, wie manches Herzeleid*, BWV 3, 68
    Cantata 21, *Ich hatte viel Bekümmernis*, BWV 21, 52, 110, 144
    Cantata 29, *Wir danken dir, Gott, wir danken dir*, BWV 29, 175
    Cantata 47, *Wer sich selbst erhöhet*, BWV 47, 69-70
    Cantata 52, *Falsche Welt, dir trau ich nicht*, BWV 52, 143
    Cantata 65, *Sie werden aus Saba alle kommen*, BWV 65, 188 n.47
    Cantata 71, *Gott ist mein König*, BWV 71, 103
    Cantata 97, *In allen meinen Thaten*, BWV 97, 62
    Cantata 131, *Aus der Tiefe rufe ich, Herr, zu dir*, BWV 131, 103
    Cantata 140, *Wachet auf ruft uns die Stimme*, BWV 140, 68
    Cantata 146, *Wir müssen durch viel Trübsal in das Reich Gottes eingehen*, BWV 146, 175
    Cantata 152, *Tritt auf die Glaubensbahn*, BWV 152, 98, 119, 144
    Cantata 153, *Schau, lieber Gott, wie meine Feind*, BWV 153, 62
    Cantata 183, *Sie werden euch in den Bann tun*, BWV 183, 143
    Cantata 194, *Höchsterwünschtes Freudenfest*, BWV 194, 146
    Canzona in d for Organ, BWV 588, 4 n. 12
    Capriccio in B♭ "sopra la lontananza del suo fratello dilettissimo," BWV 992, 95
    Christ, der du bist der helle Tag, BWV 766, 94
    Chromatic Fantasia & Fugue in d for Clavier, BWV 903, 85-86, 170-71

Clavierbüchlein für Anna Magdalena Bach. See Berlin, Deutsche Staatsbibliothek, *P 224*
Clavierbüchlein für Wilhelm Friedemann Bach, uncompleted pieces in, 88-89
Clavierübung I, 14
Clavierübung II, 14, 76
Clavierübung III, 6, 14, 76, 167
Clavierübung IV. *See* Goldberg Variations
Concerto in a for Organ, BWV 593, 169
Concerto in a for Flute, Violin, and Clavier, BWV 1044, 22
Concerto in d for Organ, BWV 596, 10, 204 n.10
Concerto in d for Two Violins, BWV 1043, 80
Ein feste Burg, BWV 720, 155
English Suite No. 6 in d, BWV 811, 61
Fantasia in a for Organ, BWV 561, 4
Fantasia in C for Organ, BWV 570, 33-34, 99, 230
Fantasia in C (incomplete) for Organ, BWV 573, 5, 12, 13, 87-89, 115, 231
Fantasia in G for Organ, BWV 571, 4
Fantasia in G for Organ, BWV 572, 41-42, 108-9, 230-31
Fantasia & Fugue in c for Organ, BWV 537, 81-84, 118, 135, 213
Fantasia & Fugue (incomplete) in c for Organ, BWV 562, 6, 12, 22, 33-34, 120, 226
Fantasia & Fugue in c for Organ, BWV 562/1a & BWV 546/2a, 106-7, 226-27, 233-45
Fantasia & Fugue in g for Organ, BWV 542, 12, 84-87, 109-10, 195 n.12, 217-18
Fantasia con Imitazione in b for Organ, BWV 563, 14, 33-34, 99-100, 227
Fantasia super *Komm heiliger Geist, Herre Gott,* BWV 651, 170
French Ouverture for Clavier, BWV 831, 22
Fugue in b on a theme by Corelli for Organ, BWV 579, 130
Fugue in c on a theme by Legrenzi for Organ, BWV 574, 130
Fugue in c for Organ, BWV 575, 130
Goldberg Canons, BWV 1087, 22

Goldberg Variations, BWV 988, 14
Gottes Sohn ist kommen, BWV 600, 155
"Great Eighteen" Chorales, BWV 651-668, 15
Italian Concerto, BWV 971, 166
Komm, Jesu, komm!, BWV 229, 69-70
Little Harmonic Labyrinth for Organ, BWV 591, 121
Musical Offering, BWV 1079, 185 n.13
O Gott, du frommer Gott, BWV 767, 94
Orgelbüchlein, 10, 28
Partita in a for Clavier, BWV 827, 19, 62
Partita in c for Lute, BWV 997, 119
Partita in d for Unaccompanied Violin, BWV 1004, 36
Partita in e for Clavier, BWV 830, 19
Passacaglia in c for Organ, BWV 582, 6, 20, 35-37, 107-8, 231-32
Prelude in a for Organ, BWV 551, 177 n.7, 40, 100-101, 225
Prelude in a for Organ, BWV 569, 34-35, 100, 229-30
Prelude in C for Organ, BWV 567, 4
Prelude in G for Organ, BWV 568, 55-57, 121, 229
Prelude & Fugue in A for Organ, BWV 536, 21, 37-40, 119, 144, 212-13
Prelude & Fugue in A for Organ, BWV 536a, 6, 97-98, 213
Prelude & Fugue in a for Organ, BWV 543, 37, 120, 130-31, 218
Prelude & Fugue in a for Organ, BWV 543a, 105-6, 218-19
Prelude & Fugue in a for Clavier, BWV 894, 22
Prelude & Fugue in b for Organ, BWV 544, 5, 12, 18, 61-69, 117, 134, 167-69, 219
Prelude & Fugue in C for Organ, BWV 531, 37-40, 101-2, 209
Prelude & Fugue in C for Organ, BWV 545, 6, 15, 20-21, 78-80, 120, 133, 220-21
Prelude & Fugue in C for Organ, BWV 545a, 78-80, 112, 221
Prelude & Fugue in C for Organ, BWV 547, 58-61, 114-15, 144, 222

Prelude & Fugue in c for Organ,
    BWV 546, 69-74, 117-18,
    221-22
Prelude & Fugue in c for Organ,
    BWV 549, 21, 37-40, 120,
    224
Prelude & Fugue in D for Organ,
    BWV 532, 41-42, 108,
    195 n.10, 209-10
Prelude & Fugue in d for Organ,
    BWV 539, 89-90, 121-22, 214
Prelude & Fugue in d for Organ,
    BWV 549a, 19, 102, 224
Prelude & Fugue in e for Organ,
    BWV 533, 37-40, 98, 210-11
Prelude & Fugue in e for Organ,
    BWV 533a, 192 n.14, 211
Prelude & Fugue in e for Organ,
    BWV 548, 5, 12, 18, 61-69,
    116, 223-24
Prelude & Fugue in E^b for Organ,
    ("St. Anne"), BWV 552, 6,
    74-77, 118, 135, 141, 165-66,
    225
Prelude & Fugue in f for Organ,
    BWV 534, 78-81, 112, 132,
    211
Prelude & Fugue in G for Organ,
    BWV 541, 5, 11, 12, 23, 51-
    55, 114, 144, 216
Prelude & Fugue in G for Organ,
    BWV 550, 37-40, 105, 152,
    225
Prelude & Fugue in g for Organ,
    BWV 535, 21, 37-40, 119,
    152, 212
Prelude & Fugue in g for Organ,
    BWV 535a, 6-7, 12, 38-39,
    96-97, 212
Prelude, Fugue, & Allegro in E^b for
    Lute, BWV 998, 119
St. Matthew Passion, BWV 244, 61
"Schübler" Chorales, BWV 645-50,
    203 n.4
Sonata in g for Unaccompanied
    Violin, BWV 1001, 121
Toccata in c for Clavier, BWV 919,
    170
Toccata in D for Clavier, BWV 912,
    170
Toccata in d for Organ, BWV 565,
    40, 98-99, 228
Toccata in d for Clavier, BWV 913,
    170
Toccata in E for Organ, BWV 566,
    11, 21, 40-41, 102-3, 228-29

Toccata in e for Clavier, BWV 914,
    80, 170
Toccata in f for Clavier, BWV 910,
    170
Toccata in G for Clavier, BWV 916,
    45, 170
Toccata, Adagio, & Fugue in C for
    Organ, BWV 564, 42-46, 109,
    227-28
Toccata & Fugue in d for Organ
    ("Dorian"), BWV 538, 17,
    57-58, 113, 133, 148, 161-65,
    213-14
Toccata & Fugue in F for Organ,
    BWV 540, 46-51, 113-14, 195
    n.11, 215
Trio Sonatas for Organ, BWV 525-30,
    10
Well-Tempered Clavier I, 10, 14
Well-Tempered Clavier II, 15
Bach, Wilhelm Friedemann, 9, 10
beaming of notes as indication of manual
    change, 162-63
Becker, Nicolaus, 146
Bellermann, Constantin, 148
Berlin
    as center of manuscript copying, 9
    Deutsche Staatsbibliothek:
        *P 224 (Clavierbüchlein für Anna
            Magdalena Bach)*, 5, 12, 14
        P 801, 7
        P 802, 7
        P 803, 7
    Staatsbibliothek Preussischer
        Kulturbesitz:
        Mus. ms. 40644 (Möller Handschrift),
            6, 7, 12
        P 274, 5, 178 n.2, 8, 12
        P 320, 8
        P 421, 171
        P 490, 6, 12, 22, 120
        P 517, 90
        P 577, 171
        P 804, 8
        P 1009, 8
        P 1107, 121
        P 1210, 152
Beyer, Johann Samuel
    definition of prelude by, 2
Bitter, Carl Heinrich, 1
Blumen Strauss. See Fischer, J.K.F., works
Böhm, Georg
    influence on Bach, 39-41, 94
    Praeludium in C, 39-40
Bologna School, 105, 192 n.20
Borsch, Johann Stephen, 9

brackets as indication of manual change, 166
Bruhns, Nikolaus, 1
  influence on Bach, 37-41
Buxtehude, Dietrich, 1
  Bach's visit with, 94
  influence on Bach's style, 39, 127-29
  works:
    Ciacona in c, BuxWV 159, 35
    Ciacona in e, BuxWV 160, 35
    Passacaglia in d, BuxWV 161, 35
    Praeludium in e, BuxWV 142, 127-28
    Praeludium in f , BuxWV 146, 40
    Praeludium in g, BuxWV 150, 48

C minor, affective nature of, 71
cadenza, Bach's treatment of, 81
Canonic Variations on *Vom Himmel hoch.* See Bach, J.S., works
cantatas
  chorale as stylistic model, 67-69
chorale preludes, improvisation of, 153
Chorton, 144
chronologies, prelude
  Keller, 122-25
  Klotz, 26, 201 n.49
  Schmieder, 25-26, 122-25
  Spitta, 25, 122-25
  Stauffer, 26-29, 91-93, 122-25
ciacona, 35
Clauss, Konsul, 6
Clavierbüchlein für Anna Magdalena Bach. See Bach, J.S., works
Clavierübung, See Bach, J.S., works
clefs, Bach's use of, 13-16
Cöthen
  Bach's activities in, 111-12
Collegium Musicum, 115
communion, use of preludes during, 138, 196 n.5
compass, manual and pedal, as basis for chronology, 201 n.49
concerto form, 42-77
Corelli, Arcangelo, 104-5
Cuncius, Christoph, 145

da capo fugue, 84
Dadelsen, Georg von, 25
decoratio, 31
dispositio, 31-32
dorian notation, Bach's use of, 27
double-chorus writing, 69

Dresden
  Bach's competition with L. Marchand, 104
  Bach's concerts in, 149-50
Dröbs, Johann Andreas, 9
Dürr, Alfred, 25

elaboratio, 31
Emery, Walter, 26
episode, Bach's treatment of, 58, 65
Erfindungskunst, 31
Erfurt, 146
Ernst August, Duke, 104, 174
L'Estro armonico. See Vivaldi, works
examinations, Bach's organ, 145-48
exclamatio, 83
executio, 31

fantasia, 33, 189 n.70, 86-87, 88
Finke, Johann Georg, 146
Fischer, J.K.F.
  fantasia style, 33
  influence on Bach's writing, 128
  works:
    Ariadne Musica, 79, 128
    Blumen-Strauss, 128
Fischer, Michael Gotthard, 9, 201 n.46
Forkel, Johann Nikolaus, 1
  on function of preludes, 137
  on registration of preludes, 158
forms, prelude
  as chronological criterion, 27
  used by Bach
    A B A B, 77-84
    concerto, 55-77
    concerto, hybrid, 42-55
    miscellaneous, 84-90
    ostinato-variation, 34-37
    through-composed, continuous, 33-34
    through-composed, sectional, 37-42
free prelude, defined, 2
French Ouverture. See Bach, J.S., works
French style, in Bach's works, 33-34, 41
Friedrich II, Count, 148
Frischmuth, Leonard, 8
fugue
  Bach's treatment of, 130
  da capo, 84
Fuhrmann, Martin Heinrich, 151-52

Gebhardi, Johann Nicolaus, 9
Gera, 146

Gerber, Ernst Ludwig
  on Bach's teaching, 203 n.63
German style, in Bach's works
  middle-German, 33
  north-German, 39-41, 103
Görlitz, 146
Görner, Johann Gottlieb, 115, 147
Goldberg Variations. *See* Bach, J.S., works
Gräbner, Christian, 115
Grasnick, Friedrich August, 9
Griepenkerl, Friedrich Conrad
  on function of preludes, 137
Grigny, Nicolas de, 33-34
Gurh, Karl, 6

Halle, 104, 145, 148
Hamburg
  Bach's recital in the Katharinenkirche, 174-75
  as center for copying, 7
  as center for organ concerts, 148, 149-50
harmonic design, of preludes, 29
Hauptgottesdienst, role of preludes in, 137-46
Heinichen, Johann David, 194 n.43
Hildebrandt, Zacharias, 146, 147
Hilgenfeldt, C.L., 1

idiom, keyboard, defined, 28
improvisation, of preludes, 173
incomplete pieces, 89
Italian style, in Bach's works, 34, 42-60

Johann Ernst, Prince, 104

Kammerton, 144
Kassel, 146, 147
  Bach's recital in Martinskirche, 147-48
Kellner, Johann Peter, 8
keys, parallel, Bach's use of, 59
Kirnberger, Johann Philipp, 9
Kister, Johann, 145
Kittel, Johann Christian, 7, 8-9
Klotz, Hans, 26, 201 n.49
Königsberg, 148
Kräuter, Philipp David
  on Bach's activities in Weimar, 104, 151
Krebs, Johann Ludwig, 8
Krebs, Johann Tobias, 7-8
Kuhnau, Johann, 145

Langewiesen, 145
Leipzig
  Bach's activities in, 115-16, 146-47
  Bach-Archiv: *Mus. ms. 2,* 178 n.2
  Easter Fair concerts, 151-52
  liturgy, 138
  Musikbibliothek der Stadt Leipzig:
    III.8.4 (Andreas Bach Buch), 7
    III.8.7, 152
Legrenzi, Giovanni, 56
Leopold, Prince, 111
Lübeck, 148
Lüneburg, 94

manual change, in preludes, 161-71
manuscript traditions, 7-10
manuscripts, prelude. *See* specific location and library
Marchand, Louis, 104, 204 n.14
Marpurg, Friedrich Wilhelm
  on *plenum* registration, 161
Mattheson, Johann
  on *dispositio,* 31-32
  on improvising preludes and fugues, 139
  on *plenum* registration, 159
melodic material, as chronological criterion, 28
Mempell, Johann Nicolaus, 8
Mey, Wolfgang Nicolaus, 8
Michel, 9
modulation, as chronological criterion, 29
Möller, Carl, 146
Möller Handschrift. See Berlin, Staatsbibliothek Preussischer Kulturbesitz, *Mus. ms. 40644*
motets, Bach, as stylistic model, 69-70
motoric pulse, 47
Mühlhausen, 103
  Bach's activities in, 103
  Bach's recitals in, 146, 200 n.40
Musical Offering. See Bach, J.S., works

Naumburg, 147
Nekrolog of 1754, 10, 95
New Haven
  Library of the School of Music, Yale University, *LM 4839e,* 201 n.46
New York
  Hinrichsen Collection, 5
Niedt, Friedrich Erhardt
  on registration, 158
Nuremburg, 9

Ohrdruf, 94
organ concerts, 148-52
organs tested by Bach, 145-48
organum plenum, 155-61
Orgelbüchlein. See Bach, J.S., works
Orgelprobe, 145-48
ostinato-variation, 34-37
ouverture, French, 74
Oxford
    Rosenthal Collection, 5, 12, 184 n.10, 167-68

Pachelbel, Johann
    as model for A B A B form, 79
    as prelude writer, 2
    as proponent of fantasia style, 33
    works:
        Ciacona in d, 35
        Toccata in C, 56
Pachelbel, Wilhelm Hieronymous, 9
pairing of prelude and fugue, 77, 127-36
part writing, as chronological criterion, 28
passacaglia, 35-37
passaggio, 37, 43, 47, 51
pedal, 12-13
pedal points, Bach's use of, 78-79
pedal solo, Bach's treatment of, 39, 44, 48
permutation fugue, 103, 107-8
Petri, Johann Samuel
    on function of preludes, 140
    on tuning, 142
Pitschel, T.L.
    on Bach's improvisations, 89
plenum registration, 159-61, 170-71
postludes, 138-42
Potsdam, 149
Praeambulum, defined, 2
Praeludium, defined, 2
Praeludium Pedaliter
    defined, 2
    north-German, as stylistic model, 40-41, 85
Preller, Johann Gottlieb, 8, 192 n.14
prelude, organ
    as concert piece, 149-51
    defined, 2
    function of, 173-75
    as preface to worship service, 138-42
    registration of, 155-59
    as sinfonia, 143-44
    sources of, 209-32
prelude and fugue
    pairing, 127-36
    unification of, 132-35
pro Organo Pleno, 157

quartets, organ, 204 n.14

Raison, André, 35
recitative, 85-86
registration, of preludes, 155-59
repercussio, 102, 105
revisions, Bach's
    of earlier works, 119-22
    of preludes, 19-23
rhythmic flexibility, 83
Rinck, Johann Christian, 9
Ringk, Johannes, 8
ritornello
    Bach's treatment of, 42-77
    modulating, 58
Rolle, Christian Friedrich, 145

Scheibe, Johann Adolph, 146, 147
    on improvisation of preludes and fugues, 139-40
    on registration, 157
Scheidemann, Heinrich, 2, 127
Schmid, Balthasar, 167
Schmieder, Johann Christoph, 146
Schmieder, Wolfgang, 25
Schneider, Johann, 115
Scholz, Leonard, 10
Schröter, Johann Georg, 146
"Schübler" Chorales. *See* Bach, J.S., works
Schweitzer, Albert, 155
Schwanenberger, G.H.L., 151
Schwencke, C.F.G., 9
Sichart, Lorenz, 10
sign motif. *See* suspiratio
Silbermann, Gottfried, 147
Silbermann, Johann Georg, 146
sinfonia, prelude as, 143-44
Spitta, Philipp, 1
    chronology, 25
    on function, 137
Stettin, 148
stile fantastico, defined, 1
Stockholm
    Musikkulturens främjande, 178 n.2
Stöntzsch, 146
Störmtal, 146
Straube, Karl, 155
suspiratio, 71, 83

tablature, Bach's use of, 180-81 n.44
Taubach, 145
titling of preludes, 17-19
Torelli, Giuseppi, 104-5

transposition, of preludes, 21
Trebs, Heinrich Nicolaus, 145
trio texture, Bach's use of, 49
Trost, Gottfried Heinrich, 146
Türk, Daniel Gottlob
   on function of preludes, 140
   on tuning, 142
Tunder, Franz, 2, 127
tuning, 142-44

Überschrift, 18

variants, of preludes, 19-23, 119-20
Vespergottesdienst, role of preludes in, 138
Vivaldi, Antonio
   influence on Bach, 47-58, 78-81, 111-12
   works:
      Concerti a cinque stromenti, 47
      Concerto in a for Two Violins, 66
      Concerto in d for Two Violins and Cello, 48
      Concerto in E for Violin, 52
      L'Estro armonico, 47, 187 n.34, 111, 193 n.29
      La Stravaganza, 47
Vogelsänger, Siegfried, 35-36

Walther, Johann Gottfried, 7-8, 22
   on *stile fantastico*, 1
Wechmar, Johann Anton, 8
Weigel, Christoph, 167
Weimar, 7, 174-75
   Bach's activities in, 104-5, 111-12
   Bach's concerts in, 151
Weise, Johann Anton, 146
Wender, Johann Friedrich, 145
Widor, Charles-Marie, 155
Wittemberg, 148
Wolff, Christoph, 36
worship service, role of preludes in, 137-44

Zschortau, 147

Cover illustrations: watermark examples selected from the *French Harpsichord Music of the 17th Century* by Bruce Gustafson, published by UMI Research Press.

LIBRARY OF DAVIDSON COLLEGE

Books on regular loan may be checked out for **two weeks**. Books must be presented at the Circulation Desk in order to be renewed.

A fine is charged after date due.

Special books are subject to special regulations at the discretion of the library staff.

DEC 23 1963

APR 25 19